The Rise of the Goddess
in the Hindu Tradition

The Rise of the Goddess in the Hindu Tradition

Tracy Pintchman

STATE UNIVERSITY OF NEW YORK PRESS

Front cover: *Painting of Durga Slaying the Demon Mahisa,* miniature painting, India 1800–1825, artist unknown. The Brooklyn Museum 36.245, given by Ananda K. Coomaraswamy, reproduced courtesy of the Brooklyn Museum.

Published by
State University of New York Press, Albany

Printed in the United States of America

For information, address State University of New York Press,
State University Plaza, Albany, NY, 12246

Production by Cathleen Collins
Marketing by Nancy Farrell

Library of Congress Cataloging-in-Publication Data

Pintchman, Tracy.
The rise of the Goddess in the Hindu tradition / Tracy Pintchman.
p. cm.
Includes bibliographical references and index.
ISBN 0-7914-2111-2. — ISBN 0-7914-2112-0 (pbk.)
1. Goddesses, Hindu. 2. God (Hinduism) I. Title.
BL1216.2.P56 1994
294.5'2114—dc20 93-40617
CIP

10 9 8 7 6 5 4 3 2

For My Parents,
Mildred and Charles Pintchman

Contents

TWO
Prakṛti, Māyā, and *Śakti*: The Feminine Principle in Philosophical Discourse 61

THREE
The Feminine Principle in Purāṇic Cosmogony and Cosmology 117

FOUR
Concluding Remarks 185

Acknowledgements

Many institutions, colleagues, and friends have helped me both professionally and personally during the years that I put into preparing this book, and I would like to thank them. I am deeply indebted to the Department of Religious Studies at U. C. Santa Barbara for the intellectual, moral and financial support that I was generously accorded throughout my years of graduate study. Gerald J. Larson and Barbara A. Holdrege mentored me during these years, and I wish to express my deep appreciation to them for their guidance and continued support. Special thanks are also due to Professors Walter Capps, Bob Michaelsen, Ruth Majercik, Birger Pearson, and Ninian Smart, who have assisted me both professionally and personally in numerous ways. Michael and Gail Towbes helped fund the fellowship that supported me through graduate school, and Rotary International sponsored my year of study in Banaras, India. I am thankful for their assistance.

I am grateful to Macmillan Press for kindly granting me permission to reproduce portions of my article, "The Ambiguous Female: Conceptions of Female Gender in the Brahmanical Tradition and the Roles of Women in India," in *Ethical and Political Dilemmas of Modern India*, edited by Ninian Smart and Shivesh Thakur (London: Macmillan Press; New York: St. Martin's Press, 1993), pp. 144–159.

I wish to express my gratitude to C. Mackenzie Brown, Thomas Coburn, and two other, anonymous readers for the State University of New York Press who read my manuscript and offered helpful suggestions for improvement. Steve Heim cheerfully debated me on a variety of esoteric subjects and read over sections of the text, as did Paul Muller, David Pinault, Jody Pinault, and Stanley N. Kurtz. I also wish to thank William Eastman, the director of State University of New York Press, Cathleen Collins, who oversaw the production of this book, and Maria denBoer, who copyedited the manuscript.

Numerous individuals have provided me with invaluable personal support and assistance. Several of my colleagues at Loyola University of Chicago have cheered me on, and I am grateful for their help and friendship. I would also like to thank my students, whose appreciation for the traditions that I love has made teaching enjoyable. Don Fredericksen, Gary Laderman, Phillip Lucas, Lloyd Pfleuger, Joseph Schaller, Lola Skarbnik, Terri Smith, Marji Stone, Tracey Weisler, Janet Wilson, and several other friends have stood by me year after year, and I could never thank them enough. Ubu and Shayna have entertained and comforted me on countless occasions. Bill is an endless source of happiness and delight, and my life would not be the same without him or my sisters, Lisa Pintchman and Marcia Andreu, who are and will always be my dearest friends. My grandmother, Pearl Lavender, has been a strong role model for me and the other women in her family, and I have drawn much inspiration from her. Finally, I wish to thank my parents, who have supported me through thick and thin. They are two of the finest people that I have ever met, and it is to them that I have dedicated this book.

Introduction

Setting the Stage

Scholars studying the religions of India have long been intrigued by the important roles that goddesses and goddess worship play in diverse strands of the Hindu tradition. Although the centrality of female divinities and their worship in India is asserted most vigorously in Tantric and non-Brahmanical Śākta traditions, which reject the claims of Brahmanical authority, the various formulations of goddesses and conceptions pertaining to goddesses in Brahmanical Hinduism are nevertheless of particular interest due to the hegemony of Brahmanical discourse and its pan-Indian appeal.

For the last 2500 years, the Indian subcontinent has been peppered with numerous religious and spiritual tendencies, movements, and groups that have often upheld competing beliefs and practices. Divergences among these groups have been dictated by social, political, historical, and geographical factors as well as ideological differences. The diversity of religious life on the subcontinent has led many scholars to reject the notion that there is any real entity that can be referred to generally as "Hinduism" or the "Hindu Tradition." Rather, scholars argue, what exists is essentially a loosely constructed web of disparate religious, social, and political threads that may or may not be related and may or may not intersect. Yet despite this enormous variety, forces that pervade many of the disparate elements constituting Indian spirituality and provide broad and encompassing orientations are nonetheless present in India. One of the most important such unifying forces is the Brahmanical tradition, which is considered by many to be central and authoritative.

Brahmanical Hinduism upholds itself as the orthodox standard against which all other traditions and orientations are measured; those that accept its authority are embraced, whereas those that do not are rejected. The status of the Brahmanical tradition transcends cultural and geographic boundaries and is understood throughout the various regions of the Asian subcontinent. Sanskrit, the language in which the texts of the Brahmanical tradition are recorded, is studied by Brahmins from Kashmir to Kerala, as are the various texts that constitute the Brahmanical Sanskrit canon. The influence of Brahmanical Hinduism is pervasive and touches a wide variety of religious phenomena all over the subcontinent. Given the status of the Brahmanical tradition, it is important to explore the ways in which it represents female divinity in order to understand what is one of the most pervasive and authoritative formulations of the feminine in Hindu India.

The Brahmanical tradition proposes the existence of a Great Goddess. Different texts present this Goddess in different ways and ascribe to her an enormous variety of identities and traits. Despite this diversity, there are nonetheless discernible patterns underlying many of the disparate elements. On the most abstract level the Great Goddess is identified with principles that are impersonal and cosmic, transcending all particularities. In short, she is represented as both materiality, usually designated in post-Vedic texts by the term *prakṛti,* and a principle of energy, usually designated by the term *śakti.* The principles with which the Goddess is equated are embodied on the divine level in different individual goddesses, who are also said to be the multifarious expressions of the Great Goddess, and on the human level in the essential nature of women. The category "feminine" or "femaleness" encompasses all of these levels.

The term *prakṛti* has several meanings, including "original or primary substance," "nature, character," "fundamental form, pattern, standard," "the original producer of the material world, Nature," and "a goddess, the personified will of the Supreme in the creation."[1] Thomas Coburn observes that the best way to circumscribe the primary meanings of the term is to describe it as "a word that has been used to designate the material world in varying relationships to the divine."[2] *Prakṛti* refers to an abstract, cosmic principle of materiality as well as manifest matter itself. The term *śakti,* from √*śak,* "to be able," means "power," "ability," "strength," "energy," and so forth.[3] The term *śakti* often denotes a cosmic principle of energy that is described as the active dimension of Brahman, the Absolute. As a cosmic principle, *śakti* both causes creation to come into existence and sustains it.

The presentation of the Goddess as both *prakṛti* and *śakti* implies that underlying the Brahmanical Hindu understanding of the feminine is some deeper connection between the two. There is in fact yet another principle, *māyā,* that serves to link them. The term *māyā* comes from √*mā,* "to measure," and can denote Brahman's creative yet delusive power or the material form that results from the activation of such a power. As the first, *māyā* is often equated with *śakti*; as the second, with *prakṛti.* Like the other two, *māyā* is often understood to be a cosmic feminine principle, and the use of the term tends to stress the illusory, impermanent, and/or changeable nature of creation in relation to the fully real, eternal, and unchanging nature of the Absolute.

Many scholars have noted the associations between some or all of these principles and female gender in Hindu thought in different contexts. Susan S. Wadley, for example, asserts that in the Hindu tradition "The female is first of all *śakti* (energy/power), the energizing principle of the universe. The female is also *prakṛti* (Nature)—the undifferentiated Matter of the universe."[4] Wadley touches upon the link between *śakti/prakṛti* and female gender in mythico-religious and philosophical contexts, but her main concern is the way in which the association of these principles with femaleness is reflected on the social level in the expectations established for the behavior of women. David Kinsley briefly discusses these three principles in relation to the goddess Kālī in particular and to the Hindu Great Goddess in general. P. G. Layle looks at the way in which these and other terms are used as epithets of the Goddess in the Devī-Bhāgavata Purāṇa, and Coburn does the same with respect to the Devī-Māhātmya.[5] None of these scholars, however, has explored the origins and nature of this symbolic complex across a wide range of scriptures.

The development of these various principles in Brahmanical Hinduism and their association with female gender can be traced historically through the various layers of Brahmanical texts. In the earliest scriptures of the Brahmanical tradition, the Vedas (ca. 1500 B.C.E.–ca. 300 B.C.E.), different goddesses are linked with materiality and/or power but not in a systematic or normative manner. Rather, there are several narrative and speculative strands that adumbrate such associations but do not articulate them clearly or directly. In the post-Vedic era up to the end of the classical period in India (ca. 300 B.C.E.–ca. sixth century C.E.), we find an increasing preoccupation with systematic formulations of beliefs and increasingly standardized articulations of cosmic structures and processes as distinct philosophical schools emerge. In this period, a normative conception of the meaning of the term *prakṛti* emerges within the context of Sāṃkhya philosophy. An understanding of *śakti* as a cosmic power also begins to emerge, although the most elaborate formulation of this notion is fully articulated only in the ninth century and later, when Tantric literature begins to appear.[6] The concept of *māyā*, too, begins to come into its own. These three principles are not identified with any particular goddess or goddesses during this period; in fact, they are not even necessarily conceived to be female in gender.

Toward the end of the classical period and in the post-classical and medieval periods (ca. fifth/sixth century C.E.–sixteenth century C.E.) different conceptual and mythological threads are woven together in the Purāṇas, and there emerges a notion of a Great Goddess, Devī (Goddess) or Mahādevī (Great Goddess), who is consistently identified as *prakṛti*, *śakti*, and *māyā*. The symbolic complex that is formulated in these texts participates in the medieval Brahmanical tendency to synthesize divergent elements and represents the confluence of various streams of thought already present in diverse conceptual and narrative environments. Vedic narrative themes in which different goddesses are associated with matter and energy come together with systematic formulations of the principles *prakṛti*, *śakti*, and *māyā* in later literature, and a new narrative emerges.

This study fills a gap in the available scholarly literature on the Goddess by exploring the rise of the Great Goddess historically in relation to these three cosmic principles and the ways in which the Goddess is formulated and elevated in Brahmanical Hindu discourse from Vedic times to the late Purāṇic period. There are five main purposes of this study: (1) to trace the origins and development within the Vedic-Brahmanical tradition of motifs that associate goddesses with materiality and power; (2) to examine the formulation of the principles *prakṛti*, *śakti*, and *māyā* individually; (3) to illuminate the development of the mutual association of all these elements; (4) to explore the resulting formulation of a Great Goddess characterized specifically as *prakṛti*, *śakti*, and *māyā*; and (5) to probe the cultural implications of this material with respect to gender issues.

We have referred to these principles as "cosmic," but it may not be clear what is meant by this term. *Prakṛti*, *śakti*, and *māyā* are often portrayed as cosmological principles, that is, structures inherent within creation. But they are also essentially cosmogonic, and they play key roles in the many accounts of creation found throughout the various scriptures constituting the Brahmanical Sanskrit canon.[7] One finds some of the richest descriptions of the nature and function of *prakṛti, śakti,* and *māyā* in the context of these creation accounts. It is in this context also that we often see the assimilation of these principles to one or more goddesses. Apart from the cosmogonic accounts, descriptions of cosmology that mention these principles usually offer rather thin descriptions of their nature and often appear to assume that their cosmogonic functions are understood. This study, then, will focus somewhat heavily on cosmogonies not by design but simply because much of the relevant data is found in the accounts of creation that appear throughout the various texts that constitute the Brahmanical canon.

Apart from questions of data, however, detailing the mechanisms of cosmogony and the resulting cosmology appears to be one of the central concerns of the tradition. Much attention is given to these topics, and one finds a great number and variety of cosmogonic hypotheses and narrative accounts across a broad range of different Brahmanical philosophical and mythological texts. One of the primary reasons for this emphasis on reflection about cosmic processes may be that cosmogony and cosmology in and of themselves are rich and meaningful categories. Cosmogonies describe fundamental categories and forces that are assumed to shape creation; these then help determine the essential nature of the universe, its structure, and the laws that govern it. In proposing to articulate truths about the world, descriptions of cosmogony and cosmology detail the confines within which it is assumed that humans as well as other kinds of beings must function. The centrality of our three principles and the Goddess with whom they are identified in descriptions of cosmogony and cosmology indicates their fundamental importance in Brahmanical Hindu conceptions about reality.

Since the symbolic complex that this study explores is largely related to issues of cosmogony and cosmology, we will focus only on those aspects and functions of the Great Goddess that are most clearly and directly related to such issues. Some may object that the present study does not pay enough attention to the Goddess's important soteriological functions. The Goddess's role as the dispeller of illusion who helps one achieve liberation (*mokṣa*) is indeed fundamental to her identity. Yet this role is essentially epistemological, for in such contexts the Goddess's salvific power is related to her identity with spiritual knowledge (*vidyā*) or her ability to grant or lead one to such knowledge. The principles with which this study is concerned, on the other hand, are not primarily epistemological but are, generally speaking, ontological; that is, they are structures that are portrayed as structures of being, not knowing. This study will therefore address the soteriological functions of the Goddess only when they are relevant to the project at hand.

It is also important to note that all three of the terms that we will explore—*prakṛti*, *śakti*, and *māyā*—are grammatically feminine terms. One might argue, therefore, that the association of these principles with female gender rather than male gender is rooted in their linguistic valence. It is evident, however, that no matter what the origin of the association of these principles with femaleness, they are identified clearly in the Purāṇas as feminine not only in their grammatical values but in their very essences. The gender-specific nature of these principles is important, for it may have implications with respect to the treatment of women in Indian society, as we shall see.

Textual Issues

Underlying the structure of this study are also several theoretical and historical presuppositions regarding the nature of Brahmanical scripture in the Indian environment that inform not only the approach that is used but also the formulation of the central problem itself. The Brahmanical Hindu tradition makes a distinction between texts that are considered orthodox (*āstika*), and are thus accepted as scripture by the Brahmanical tradition, and those that are considered heterodox (*nāstika*). The orthodox Brahmanical tradition includes the Vedic texts, Dharma-Śāstras (legal codes), epics (Mahābhārata and Rāmāyaṇa), Darśanas (philosophical systems), and Purāṇas (mythological compilations). As the Dharma-Śāstras treat mainly legal and social matters and thus contain little cosmogonic or cosmological material, the present study does not treat them in great detail. The Rāmāyaṇa, one of the two great epics of ancient India, also contains little material relevant to the subject at hand.[8]

The Vedas represent the earliest and most symbolically important layer of the orthodox Brahmanical canon. There are four main classes or genres of Vedic literature that emerge in more or less chronological order: Saṃhitās (ca. 1500–800 B.C.E.), Brāhmaṇas (ca. 1100–800 B.C.E.), Āraṇyakas (ca. 1100–800 B.C.E.), and Upaniṣads (ca. 800–300 B.C.E.). There are four Saṃhitās—Ṛg, Yajur, Sāma, and Atharva—each of which is associated with a different school. The many different Brāhmaṇas, Āraṇyakas, and Upaniṣads are all based on one of the four schools of the Saṃhitās. The term "Veda" in its most limited sense designates the four Vedic Saṃhitās or the four Saṃhitās along with the Brāhmaṇas, Āraṇyakas, and Upaniṣads associated with them.

The Vedic Saṃhitās are largely Aryan in origin, and much of their content was probably brought into India by invading Indo-European tribes during the middle of the second millennium B.C.E. Each of the four Vedic Saṃhitās has contents and concerns that differ from those of the other Saṃhitās. The Ṛg-Veda Saṃhitā is a collection of hymns (*ṛc*s) to different gods and goddesses and contains a great deal of important mythological material. The Sāma-Veda Saṃhitā, which is a collection of chants (*sāman*s), is based largely on Ṛg-Vedic materials. The Yajur-Veda Saṃhitā is composed mainly of prayers and sacrificial formulas (*yajus*es) and has been handed down in two basic forms, black (*kṛṣṇa*) and white (*śukla*). The black Yajur-Veda Saṃhitā has four different recensions, the most important of which is the Taittirīya Saṃhitā. All of the recensions of the black Yajur-Veda contain explanations and discussions of the sacrificial rites to which the different formulas belong, whereas the white Yajur-Veda Saṃhitā does not. Finally, the Atharva-Veda Saṃhitā contains mostly charms and spells.[9] Later genres of Vedic literature also have distinct orientations. The many different Brāhmaṇas largely provide the instructions for Vedic sacrifice, explain its meaning, and reflect on its larger significance. The Āraṇyakas focus on the more esoteric significance of Vedic ritual. Finally, the Upaniṣads develop further the reflective tendencies of the Brāhmaṇas and Āraṇyakas and give them independent expression apart from ritual concerns.

Although the earliest portions of the Vedas appear to be relatively free from the influence of the indigenous Indian cultures, the impact of these cultures becomes increasingly evident in the later portions of the Vedas. Thus, by the time of the Upaniṣads, the influence on the Aryan tradition of various ascetic and meditative groups generally held by most scholars to be indigenous to India—as well as the contemplative and philosophical orientations of these groups—is quite apparent. As the Aryan and non-Aryan strands of the tradition continue to intermingle during the post-Vedic period, different philosophical systems come to be formulated systematically. Those that are welcomed by the orthodox tradition accept the validity and authority of the Vedas. Eventually, six different systems emerge: Nyāya, Vaiśeṣika, Pūrva-Mīmāṃsā, Vedānta, Sāṃkhya, and Yoga. While the philosophical systems express the tradition's reflective tendencies in the post-Vedic period, its narrative dimensions are given expression in the epics (ca. 400 B.C.E.–400 C.E.) and Purāṇas (ca. 200–300 C.E. and later).

There is a remarkable amount of borrowing and sharing of elements in the post-Vedic Brahmanical tradition, both from genre to genre and from period to period. Thus we find, for example, long discourses in the epics and Purāṇas that pertain to the authority of the Vedic tradition or others that are clearly influenced by the concerns of various Brahmanical philosophical schools. There are at least two factors that contribute to this kind of phenomenon. First, canonical texts recorded in written form in later centuries borrowed heavily from their predecessors. Second, what eventually came to be recorded in written documents was developed, elaborated, and maintained in a strictly oral medium for many centuries before being committed to writing.[10]

Both the Vedas and post-Vedic Brahmanical texts were originally oral, not written. With respect to the Vedas, writing was felt to be polluting and was thus an improper medium for the transmission of such sacred scriptures. Yet the Vedas represent a fixed canon and are meant to be maintained in a strictly unaltered form. The orality of the Vedic tradition therefore does not lend itself to any kind of variation or recombination. The strictness with which the exact structure of the Vedas is meant to be preserved is due at least in part to the efficacy attributed to the sound-values of the Vedas; the sounds themselves are felt to be constitutive of reality, and precise recitation of these sounds contributes to the maintenance of the existing cosmic order. Any alteration in the recitation of the Vedic utterances would therefore have cosmic ramifications.[11] Post-Vedic texts, like the Vedas, were also originally oral, yet the post-Vedic tradition is alterable and allows for human elaboration.[12] It appears that a great deal of what was eventually systematized and recorded in post-Vedic Brahmanical documents thus found its way into diverse environments in a variety of forms.

The influence of such borrowing and sharing of elements is most conspicuous in the Purāṇas, which draw in materials from a wide variety of systems and ages. C. Mackenzie

Brown has noted that the Purāṇas are essentially assimilative texts to which "much has been added over the millennia, and relatively little has been lost":[13]

> These Purāṇic works are rooted in an ancient oral bardic and priestly culture, and even when committed to writing, they continued to interact with the ongoing oral traditions. They were not static texts but remained fluid, continuously expanding, incorporating an ever-increasing body of traditional lore. They thus came to include a vast variety of materials from widely different ages.[14]

The Purāṇas also borrow heavily from one another, and entire sections of one are sometimes found in another in identical or almost identical form. Yet through it all, the Purāṇas are careful not to lose contact with the essential values of the Vedic-Brahmanical tradition. As Brown also notes, the Purāṇas are seen not as innovations of the tradition but as elucidations and interpretations of the Vedas. It is their adherence to the ancient traditions that makes them religiously authoritative, since "truth, in the Hindu tradition, is not something so much to be newly discovered as to be recovered."[15]

In exploring the history and formation of the canon in the Brahmanical tradition, it is helpful to evoke what many contemporary scholars call "intertextuality," if we understand the term "text" in a broad sense to include both the oral and written dimensions of Brahmanical scripture. Intertextuality indicates that a given text produced in a given culture is always grounded in a textual tradition of which it is aware and of which it is itself a self-conscious product. In other words, texts are highly self-referential and are created largely in response to other texts.

> The text is not an autonomous or unified object, but a set of relations with other texts. Its system of language, its grammar, its lexicon, drag along numerous bits and

> pieces—traces—of history. . . . The "genealogy" of the text is necessarily an incomplete network of conscious and unconscious borrowed fragments. Manifested, tradition is a mess. Every text is an intertext.[16]

The term "intertextuality" is often used to describe the repetition from text to text of unarticulated yet formative rules and regulations that determine the general nature of language and textuality in a given tradition. Yet intertextuality also includes the self-conscious adaptation of literary structures and devices found in one text or textual tradition by another text or tradition. In this sense, the notion of intertextuality is helpful in describing the continuity of certain narrative structures and ideas from text to text and in a sense helps explain how tracing the history of an idea is even possible. Such notions are especially applicable to scripture in the orthodox Brahmanical tradition, for the texts constituting the Brahmanical canon are heavily self-referential.[17]

This intertextual emphasis reflects in part the importance of scripture as a symbol of authority in Brahmanism. The Brahmanical tradition defines itself in relation to a body of sacred, orally transmitted texts, the Vedas—or, collectively, the Veda—which are seen to be the unquestionable foundation of the scriptural tradition. Yet, as a number of scholars have emphasized in recent years, the status of the Veda as a symbol of authority has less to do with its contents than one might suspect. J. C. Heesterman, for example, notes that "the high prestige of the Vedas is paralleled by an equally high disregard for its contents."[18] Brian K. Smith also notes the symbolic function of the Veda:

> The great paradox of Hinduism . . . is that although the religion is inextricably tied to the legitimizing authority of the Veda, in post-Vedic times the subject matter of the Veda was and is largely unknown by those who define themselves in relation to it. Its contents

> (almost entirely concerning the meaning and performance of sacrificial rituals that Hindus do not perform) are at best reworked (being for example, reconstituted into ritual formulas or mantras for use in Hindu ceremonies), and in many cases appear to be totally irrelevant for Hindu doctrine and practice. . . . Although it appears to be the case that Hindus do acknowledge the absolute authority of the Veda for legitimizing post-Vedic Hindu beliefs and practices, the relationship to the Veda often seems to be, as Renou writes, like "a simple 'raising of the hat' in passing to an idol by which one no longer intends to be encumbered later on."[19]

The authoritative status of the Veda is also reflected in Brahmanical Hinduism's traditional designation of the Veda as *śruti*, "that which is heard," or revelation, as opposed to the rest of Brahmanical scripture, which falls under the category of *smṛti*, "that which is remembered," or tradition. *Śruti* is affirmed as having a transcendental, divine, non-human origin, whereas *smṛti* texts can be attributed to personal authorship.[20] Some would claim that, as revelation, the Veda is not only scripture but represents the concrete expression of the subtle structures of creation. It is said that the sound-vibrations of creation were seen and heard by ancient seers called *ṛṣis* who then sent forth these sounds in their own speech; these sounds became the words of the Vedas. In a recent study, Barbara Holdrege has explored these mechanisms and the larger issues surrounding the cosmological status of the Veda as a transcendent reality represented as eternal, uncreated knowledge that is the essence of ultimate reality and the source and foundation of creation.[21]

The importance of Veda as a symbol of authority in Brahmanical Hinduism extends not only to the actual Vedic scriptures themselves but also to the entire Brahmanical tradition of scripture. Although the Vedas enjoy special status as that in reference to which the Brahmanical tradition defines itself, the Veda becomes a symbol under which the entire orthodox canon can be subsumed. The authority of any text increases when it relates itself to the Vedic tradition. Holdrege notes four ways in which post-Vedic texts assimilate themselves to the Veda and thus participate in its authoritative status: (1) by explicitly claiming the status of Veda, as do the epics and some of the Purāṇas, which call themselves the fifth Veda; (2) by establishing a genealogy that links the teachings of the given text to the Veda; (3) by claiming that the text's teachings derive from lost Vedic texts; or (4) by otherwise conforming to the paradigm of Veda.[22]

It should be emphasized that although the Veda's value as a symbol irrespective of content plays an important role in the tradition, nevertheless its authority also operates to some extent on the level of content as well. Narrative structures and teachings found not only in the Vedas themselves but also in post-Vedic Brahmanical texts are granted authority by virtue of being part of the Vedic tradition; when such structures are then absorbed into subsequently recorded scriptures, they help lend the newer texts an air of authority as well. So, for example, the essential teachings of the orthodox philosophical schools, which accept the authority of the Vedas and thus present themselves as a continuation of the Vedic tradition, also enjoy authoritative status. Because of their status, these teachings are simply accepted as valid and are then absorbed into later Brahmanical discourse without ever being seriously called into question. Both concepts and narratives found in earlier layers of Brahmanical scripture are in fact frequently adopted by later Brahmanical scriptures. The ability of a particular teaching or narrative to help convey authority simply by virtue of its inclusion in a previously existing authoritative text is probably one of the primary motivating factors behind such borrowings and thus may help contribute to the Vedic-Brahmanical tradition's intertextual richness.

One must also stress the role in intertextual discourse of not only texts, both oral and written, but also the transmitters of texts. Although we know very little about authorship with respect to Brahmanical scriptures, it is apparent that this genre is more or less the exclusive product of Brahmins who were educated in the tradition of Brahmanical Sanskrit literature. The epics and Purāṇas contain many strands that are non-Brahmanical in origin, but these strands appear to have been appropriated by Brahmins and reworked to conform at least to some extent to Brahmanical values. The traditional system of Brahmanical education entails the apprenticeship of a Brahmin student to his Brahmin teacher, who educates him in the Brahmanical Sanskrit tradition. In such a context, knowledge of the tradition is the primary sign of scholarly authority. The self-enclosed, elitist system of Sanskritic learning combined with the emphasis on memorizing traditional texts probably reinforces the tendency within Brahmanical Hinduism to invoke earlier narrative structures in subsequent narrations.

Given this general framework, it is not surprising that the presentation of the particular configuration surrounding conceptions of a single Great Goddess that ultimately emerges in the Purāṇas draws heavily from mythic and philosophical themes found in earlier Brahmanical texts, and its roots can be traced back to Vedic materials. Paradigmatic narrative and conceptual structures, especially with respect to cosmogony, are maintained. This conservative aspect of the development of the Goddess represents the attempt to preserve essential tenets of Brahmanical orthodoxy by utilizing elements that are already present in and accepted by the core tradition.

Despite strong continuities, however, there are also important discontinuities that cannot be ignored. By the time of the Purāṇas, the influence of non-Brahmanical elements on Brahmanical orthodoxy is highly evident, and outside elements are absorbed more and more into the core tradition. The impulse to revere goddesses very highly, for example, seems to represent primarily an originally non-Brahmanical impulse whose influence becomes increasingly apparent in the Purāṇas. Devotion to a personal god, which is of rather little importance in the Vedic and philosophical traditions, also becomes much more important during the Purāṇic period and is thus absorbed into Brahmanical values. The conservative tendency to retain orthodox narrative and philosophical structures is challenged by a countervailing tendency to absorb nonorthodox elements into Brahmanical orthodoxy. The older formulations that are incorporated into the Purāṇic texts are then greatly elaborated or varied to conform to the orientation of the new textual environment.

Summary of the Book

Taking into account these various factors, this study argues that the Great Goddess, like other gods and goddesses of the Hindu pantheon, develops over time as a result of the blending of Brahmanical and non-Brahmanical religious tendencies and divinities. Yet the essential identity of the Great Goddess as "Great" appears to be constructed at least initially largely in and by the Brahmanical tradition, which provides the context for her definition. The conflation of mythological and philosophical categories that we find in the Purāṇas provides the framework for the equation of goddesses with principles. Many of the goddesses and stories are not originally Vedic-Brahmanical, but the framework and the principles are both taken straight from the Vedas and the orthodox Brahmanical philosophical systems. The various aspects of the Goddess's identity are then placed in a logical cosmogonic sequence and are viewed as different levels of manifestation of a single, inherently female cosmogonic power. The result is the postulation of a unique, all-encompassing principle that is expressed on different levels of creation in diverse ways but that can be understood theistically as a Great Goddess no matter what the sectarian allegiance of the given text. One might even argue that the identity of the Great Goddess as a cosmogonic principle manifest in stages as *śakti, māyā,* and *prakṛti* is in fact not only her defining characteristic, but also the sine qua non of her very existence. It is only through the synthesis of philosophical and mythological cosmogonic categories and structures that diverse notions of female divinity become combined and the notion of a single Great Goddess emerges.

The rise of the Great Goddess in the Brahmanical tradition is probably tied to issues of Brahmanical hegemony. In order to maintain its status and acceptance in and by society at large, the Brahmanical tradition had to incorporate elements from the popular traditions. In the case of the Great Goddess, although the impulse to elevate female divinities to supreme status probably originates primarily from non-orthodox, autochthonous religious systems, as other scholars have argued, the mechanisms by which the feminine principle is elevated in orthodox literature are borrowed from the orthodox tradition itself. Thus Brahmanical orthodoxy is able to maintain its essential authority while adapting itself to suit the changing religious orientation of the population at large.

The first two chapters of this study clarify the historical background from which the relevant associations emerge. Chapter one explores the mythology of the Vedas, in which different goddesses are associated with cosmogonic and cosmological notions of power and materiality, although such associations are not articulated formally. Chapter two turns to the early philosophical schools and explores the relevant philosophical conceptions with respect to systematic formulations of cosmogony and cosmology. This chapter also explores some of the ways in which relevant philosophical and mythological themes come together in certain environments.

The third chapter of this study focuses on the Purāṇas. In the Purāṇas, different goddesses come to be identified with the cosmogonic and cosmological principles *prakṛti, śakti,* and *māyā.* This chapter examines diverse accounts of creation in several different Purāṇas and details both the essential cosmogonic patterns that are articulated and the variable elements that are introduced according to the unique perspective of the individual texts. The notion of a Great Goddess who is *prakṛti/śakti/māyā* emerges in these materials as a synthesis of concepts already present in the different strands of the tradition explored in the first two chapters.

The conclusion summarizes the observations made in this study before exploring the larger implications of the material as a whole and assessing in particular some of the historical, political, and interpretive issues that emerge from the data. Finally, we turn to the social implications of the observations made in this study and explore how structures pertaining to the Goddess may help shape conceptions of female gender, the treatment of women in Hindu society, and the roles that women are assigned. The conclusion argues that the formulation of the Great Goddess may well have implications with respect to notions about gender and gender roles in Hindu society. In Brahmanical Hinduism, femaleness as a category is defined at least in part according to the principles embodied in the Goddess. Although principles in and of themselves are essentially neutral, one can interpret them in various ways. In the Brahmanical tradition, there is a strong tendency to portray *prakṛti, śakti,* and *māyā* on one level as positive and creative yet at the same time inherently ambiguous and potentially dangerous. Therefore, they must be monitored and controlled so that they manifest their positive tendencies rather than their negative ones. Such representations may in fact help support social practices that restrict the choices women, who embody *prakṛti, śakti,* and *māyā,* have.

CHAPTER ONE

The Feminine Principle in the Vedas

Cosmogony, Cosmology, and Goddesses in the Vedas

Our investigation begins with the Vedas. In their portrayals of goddesses, many Vedic passages articulate motifs that help lay the foundation for later formulations of the Great Goddess as *prakṛti* and *śakti.* The idea of an abstract female principle or principles, although not fully articulated, begins to take form in these texts, particularly in Vedic accounts of cosmogony.

In the Vedas, many goddesses are described as playing a role in the process of creation and therefore have cosmogonic significance. There are a variety of myths in the Vedas that are explicitly cosmogonic or that contain cosmogonic elements, and the roles of individual female divinities and principles in the process of creation differ in the individual accounts. In this regard, it is helpful to distinguish between different phases in the unfolding of creation, and different types of creative principles. Regarding the first point, F. B. J. Kuiper has suggested that there are essentially two different stages in Vedic cosmogony: (1) the postulation of an undivided unity that represents the primordial state of the cosmos and in which there is no fixed or stable point of support, followed by (2) the differentiation of the originally undifferentiated primordial unity and the division of the worlds.[1] In the first stage, the cosmos exists in an unmanifest, subtle, potential state; it is only through some kind of transformative action that this primal unity is impelled into manifestation and differentiation (the second stage). The transition from the first to the second phase of creation requires some sort of catalyst capable of effecting a transformation. W. Norman Brown distinguishes between an animate, psychical, or willful being who is an active agent in creation, and an inanimate, material, insentient, nonpsychical, and nonwillful substance that can be identified as the object upon which the first being acts.[2] These two principles represent in philosophical terms an efficient and a material cause. It is often, although not always, through the agency of an active, willful being that the transformation from the first to the second stage occurs. In our analysis we will distinguish between stages and types of causal principles when referring to the role of female divinities in creation.

One must also be careful to distinguish between the cosmogonic roles of certain Vedic goddesses and their cosmological significance. Many passages ascribe to certain goddesses an active role in the process of creation; others assimilate goddesses to general structures inherent within the created universe either in conjunction with or apart from descriptions of cosmogonic events. With respect to both cosmogony and cosmology, some goddesses seem to be associated largely with materiality, the "stuff" of creation, whereas others are associated more with cosmic energy, the "life force" that generates the creative process and/or enlivens creation. The lines are often blurred, however, and many goddesses are affiliated with both. Such associations imbue these divinities with meaning beyond their individual identities and personalities.

It is also helpful in this regard to differentiate between these goddesses' concrete/personal identities and their abstract/impersonal significances. Just as there are different levels of the cosmogonic process and different kinds of principles of creation, so too there are distinct levels of manifestation of divinity. These can be chronological, conceptual, or both. Of the Vedic goddesses that we will examine, each has a personal identity, yet each also has or acquires an impersonal level of meaning that transcends the individuality of that particular goddess. In fact, although the various Vedic goddesses that we will discuss have distinct personalities and attributes, their individual identities are actually quite fluid. In the Saṃhitās, certain notable characteristics, both personal and impersonal, are consistently "cross-identified," that is, associated with more than one goddess. The tendency toward cross-identification is further accentuated in the Brāhmaṇas and the Upaniṣads, where different goddesses who are depicted in the Saṃhitās as sharing traits and functions come to be explicitly equated with one another.

All of these tendencies—the association of goddesses with cosmogonic processes and cosmological structures, the attribution of abstract/impersonal levels of meaning to individual goddesses, and the cross-identification of traits and identities—represent seeds of the Great Goddess idea, seeds that will then sprout and develop in later scriptures. As we shall see, post-Vedic materials pick up and elaborate on these tendencies, and they become major ingredients in later formulations of the Goddess. Thus although there is no systematically articulated theology of a single Great Goddess in the Vedas, there are some important factors at work that influence the way in which the Great Goddess eventually comes to be formulated.[3]

In order to clarify the lines of continuity between the characteristics of various Vedic goddesses and those of *prakṛti* and *śakti* as these concepts are developed later in the tradition, we will explore in each layer of the Vedic texts some of the characteristics of six Vedic goddesses and goddess groups: the waters (*ap*), the goddess earth (Pṛthivī/Bhūmi), Aditi, Virāj, Vāc (and Sarasvatī, with whom she is identified), and Śacī/Indrāṇī. By examining the Vedic texts layer by layer, one can trace the development of certain aspects of these goddesses' identities and traits. The deities that we will examine can be divided into two groups: those whose fundamental nature is primarily connected with materiality (*ap*, Pṛthivī, and Aditi), and those whose nature is more connected with the idea of a principle of energy (Virāj, Vāc, and Śacī/Indrāṇī). We will begin our analysis of each group with the most abstract member, namely, the waters (*ap*) in the first group and Virāj in the second, and take each goddess or group of goddesses into account, exploring both the concrete, explicit nature of the deity according to the text, including all levels of expression of that deity, and the symbolic, implicit significance of each divinity. We do not wish to read anything "into" the text from outside it; our aim is rather to read "with" the text but also beyond it, attempting to interpret certain mythological constructs and suggest their possible significances in a larger context.

Saṃhitās

THE WATERS

In the Vedas, there appear to be two different levels of manifestation of the goddesses collectively referred to as the waters. On one level, the waters are concrete and are represented in personal terms as goddesses. At this level, they appear in three different forms: (1) atmospheric, where the waters are generally identified as celestial and are associated with natural phenomena like clouds and rain; (2) subterranean, flowing under the earth's surface; or (3) elemental, where the waters are concretely manifest, often as the water contained in rivers and streams or as the water employed by the Vedic priests in sacrifice. On another level, the waters are described as abstract and impersonal. They function at this level as the primordial, unmanifest foundation of physical creation. In this capacity, the waters serve as either the medium in which creation gestates or the subtle material matrix from which gross creation is derived. All of these categories represent different aspects or manifestations of the waters. The same naming term (*ap*) is generally used in all cases except for the most abstract level of demarcation, where the terms *ambhas*, *salila*, and *samudra* are sometimes used to denote the function of the primordial waters as the material matrix of creation. Only the term *ap* is feminine. *Ambhas* and *salila* are neuter nouns and *samudra* is masculine, suggesting that the waters thus described shed their specifically feminine identification.

As personal deities with qualities, the waters (*ap*) are depicted primarily as healing, purifying, life-giving, life-affirming, abundant, maternal goddesses, manifest as atmospheric, terrestrial, sacrificial, or in some other way tangibly liquid water. They are beneficent and are invoked often for aid, protection, strength, healing, or removal of impurity;[4] they are revered also as divine and immortal (*amṛta*).[5] In Ṛg-Veda 1.23.18–19 the waters are described as the source of medicinal elixir:

> I call the waters (*ap*), goddesses (*devī*), where our cows drink: may oblations be given to the streams.
> Elixir (*amṛta*) is in the waters: healing balms are in the waters; gods, be swift to praise (them).[6]

In Ṛg-Veda 10.17.10 they are invoked as mothers who are the source of purification:

> May the waters (*ap*), mothers (*mātṛ*), purify us; clarifiers of ghee, may they clean us with ghee, for the goddesses (*devī*) carry off all impurity: So I arise from them purified and bright.

Ṛg-Veda 10.9.1–6 also praises and invokes many of their auspicious qualities, such as their protective, nourishing, and healing capacities:

> These waters, indeed, are refreshing: help us to look upon strength and great joy.
> Like loving mothers (*mātṛ*), give us here (a portion) of your most auspicious fluid. . . . Oh waters, you refresh and rejuvenate us.
> May the waters, goddesses, be for our happiness and protection, and for drinking. May they pour forth happiness and welfare.
> I beg the waters, sovereigns ruling over wealth and human beings, for healing balm (*bheṣaja*).
> Soma told me that within the waters are all healing balms and Agni, (who is) benevolent to all.

Other passages lauding the waters also praise their divine, maternal aspects.[7]

The reference to Agni-in-the-waters in Ṛg-Veda 10.9.6 hints at the waters' motherly role. They are referred to as the mothers of Agni,[8] who is frequently called the "Son of Waters," or as mothers of Savitṛ,[9] and they are described along with Aditi and the earth as the source of all the gods.[10] Yet they are also assigned a more universal parental role as the "very motherly ones of all that stands and moves" or "mothers of the world" and sovereigns who have supreme control over human beings (above).[11] Besides their identity as goddesses or the maternal source of individual divinities, they are thus also lauded collectively as the mothers of all that exists.

The waters are also described in terms that hint at a more abstract level of functioning in cosmogony. The cosmogonic role of the waters has been noted by many scholars, including Kuiper, who associates the primeval waters with the first stage of Vedic cosmogony described above.[12] In many passages of the Saṃhitās, the waters assume the role of an undifferentiated, primordial matrix that serves as the support of and potential for material formation. This matrix is portrayed as womb-like, emphasizing the maternal, nurturing, motherly aspect of the waters, and usually represents the unmanifest, abstract, subtle stage of creation that is the potential state of the material, manifest cosmos. In this capacity, the waters also function as the material cause of creation.

The waters are the maternal medium in which either the gods or manifest creation itself is said to gestate until it is ready to be born. In Ṛg-Veda 10.82.5–6, for example, the waters are described as the primordial matrix receiving the embryo/germ (*garbha*) in which all the gods are gathered at the dawn of creation:[13]

> That which is beyond heaven, beyond this earth, beyond the gods and *asuras*—what first embryo/germ, wherein all the gods beheld each other,[14] did the waters (*ap*) hold?
> The waters held that very first embryo/germ where all the gods came together, that one in which all worlds abide, placed on the navel of the Unborn.[15]

Here, the waters function as a kind of primordial womb in which the gods develop and from which they arise. This motif is also found in Ṛg-Veda 10.121.7–8, where the waters are the matrix that contains the universal *garbha*; they give birth to Agni, and simultaneously the one "life-breath" (*asu*) of the gods (probably the creator Prajāpati) is produced:

> Indeed, when the great waters (*ap*) came, bearing the universe as an embryo/germ, producing Agni, then arose the gods' one life breath . . . who with might surveyed the waters containing power (*dakṣa*) and producing sacrifice.

A similar role is described in Atharva-Veda 4.2, a variant on Ṛg-Veda 10.121:

> The waters (*ap*), producing an offspring, set into motion in the beginning an embryo/germ (*garbha*).[16]

In these instances, the role of the waters is clearly feminine, for the waters act as the womb that bears creation in its potential form. The maternal nature of this role is underscored by the fact that in all these cases a feminine term (*ap*) is used to designate the waters.

In other passages, the role of the waters in the dawn of creation is somewhat different. In Ṛg-Veda 10.129.1–3, for example, the cosmic, primeval waters seem to act less as a womb and more as a kind of primal soup:

> There was not nonexistence (*asat*) nor existence (*sat*) then: there was not air nor the heaven that is beyond. What did it cover up? where? In whose protection? Was water (*ambhas*) there, unfathomable, profound?
> There was not death nor immortality then. There was not a beacon of night or day. That One, having no wind, breathed by its own power. Other than that, there was not anything beyond.
> In the beginning, darkness was hidden by darkness. All this was water (*salila*), indistinguishable.

This hymn is extremely obscure, and it is difficult to understand clearly the relationships among the various elements in the text. Nevertheless, the waters are cited as existing before differentiated creation, when everything is water (10.129.3). At this time, there is only darkness hidden by darkness, indistinguishable (10.129.3); there is not yet even any distinction between *sat* and *asat* (10.129.1). The relation between the waters and "That One" (*tad ekam*) mentioned in verses two and three is an enigma. It may be that *tad ekam* emerges from the waters, but the connection is not clearly articulated. The waters are identified in this hymn as being present before the appearance of light and differentiated form but, although appearing to be some kind of primordial material principle, are not explicitly identified as the source itself of any further material creation. Whether or not the waters are manifest or unmanifest is also not articulated. The enigmatic nature of the role of the waters reflects the enigmatic nature of the hymn, which presents the riddle of creation but does not attempt to solve it, preferring to pose questions without supplying answers.

Ṛg-Veda 10.129 does not use the term *ap*, preferring the terms *ambhas* (10.129.1) and *salila* (10.129.3), both neuter nouns. Different terms used to designate the waters seem to indicate not different entities but rather different aspects of the same general principle. In Ṛg-Veda 7.49.1, for example, *ap*, *salila*, and *samudra* are different but related manifestations of the waters:

> From the middle of the water (*salila*), the waters (*ap*), goddesses (*devī*), having the ocean as their chief (*samudrajyeṣṭha*), flow cleansing, restless.

Elsewhere, it is said that the streams and waters (*ap*) flow into the ocean (*samudra*). So, for example, in Ṛg-Veda 1.32.2, the waters released by Indra in his battle with Vṛtra are described as coming quickly down to the ocean.

In Ṛg-Veda 10.129, then, the use of neuter terms seems to indicate that in this context the waters are conceived of not as feminine entities but as principles devoid of gender. The use of gender-neutral terminology frustrates attempts toward personification and thus would make sense in this most abstract of hymns that emphasizes the enigmatic, inscrutable, abstruse nature of creation. Here, as in the cosmogonic hymns mentioned above, the waters are described as a kind of primordial matrix present at the undifferentiated phase of creation.

Although in Ṛg-Veda 10.129 the precise position of the waters in the unfolding of the cosmogonic drama is unclear, in Ṛg-Veda 10.190 they seem to appear at the crucial transitional phase between the primordial stage of creation and the emergence of differentiated forms:

> Order (*ṛta*) and truth (*satya*) were born from inflamed heat (*tapas*).

> From that arose night; from that (arose) the foaming ocean (*samudra*).
> From that foaming ocean was born the year, arranger of days and nights, Lord over all that blinks.
> Dhātṛ [the creator/ordainer] arranged in succession the sun and moon, heaven and earth, the midregions and light.

In this hymn, heat (*tapas*) is said to generate order (*ṛta*) and truth (*satya*), both of which are abstract principles, and night (*rātri*). This represents Kuiper's first phase—the undifferentiated, primordial state of creation. Following this, heat then generates the cosmic waters in the form of an ocean (*samudra*). From these waters is born the year, which then arranges time into days and nights and becomes the ruler over "all that blinks," that is, all living creatures. This leads to the creation of the sun, moon, heaven, earth, midregions, and light by Dhātṛ, the creator or ordainer. The first element of differentiated creation, time, is produced directly from the waters, followed by the proper arrangement of the cosmos effected by Dhātṛ, who is the efficient cause of the manifest, ordered universe.

A similar position at the dawn of differentiated creation is attributed to the waters in the Taittirīya Saṃhitā, where the waters act as a kind of primal matter. They are transformed into earth through the mediation of fire:

> In the beginning, this was the waters (*ap*), water (*salila*); He, Prajāpati, becoming wind, hovered (√*lī*) on a lotus leaf. He found no support. He saw that nest (*kulāya*) of the waters (*ap*); he piled fire (*agni*) on it; that became this (*iyam,* namely, the earth). Then indeed he stood firm.[17]

The primordial state of the undifferentiated cosmos is represented as formless water, which is the material matrix present at the dawn of creation, the unmanifest potential of the cosmos that must be disturbed in some way in order for differentiated creation to come about. When the waters are transformed, they become the earth. This theme is echoed in Taittirīya Saṃhitā 7.1.5.1:

> In the beginning, this was the waters (*ap*), water (*salila*). Prajāpati, becoming wind, moved in it. He saw her; becoming a boar, he seized her. Becoming Viśvakarman, he rubbed (*vi* √*mṛj*) her. She extended (√*prath*); she became the earth (*pṛthivī*); hence the earthness of earth. Prajāpati made effort in her. He created the gods, Vasus, Rudras, and Ādityas.

In this version, the waters are identified again not only as a kind of primal matter, but also as the source of the manifest earth from which Prajāpati then furthers his creation. The waters are the original, primordial "stuff" from which other "stuff" is created. The waters are also affirmed as the basis of the manifest world in Taittirīya Saṃhitā 2.1.5.4:

> The plants (*oṣadhi*) are the waters (*ap*), man is what is not; the waters indeed give him existence (*sat*) from nonexistence (*asat*); therefore they say, both he who knows thus and he who does not, the waters, indeed, give existence from nonexistence.

As cosmogonic principles or as personal deities the waters are also attributed special powers, especially healing and procreative powers, and are invoked for strength.[18] In Ṛg-Veda 10.121 (above), the waters are said to contain *dakṣa*, meaning "energy," "strength," or "power," which is also personified and associated with the goddess Aditi. Even Agni is said to have absorbed his powers (*svadhā*) from the waters when he dwelt in their lap.[19] Although one cannot draw any definite conclusions about the nature of the capabilities attributed to the waters in the Saṃhitās, it is important to note that the waters are conceived to be imbued with some sort of inherent abilities or powers that are mentioned in passing but not developed.

EARTH

In the Saṃhitās, the goddess earth, Pṛthivī or Bhūmi, is less abstract than the waters. There appear to be three different aspects of Pṛthivī's nature in the Saṃhitās: (1) the physical earth that sustains living creatures and upon which we live; (2) the universal mother of physical creation; and (3) manifest matter itself that is formed in the cosmogonic process and, like the waters, is part of the narrative of creation. This last aspect is elaborated only in the Yajur-Veda Saṃhitā and thus appears to have been developed later than the other two.

Pṛthivī is addressed as "mother" (*mātṛ*) in several hymns,[20] and her maternal nature appears to be her dominant quality. As a motherly figure, she is depicted primarily in the first two roles mentioned above, that is, as the abundant, life-supporting physical earth that is the mother of living creatures and as the maternal source of the manifest world. Although such depictions are found in the Ṛg-Veda, one of the most elaborate expressions of these aspects of Pṛthivī appears in Atharva-Veda 12.1:

> May Pṛthivī, who bears plants (*oṣadhi*)[21] having varied powers, spread forth and accommodate us . . . may this earth on which what breathes and moves is active assign us precedence in drinking. There are four regions of this earth, on which food and men have sprung up and which bears abundantly breathing and moving (creatures); may this earth bestow on us cattle, indeed, inexhaustibleness. . . . May she [earth] yield precious nectar; may she sprinkle us with vital power (*varcas*). . . . May this earth having many streams yield milk for us . . . may this earth, a mother to me her son, pour forth milk for us. . . . Let us always move along on the firm earth, Pṛthivī, all-producing mother of plants, sustained by order (*dharma*), all-gracious.[22]

As the physical earth, Pṛthivī is a bountiful goddess described as the source of plants and herbs and is called the all-producer (*viśvaṃsū*).[23] She is invoked to pour out nectar and milk to feed her children and is said to have golden breasts.[24] As a giver of life, Pṛthivī also appears to be elevated to a more abstract level of conception where her maternal nature is emphasized in a general sense. She is perceived to be the universal mother and sovereign of manifest creation described as conceiving the germ of all things that exist and bearing all things in her womb,[25] and she reigns as the mistress of whatever is and whatever is to be.[26] In this capacity, she shares certain qualities with the waters, but Pṛthivī is never described as subtle or unmanifest.

In addition to her aspect as the physical earth, Pṛthivī is also portrayed as the universal mother coupled with the universal father Dyaus, the male deity of the heavens. This portrayal of earth is particularly prevalent in the Ṛg-Veda. Together, Pṛthivī and Dyaus are invoked as the parents of the world and of the gods.[27] Pṛthivī is described as supporting the moving world that dwells upon her and, along with Dyaus, is praised as all-sustaining:

> May that blessed, very victorious pair that supports (us),
> Dyaus-Pṛthivī, protect us from terrible danger.[28]

The coupling of Pṛthivī and Dyaus is one of the earliest expressions in Vedic literature of consort pairing, which, as we will see, pertains also to other goddesses in the Saṃhitās and becomes even more prevalent in the Brāhmaṇas. Pṛthivī and Dyaus supply the prototype for the universal male/female parental pair.

Pṛthivī's place in cosmogony is articulated especially in the Yajur-Veda Saṃhitās, where Pṛthivī's relationship to the cosmogonic waters becomes particularly important and she is sometimes described as lifted out of the primordial waters or derived from water. In some Yajur-Veda narratives, for example, the waters are said to cover the earth in the beginning of creation; a boar dives down and brings up the earth, which then floats on the surface of the waters.[29] Taittirīya Saṃhitā 7.1.5.1 cited above describes the earth as actually created from the waters, and Atharva-Veda 12.1.8 states that Pṛthivī was water (*salila*) in the beginning of creation. Thus it appears that the waters may be said to represent the most abstract level of materiality, and earth the next stage of formation. The waters are the fundamental material cause of the cosmos, often described as being manipulated by a creator figure who acts as the efficient cause of creation, and the earth is what is first formed.

Like the waters, Pṛthivī is also thought to have special powers, especially procreative powers. She is described as having great inherent might (*mahī svatavas*)[30] and as having forces (*ūrj*) that flow forth from her body.[31] As is also the case with the waters, this particular aspect of Pṛthivī is mentioned in passing but not further developed.

ADITI

Literally, *aditi* is an adjective meaning "unbounded." As a goddess in the Vedas, Aditi seems to have many different aspects, but she is depicted primarily in three ways: (1) as a mother figure; (2) as similar or equivalent to the earth; and (3) as a universal, abstract goddess, representing physical creation itself or aspects of physical creation.

Above all, Aditi is the mother of the seven Ādityas. The story of her children's birth is recounted in Ṛg-Veda 10.72, where Aditi is said to have given birth to eight sons. She threw away the eighth, Mārtāṇḍa, but later brought him again to life. As a mother, Aditi is also depicted in more nearly universal terms, and in her great nurturing capacity is often identified as a cow.[32] She is called "our birthplace," the great mother, or the mother of kings.[33] She shares her maternal nature with the waters and the earth, and in Ṛg-Veda 10.63.2, all three (Aditi, the waters, and the earth) are said to give birth to the gods:

> Indeed, all your names, oh gods, are to be honored, praised, and worshiped; (you) that are born here of Aditi, the waters (*ap*), and earth (*pṛthivī*), hear my call.

This verse suggests that Aditi, the waters, and earth may on some level be different aspects of one another, for they are homologized by being cited collectively as mother of the gods. In this vein, Aditi is at times equated with the earth[34] and is often presented in terms that are reminiscent of descriptions of Pṛthivī. She is described, for example, as having unrivaled bounteousness[35] and as being extended or broad (*urūvī*).[36]

On an abstract level, Aditi seems to be represented in ways that suggest she is more than an individual goddess. On this level, she is equated with aspects of the cosmos:

> Aditi is the heaven, Aditi is the middle region (*antarikṣa*), Aditi is the mother, she is the father, she is the son; all the gods are Aditi, and the five clans; Aditi is what has been born (*jāta*) and what will be born (*janitva*).[37]

In Atharva-Veda 7.6.4, she is described as the great mother in whose lap lies the atmosphere. Similarly, in Vājasaneyi Saṃhitā 9.5, she is represented as the support of the cosmos:

> In conception of strength[38] we call with speech the great mother, Aditi, on whom this whole world has settled.

In such passages, Aditi is imbued with a cosmic significance, suggesting that she is identified with the unbounded physical realm. This aspect of her nature is noted by F. Max Müller, who characterizes Aditi in her cosmic role as "the Beyond, the unbounded realm beyond earth, sky, and heaven."[39] He describes Aditi as

> the visible Infinite, visible, as it were, to the naked eye, the endless expanse beyond the earth, beyond the

> clouds, beyond the sky. That was called A-diti, the unbound, the un-bounded . . . and meant therefore originally what is free from bonds of any kind, whether of space or time, free from physical weakness, free from moral guilt.[40]

Although Müller's assessment of Aditi's significance may stretch the limits of the textual evidence somewhat, she certainly has some kind of abstract, universal significance associated with physical creation even though her precise nature is not clearly articulated.

In Ṛg-Veda 10.72, Aditi also appears to be associated with *dakṣa,* which the waters are said to contain in Ṛg-Veda 10.121.8, but here *dakṣa* is personified. In Ṛg-Veda 10.72.4, Aditi is said to give birth to Dakṣa, who in turn is said to produce her in an act of mutual procreation. Dakṣa in this case is probably a proper name referring to an individual deity, but—as noted above—the term itself can mean "energy, "strength," or "power."

VIRĀJ

Virāj is an enigmatic character whose personal identity in the Saṃhitās is less fully elaborated than that of the other deities that concern our investigation. She is mentioned only three times in the Ṛg-Veda, and in one of these instances seems to be a Vedic meter rather than a deity.[41] In Ṛg-Veda 9.96.18, Soma is compared to Virāj and is described as being "like Virāj, resplendent as a singer," but nothing further is specified.

In Ṛg-Veda 10.90, the Puruṣa-Sūkta, Virāj is attributed cosmogonic qualities. This hymn describes the sacrifice of the cosmic being, the thousand-headed Puruṣa, who is the source of all creation; different parts of his body engender the different parts of the cosmos. In this verse, Puruṣa and Virāj are said to produce each other, for "from him Virāj was born; again from Virāj Puruṣa (was born)."[42] Nothing else is said about the particular qualities of Virāj, and it is not clear from this passage that she is even identified here as female.

In the Atharva-Veda, on the other hand, Virāj in her cosmological aspect is usually described as female, although she also appears to be identified as a male being or as a hermaphrodite on some occasions.[43] Even in Atharva-Veda 8.9.7, where Virāj is called the father of devotion, the verses that follow attribute to her a female gender. It is in this Saṃhitā that her creative and cosmological significance comes to the fore.

The cosmogonic role of Virāj is described in Atharva-Veda 8.10, where Virāj is described as a divine, cosmic force that enters and enlivens all creation:[44]

> Virāj truly was here in the beginning. All were afraid of her (when she was) born, (thinking), "She alone will become this." She rose; she entered the householder's fire (*gārhapatya*). . . . She rose; she entered the fire of offering (*āhavanīya*). . . . She rose; she entered the southern fire (*dakṣina*). . . . She rose; she entered the assembly (*sabhā*). . . . She rose; she entered the meeting (*samiti*). . . . She rose; she entered consultation (*mantraṇa*). . . . She rose; she stood striding out fourfold in the middle region. The gods and men said of her, "She alone knows this. Let us invoke her that we both may live."[45]

Further on in the hymn, she is said to rise and come to the trees, the fathers (*pitṛ*), the gods, and men, by each of whom she is killed; yet she always regenerates, suggesting that she has some kind of immortal character. When Virāj again rises and approaches various groups of beings—the *asuras* and gods, fathers, men, seven *ṛṣis*, *apsarases* and *gandharvas*, other people, and serpents—they each milk from her some substance upon which they depend. In this context, Virāj is connected to notions that we will pursue in later Brahmanical literature, for in Atharva-Veda 8.10.22, Virāj is explicitly identified with the *māyā* of the *asuras*:

> She rose; she came to the *asuras*. The *asuras* called to her, "Oh Māyā, come here." Virocana Prāhrādi was her calf; an iron vessel (was) the (milking) vessel. Dvimūrdhā Ārtvya milked her; he milked that very Māyā. The *asuras* subsist on that Māyā.

The uses and connotations of the term *māyā* in the Vedic literature are quite complex and will be taken up in the next chapter. Suffice it to say for the moment that the term is used in this passage to denote that upon which the *asuras* depend for their existence.[46] For our purposes, what is most important is that a female divinity (for in this hymn Virāj is clearly female) is described in terms that suggest she is a universal creative power that is explicitly identified with the *māyā* of the *asuras*. As we shall see, the connection of a principle of energy described as feminine with the term *māyā* is of particular significance in our investigation.

The opening of the first verse of Atharva-Veda 8.10 ("Virāj truly was here in the beginning") suggests that Virāj may also be thought of as a kind of foundational material principle.[47] She is invoked as strength, yet she also has a nourishing aspect and is likened to a cow.[48] Elsewhere, Virāj is identified with speech, earth, and the midregions, suggesting a general association between Virāj and material creation, but in this passage Virāj is also identified with Prajāpati and Mṛtyu, death, and is ascribed male gender.[49] Generally, the explicitly material aspect of Virāj is not as well developed in the Saṃhitās as are the universal energizing capabilities that dominate her character.

As a cosmic energizing principle, Virāj is also described as breathless but moving by the breath of breathing—that is, living—creatures. It is by her control that the *yakṣas*, a class of supernatural beings, move, and she is described as touching (√*mṛś*) all existence.[50] Containing great power, she enters all creation:

> She is this very one that first shone forth; entered into these others, she goes about. Great powers are within

> her. The woman, the first-bearing mother, has approached.[51]

VĀC (AND SARASVATĪ)

Throughout the Saṃhitās, Vāc, "speech," is portrayed on two levels: (1) as manifest in the faculty of speech, expressed in human language, and (2) as a goddess ascribed certain universal creative powers.[52]

Vāc's manifestation in earthly speech is particularly lauded in Ṛg-Veda 10.71. In this hymn, Vāc's first utterances are said to be sent forth when names are given to objects.[53] Men following the "trace of Vāc" discover that she has entered into those who are able to best apprehend her, the seers (*ṛṣis*), who then send her forth in their own speech:

> With sacrifice they followed the track of Vāc; they found her entered into the *ṛṣis*. Bringing her near, they distributed her in many places. Seven singers chant (her) together.
>
> Many a one, seeing, has not seen Vāc; many a one, hearing, does not hear her. But to many another she has revealed herself, like a longing, well-dressed wife to her husband.[54]

Ṛg-Veda 8.89.11 asserts that the gods generated Vāc and now animals of every type speak her, suggesting that she is manifest in all earthly vocal utterances. Ṛg-Veda 1.164.45 indicates that this earthly dimension is only one quarter of the totality of Vāc, whose other three quarters are concealed and do not come forth. What humans speak constitutes only the fourth dimension:

> Vāc is measured out in four parts. Those Brahmins with insight know these (parts). Three parts, which are hidden, mortals do not activate, (but) they speak the fourth part.[55]

Atharva-Veda 9.10.13 echoes a similar sentiment, describing Vāc as abiding in the highest heaven. Thus Vāc has a divine, transcendent aspect as well as an earthly dimension.

In Ṛg-Veda 10.125, Vāc describes herself as powerful and all-pervasive:

> I am queen, gatherer of riches, knowing, the first among those worthy of being honored. I am she, having many stations (and) much-bestowing, whom the gods have distributed in many places.
>
> Through me, he who discerns, who breathes, who indeed hears what is said, eats his food. Though ignorant (of this), they dwell in me. Hear that you are heard! What I tell you is to be believed.
>
> I, myself, say this welcome news to gods and men. He whom I love, I make him powerful, (I make) him a Brahmin, (I make) him a seer (*ṛṣi*), (I make) him wise. . . .
>
> I have entered into heaven and earth. I bring forth the father at the summit of this (creation). My *yoni* (womb/origin/abode) is within the waters (*ap*), in the ocean (*samudra*). Thence I extend over all worlds, and I touch heaven with my uppermost part.
>
> I also blow forth like the wind, reaching all the worlds. Beyond heaven, beyond the earth, so great have I become through my grandeur.[56]

This hymn indicates that Vāc is immanent in creation ("distributed in many places" and "entered into heaven and earth") but also transcendent ("beyond heaven, beyond the earth"). She is that which sustains and enlivens all of creation, a principle of life-energy that pervades the universe. In verse seven, Vāc is associated with the (primordial) waters, from which she stretches forth extending throughout the worlds, and in which is located her *yoni*. The term *yoni* can mean "place of rest" or "seat," which would signify that Vāc's abode resides in the waters. Or, the term can mean "origin" or "place of birth," indicating that Vāc may be born in the waters. Finally, and perhaps most significantly, the term can mean "womb, uterus" or "vagina." If this is in fact what is meant by the term in this context, then the waters are the womb or generative organ of Vāc. Such a description of the relationship between the waters and the goddess would emphasize the above-described role of the waters as cosmic womb and thus would be in keeping with descriptions of the cosmogonic role of the waters narrated elsewhere in the Ṛg-Veda. It would also indicate that the waters are an aspect of Vāc.

Vāc's role in creation and her relationship with the cosmic waters are described somewhat differently in Ṛg-Veda 1.164.41–42, which portrays Vāc as a buffalo-cow (*gaurī*) who lows, forming the waters (*salila*) and bringing creation into existence:

> The buffalo-cow [Vāc] lowed; she fashioned the floods (*salila*), having become one-footed, two-footed, four-footed, eight-footed, nine-footed, she who in the highest heaven has a thousand syllables.
> From her flow forth the (heavenly) oceans (*samudra*), on account of which the four directions exist, and from her flows the *akṣara* (imperishable/syllable), on which the entire universe exists.[57]

In this hymn, Vāc is the source of the primordial waters that form the subtle material matrix of creation. They flow forth in differentiated streams as her utterances, and manifest creation is formed from this speech-water. The physical cosmos is born through Vāc's creative powers, which give rise to the primal floods. Here, as in Ṛg-Veda 10.125, Vāc is connected to the primordial waters.

The association between Vāc and water is in fact important. Vāc is equated with the river goddess Sarasvatī in the Yajur-Veda and in later texts.[58] As a hypostatized river, Sarasvatī is an aspect of the goddess-waters (*ap*) and shares some of their characteristics. She is associated with wealth, power, and medicine, as are the waters;[59] like them also, she is said to abound in milk and is depicted as a maternal figure who nourishes her progeny.[60] She is described as the divine one in which all living beings are situated[61] and in Atharva-Veda 7.10 is asked to nurse her children:

> Your breast, which is ever-flowing, delightful, favorable, well-invoked, granting good gifts, by which you nourish all precious things, Sarasvatī, make it be received.

Sarasvatī is also conceived as penetrating and filling the realms of the earth and the firmament, and she is said to have sprung from three sources.[62] She is called the best of rivers (*nadītamā*) and is depicted as extremely potent, surpassing all other waters in strength.[63]

Like the other goddesses that we have examined thus far, Sarasvatī also has more than one aspect in the Saṃhitās. Besides being a river goddess, she is also connected with Vedic sacrifice. Sarasvatī is often invoked and called to the sacrifice along with her two partners, Iḷa and Bhāratī (or Mahi), and it is said that the pious worship Sarasvatī during sacrifice.[64] She is also said to govern all thought and is invoked for inspiration.[65] The identification of Sarasvatī with Vāc is a highly complex problem, and the mechanisms of this equation are beyond the scope of this investigation.[66] It should be noted, however, that the descriptions of Vāc link her generally with the waters, which share with her a cosmogonic and cosmological role, and in later texts with Sarasvatī, who is a manifestation of these waters. The connection between Vāc and the maternal waters is more developed in the Brāhmaṇas, where the two appear to be different aspects of the same principle.

Vāc apparently also has a more nourishing, maternal dimension, and, like other goddesses we have examined, she is likened to a cow and is described as yielding food.[67] However, it is her all-pervading, enlivening powers rather than her maternal qualities that dominate Vāc's character.

ŚACĪ/INDRĀṆĪ

The term *śacī* is used in the Vedas primarily in two ways: (1) as a general term for the strength of the gods; and (2) as a proper name for the wife of Indra, also called Indrāṇī.

As a general term denoting strength or the divine powers of the gods, *śacī* is used several times in the Ṛg-Veda Saṃhitā and is associated especially with Indra. The term *śacīvat,* "possessed of might," is used to describe Indra and is applied to other deities on only two occasions; similarly, the epithet *śacīpati,* "lord of might," which is used to describe Indra, is ascribed to other divinities only once, when it is applied to the Aśvins (Ṛg-Veda 7.67.5).[68] The term is often used in the instrumental plural to denote the agency by means of which the gods execute their actions.[69]

The term *śacī* in the Ṛg-Veda Saṃhitā, as in later literature, is also another name for Indra's wife, Indrāṇī.[70] As his consort, Śacī is Indra's strength personified. S. K. Das argues that the terms *śakti* and *śacī* originally denoted the nature functions of divinities and sees in the hypostatized Śacī a development whereby the power of a divinity, his *śakti* or *śacī,* is conceived of in feminine terms and then deified. In this regard, Das distinguishes between *śakti/śacī* and a similar group of goddesses called Gnās, "women," who are the divine consorts of the gods.

> In the Vedic stage Gnā certainly implies in the collective sense a 'group of Divine Females' who produce or promote fertility and wealth. Thus whereas the Ṛgvedic Śacīs represent 'Divine Powers' as the deified nature functions of male gods, forming an essential element in the constitution of the latter's personalities, the Gnās are distinctly separate principles of 'female energy' acting in association with their 'male counterparts.'[71]

Unlike the Gnās, who are personified as distinct female divinities, Śacī/Indrāṇī appears to be portrayed as the energy that is an inherent aspect of her male counterpart and is identified as female. As we shall see, in later literature this image of a god possessed of a divine, female power will become a central theme in accounts of cosmogony and contributes to the way in which the Great Goddess is constructed. We do not find in Śacī the same explicit cosmogonic or cosmological implications that we have seen in Vāc and Virāj; nevertheless, by embodying the nature of divine energy presented in the Ṛg-Veda as the feminine aspect of a male deity, Śacī represents an important piece of the puzzle.

In the Vedic Saṃhitās, we can discern two important tendencies regarding the nature of female divinities. First, several different goddesses are associated in some way and on some level with materiality and/or a principle of energy. These goddesses are sometimes represented in concrete terms and associated with visible, manifest aspects of the cosmos, but they are also conceived in abstract terms and associated with nonvisible, non-manifest principles of creation. Both levels of description are present in the Saṃhitās. Second, although these goddesses are discrete divinities, they share certain traits and characteristics, and similar terms may be used to describe different goddesses. Thus there is a certain amount of cross-attribution of traits and even identity (as in the case of Aditi-Pṛthivī, Sarasvatī-Vāc). Furthermore, goddesses who are associated with materiality may also be attributed powers, and vice-versa; the principles of materiality and energy are not distinctly separate from one another. Thus goddesses associated with matter are not portrayed as entirely passive, and those connected to the principle of energy are associated also with materiality.

Brāhmaṇas[72]

The depiction in the Saṃhitās of the different goddesses that we have examined thus far leads us to conclude that the association of materiality and energy with female divinity seems to be part of the Vedic tradition from the very beginning of its existence. We have also seen that although many of the characteristics of these goddesses are shared, each goddess is portrayed as a discrete, individual deity. In the Brāhmaṇas, two further developments occur: (1) the tendency for different discrete goddesses to shed their individual uniqueness and to be identified with one another in some way is increasingly prominent; and (2) through this process of cross-identification, a more general notion of female divinity that is rather fluid in character begins to become increasingly dominant. Individual goddesses become less distinct and are associated more generally with one another and with cosmogonic and cosmological structures. Thus the personal level of identity of these divinities tends to take a back seat, while their abstract identities and functions become increasingly important.

THE WATERS

Descriptions of the waters as the matrix of creation are found scattered throughout the Brāhmaṇas even outside of any cosmogonic context. The waters (*ap*) are described as the great ocean present at the beginning,[73] the foundation (*pratiṣṭhā*) of the universe,[74] and the first-made of the universe.[75] They are said to have produced everything that exists.[76] The notion that the waters are present at the beginning of the cosmogonic process and are in some way foundational seems to be well accepted in these texts, and they are even described generally as pervading (√*āp*) all of creation.[77] The waters are also identified with the gods and are called the abode of all the gods.[78]

The role of the waters in creation is described in different cosmogonic accounts in the Brāhmaṇas, especially in the Śatapatha Brāhmaṇa. As in the Saṃhitās, the waters are described both as a kind of cosmic womb and as the material foundation from which the differentiated cosmos is derived. Yet they are also described collectively as the willing agent of creation, the efficient cause that impels the cosmos into manifestation. In all cases, their appearance marks the beginning of the transition from the primary stage of creation to the unfolding of the second phase.

The waters retain their identity as the primordial womb that receives the primeval egg (*aṇḍa*) in Śatapatha Brāhmaṇa 6.1.1.9–10. In this account of creation, the non-existent (which is also identified as the *ṛṣis* or as Indra) gives rise to seven persons, which combine to form one person, Prajāpati the creator. Prajāpati then fashions the waters (*ap*) out of Vāc, who is identified with the world (*loka*). The waters pervade and cover everything. Prajāpati then enters the waters along with the triple Veda, giving rise to an egg:

> He [Prajāpati] produced the waters out of Vāc alone, (who is) the world. That very Vāc was his; she was sent forth. She pervaded all this; and because she pervaded (√*āp*) whatever (existed), therefore she (is called) water (*ap*). Because she covered (√*var*), therefore (she is called) water (*vār*).
>
> He desired, "May I be reproduced from these waters." He entered the waters with that triple knowledge. Thence an egg arose. He touched it. He said, "May it be! May it be! May it be still more!" From it *brahman*, the triple knowledge, was first produced.

As in Ṛg-Veda 10.82.5–6 and Ṛg-Veda 10.121.7, the waters here function as a universal matrix of gestation. Vāc is described as the source of the waters, echoing the pattern found in Ṛg-Veda 1.164.41–42.[79] We will discuss the relationship between Vāc and the waters in greater detail below.

The role of the waters as the material basis of the manifest world is more prominent in Śatapatha Brāhmaṇa 6.1.3. Here, the primordial waters flow forth from Prajāpati's body when he practices *tapas*:

> In the beginning, indeed, Prajāpati, one alone, was here. He desired, "May I exist! May I be reproduced!" He exerted himself; he practiced austerity (*tapas*). From him, exhausted and heated, the waters were produced; from that heated person, the waters are born.

The term *tapas*, from the verbal root √*tap*, means both "heat" and "ascetic austerity," for ascetic practices are said to heat up the body. In this passage, the waters are produced from Prajāpati's heated (√*tap*) body; the waters are then heated to produce foam, which is then heated to produce clay, which gives rise to sand, from which is produced the pebble, and so forth. The waters that emerge from the heated body of Prajāpati are, then, the immediate source of differentiated material forms.

In other accounts, the waters are collectively the personal creative principle that toils to produce creation, as well as the womb in which the incipient cosmos gestates in the form of an egg. For example, in Śatapatha Brāhmaṇa 11.1.6.1, the waters are described in the same manner as is Prajāpati in 6.1.3:

> In the beginning, indeed, this was water (*ap*), only water (*salila*). They [the waters] desired, "How, now, might we reproduce?" They exerted themselves; they practiced austerity (*tapas*). When they were practicing austerity, a golden egg was produced.

From the golden egg is born Prajāpati, the creator and fashioner of the world. In another account, the waters practice *tapas* and conceive, later giving birth to the sun.[80] In these cosmogonic variants, the role of the waters in the birth of the cosmos is conflated with that of the personal agent of creation, who is usually identified in the Brāhmaṇas as Prajāpati.

The feminine identity of the waters is preserved throughout these texts. The waters are described as female (*vṛṣā*),[81] equated with the wives of the gods,[82] likened to an *apsaras*,[83] and are even represented in one passage as having their period favorable for conception.[84]

EARTH/ADITI/VIRĀJ

In the Brāhmaṇas, as in the Saṃhitās, the earth is less abstract than the waters but is similarly represented as a manifestation of the material matrix of creation. Earth is described in Śatapatha Brāhmaṇa 6.1.1.12ff. as being formed by Prajāpati when he compresses the shell of the primordial egg and throws it into the waters:

> He desired, "May I produce this [the earth] from these waters!" Pressing it together, he cast it into the waters. The juice that flowed from it directed outwards became a tortoise; then what was sprinkled upwards (became) that which is produced above the waters. This all dissolved in the waters. This appeared as one form only, as water only.
>
> He desired, "May it be greater! May it reproduce!" He practiced austerity. Exhausted, having practiced austerity, he emitted foam. He knew that, "indeed, this form is different; it is becoming more. I must exert myself." Exhausted, having performed austerity, he produced clay, mud, salty soil, and sand, gravel, rock, ore, gold, plants and trees. Thus he covered the earth.
>
> This was produced. . . . He said, "This, indeed, has become (√*bhū*) a foundation." Thus, it became the earth (*bhūmi*). He spread it out (√*prath*), and it became the earth (*pṛthivī*).

This phase of creation represents a further stage of development following that described in Śatapatha Brāhmaṇa

6.1.1.9–10 cited above. Elsewhere, the earth is also said to lie spread out on the waters,[85] or Prajāpati is described as the begetter of both of them.[86] Earth is no longer coupled with Dyaus but rather with Prajāpati, who is described as her mate.[87] There is no apparent evidence that the earth in this sense represents anything other than the physical, manifest earth.

The earth is also called a cow and a female buffalo (*mahiṣi*) and is identified with Vāc.[88] She retains her female identity and her place in cosmogony but loses many of the distinctive features that characterize her in the Saṃhitās. In the Brāhmaṇas, the earth is consistently identified with Aditi,[89] and the two are almost completely conflated. However, Aditi also retains her larger identity as the generally manifest cosmos and is referred to as "all this, whatever this universe is."[90] Aditi, too, is identified with Vāc.[91]

Whereas the waters represent the unmanifest complex from which creation emerges in the beginning of time, the goddess earth/Aditi represents the physically present universe that living creatures inhabit and in which they function. Virāj seems to be a specific aspect of this creation, namely, food (*anna*), with which Virāj is consistently identified.[92] As food, Virāj promotes life on the level of manifest creation but does not appear to retain any explicit cosmological significance.

VĀC/SARASVATĪ

In the Brāhmaṇas Sarasvatī is homologized with Vāc so that the two become completely identified with one another,[93] and Vāc is frequently called Sarasvatī-Vāc. She is consistently mentioned in connection with cosmogony, where she plays the role of the catalyst that in some way activates the unfolding of the cosmos. In this context, Vāc is often associated with Prajāpati, the creator, either as his mate or as the instrument with which he creates. As noted above, she is also associated with the waters and with the goddess earth/Aditi. In fact, the waters, the earth/Aditi, and Vāc all seem to represent different aspects of the same general creative principle.

In several of the accounts of creation that are found in the Brāhmaṇas, Prajāpati is portrayed as the personal creator figure who orchestrates the manifestation of the physical universe. In this capacity, he is often aided by Vāc, whom he manipulates in some way or with whom he unites to set in motion the mechanisms of cosmogony. On this level, speech is not necessarily identified as the goddess Vāc but may also refer to the faculty of speech, which is a manifestation of the goddess herself. For example, we have seen in Śatapatha Brāhmaṇa 11.1.6.1 that the waters perform *tapas,* leading to the creation of a golden egg. Prajāpati is born from the golden egg; he speaks the words, "*bhūḥ, bhuvaḥ, svaḥ,*" and thus the three worlds (earth, midregions, and sky) are born:

> After a year, he wished to speak. He said, "*bhūḥ;*" this became the earth. He said, "*bhuvaḥ;*" this became the midregions. He said, "*svaḥ;*" this became the sky.[94]

In Pañcaviṃśa Brāhmaṇa 20.14.2–5 cited below, Prajāpati creates the three worlds with the three sounds "*a*" (earth), "*ka*" (midregions), "*ho*" (heaven).[95] Elsewhere, Prajāpati is said to unite sexually with Vāc in his creative effort. In Śatapatha Brāhmaṇa 6.1.2.6ff., for example, it is stated that on four occasions Prajāpati copulates with speech (*vāc*) mentally or, literally, with his mind (*manasā*). Each time, Prajāpati becomes "filled with drops," which he emits (√*sṛj*), creating the Vasus, Rudras, Ādityas, and all-gods, respectively.

The mental union between Prajāpati and Vāc described above hints at another pattern that we find throughout the Brāhmaṇas: as the faculty of speech, Vāc is often associated not only with Prajāpati but also with his mind (*manas*) or the faculty of mind in general.[96] Speech and mind are said to rest on one another.[97] Mind is male, speech is female, and they are described as a couple;[98] together, mind and speech are said to convey the sacrifice to the gods.[99] Mind is often considered to be more subtle and more fundamental than speech, which simply gives expression to the mind's contents. It is stated, for example, that mind supports speech, going before it and preparing it, and of the two, mind is better because speech only imitates mind.[100]

Mind and speech are also paired in cosmogonic contexts, and mind is said to preexist speech and to be its source. In Śatapatha Brāhmaṇa 10.5.3.1–4, for example, mind, which is declared to be neither existent (*sat*) nor nonexistent (*asat*), is present at the beginning of the universe and sends forth speech. In Pañcaviṃśa Brāhmaṇa 7.6.1–3, Prajāpati wishes to reproduce, so he meditates, and the contents of his mind become the *bṛhat*, a kind of *sāman* or Vedic chant. He sends forth the *bṛhat* through speech, which becomes the *rathantara* (another kind of *sāman*):

> Prajāpati desired, "May I be many, may I be reproduced." He meditated silently in his mind; what was in his mind, that became the *bṛhat* (*sāman*). He thought, "This my embryo/germ (*garbha*) is hidden; I will bring it forth through speech (*vāc*)". He released speech. This speech became the *rathantara*.

In the Pañcaviṃśa Brāhmaṇa, as well as in other Brāhmaṇas, the *rathantara* is often equated with both the earth and Vāc, who are also assimilated to one another.[101] As the *rathantara*, Vāc is usually coupled with the *bṛhat*, which is equated with mind or its contents, as in the Pañcaviṃśa Brāhmaṇa passage above. It is through the interaction of mind and speech, *bṛhat* and *rathantara*, that creation comes about. At times, mind and speech are also associated with breath (*prāṇa*), or speech is coupled with breath. In Aitareya Brāhmaṇa 2.27, for example, speech is invoked together with breath, and in Śatapatha Brāhmaṇa 7.5.1.7

and 10.1.1.9, breath (*prāṇa*) is said to be the male mate of speech (*vāc*), thus taking the place of both Prajāpati and mind.[102]

In the Brāhmaṇas, the coupling of speech with Prajāpati or mind participates in a larger series of correspondences in which speech and mind are correlated with the different orders of reality established in the Brāhmaṇas and Upaniṣads: the natural order (*adhibhūta*), divine order (*adhidaiva*), human order (*adhyātma*), and sacrificial order (*adhiyajña*).[103] In the natural order, speech is said to correspond to this world or earth, and mind to "yonder" world or heaven.[104] In the divine order, speech usually corresponds to Sarasvatī (or Vāc), and mind to Sarasvat (or Prajāpati).[105] In the human order, speech (= the *rathantara*) corresponds to the human faculty of speech or, in the social order, the Brahmin caste; mind (= the *bṛhat*) corresponds to the faculty of mind or the Kṣatriya caste.[106] Finally, in the sacrificial order, speech is the Hotṛ priest or Agnihotra cow, and mind is the Adhvaryu priest or calf.[107] Different sets of correspondences and a number of variants also appear; wherever gender distinctions arise when such couplings are made, however, speech, Vāc, is always female, and her mate is always male.[108]

The connection that we have seen in the Saṃhitās between Vāc and the primordial waters gains in importance in the Brāhmaṇas and parallels the pattern that we have seen in Ṛg-Veda 1.164.41–42. In the process of cosmogony, Vāc is sometimes described as the source of the cosmic waters, which are an aspect of Vāc herself. This dynamic is recounted in Śatapatha Brāhmaṇa 6.1.1.9, cited above, where the primordial waters that Prajāpati creates and in which are placed the primeval egg are fashioned from Vāc and identified with her. In Pañcaviṃśa Brāhmaṇa 7.7.9, Vāc is likened to an ocean (*samudra*); the use of the term *samudra* resonates with the use of the term in the Saṃhitās to indicate the primordial waters, thus implying that Vāc is the waters present at the beginning of creation in an undifferentiated state. In other passages, however, Vāc flows forth as streams of water that immediately become differentiated. In Pañcaviṃśa Brāhmaṇa 20.14.2, it is stated that Prajāpati is alone in the beginning of creation. He sends forth speech, which flows upward as a stream:

> Prajāpati alone was here. Vāc alone was his own; Vāc was second to him. He thought, "Let me send forth this very Vāc. She will spread forth, pervading all this." He sent forth Vāc. She spread forth, pervading all this. She extended upwards as a continuous stream of water. Saying "*a*," he cut off a third of it. This became the earth (*bhūmi*). . . . (Saying) "*ka*," he cut off (another) third; this became the midregions (*antarikṣa*). . . . (Saying) "*ho*," he threw a third upwards; it became the sky (*dyaus*).

These waters are not the undifferentiated matrix that we have seen in other narrations of cosmogony but represent the incipient stage of differentiated creation. Prajāpati breaks off three different portions of this stream, each of which corresponds to a different syllable; these three portions then become the three manifest worlds. Creation thus results from the fullness of Vāc when she pours forth as the waters that form the material foundation of the physical universe, either as the primordial waters or as differentiated streams. Prajāpati is the male creator principle, and Vāc is the female principle that manifests itself as a primordial liquid flow.

We should note two further points about the coupling of the goddess Vāc with Prajāpati or the correlative linking of the faculty of speech with mind. First, Vāc acquires a consort or male counterpart in the Brāhmaṇas, which is not true in the Saṃhitās. When Prajāpati is described as possessing Vāc as his ability to speak or make manifest the contents of his mind, he then uses her to create.[109] In such contexts, Vāc is Prajāpati's inherent creative power in the same way that Śacī/Indrāṇī is Indra's inherent power. It is also notable that Prajāpati is at least once identified with Dakṣa,[110] with whom—or which, as a principle—Aditi and the waters are associated in the Ṛg-Veda, although little else can be said about these relations. Second, Vāc is consistently identified with the earth, and in the series of correspondences established in the Brāhmaṇas, directly correlated with earth, whereas Prajāpati is associated with mind and, correlatively, the heavens. These associations resonate with the representation of Pṛthivī and Dyaus, earth and heaven, as the primordial parental couple par excellence in the Saṃhitās.

INDRĀṆĪ

There is little in the Brāhmaṇas on Indrāṇī. One passage in the Śatapatha Brāhmaṇa, however, is particularly relevant to our investigation. We have seen above the way in which correlations among different levels of reality are recognized in the Brāhmaṇas. Such correlations establish correspondences between macrocosmic levels of reality and microcosmic levels. This applies also to Indra and Indrāṇī. In Śatapatha Brāhmaṇa 10.5.2.9–12, Indra and Indrāṇī are located on the microcosmic level in the human body:

> Now, that one is Indra who is the man in the right eye, and this one [the other person] is Indrāṇī. . . . Those two descend to the space in the heart. They copulate. When they come to the end of (their) union, then, indeed, that man sleeps; just as, having gone to the end of a union, a man (here on earth) is, as it were, not conscious, so that one [Indra] becomes as if he were not conscious. For this is a divine union; indeed, that is the highest bliss. Therefore, the mouth of a sleeping man is phlegmy, for those two deities then emit seed (*retas*) from which all this, whatever exists, springs.

Indra is identified here with *prāṇa*,[111] vital breath, although Indrāṇī is not correlated with any other faculty. This union is also recounted in the Bṛhadāraṇyaka Upaniṣad, but in this account Indra, the person in the right eye, is mated with Virāj, who is identified as his wife.[112]

There are two important points to be noted regarding this passage. First, the coupling of Indra/Indrāṇī is presented in terms that interpret the divine sexual union of the two deities on the level of human physiology. Thus Indra/Indrāṇī, like Prajāpati/Vāc (= Sarasvat/Sarasvatī), are correlated with the human order (*adhyātma*). The establishment of a macrocosmic/microcosmic correspondence between the sexual union of divinities and aspects of human physiology becomes important in the later development of Tantric notions concerning the concept of *śakti*. Second, the divine coupling of these two divinities is represented in this passage as having cosmogonic significance. It is from their union that "all this" (*idam sarvam*), that is, the manifest world, comes into being. Thus we see in this passage a repetition of the theme of cosmogonic sexual union characteristic of the portrayals of Prajāpati/Vāc. Here, however, it is Indra and Indrāṇī who are the primordial creative couple.

In the Brāhmaṇas, there is an increasing tendency toward abstraction of what are clearly identified in the Saṃhitās as female divinities. Elements are combined in different ways in different accounts of creation. The pattern that emerges reveals two distinct phases within the first stage of creation that Kuiper describes: (1) creation is impelled into motion by the interaction of a male creator figure, Prajāpati, with his female counterpart or mate, Vāc; (2) this interaction leads to the production of the primordial waters from or as Vāc. The waters are then manipulated, and the manifest cosmos or earth is formed (Kuiper's second stage). Vāc, the waters, and earth/Aditi are not clearly distinguished but rather seem to be different aspects of the same feminine principle.

Upaniṣads

In the Upaniṣads, the basic framework established in the Brāhmaṇas is affirmed, but—consonant with the more reflective, rather than mythological, character of the Upaniṣads—the abstract aspect of these structures is emphasized even more. Thus the same elements are in place but often devoid of gender distinction.

The emphasis in these texts is placed on speculation regarding an underlying substratum of all existence, Brahman or Ātman. Brahman represents the ultimate principle of objectivity, and Ātman represents the same principle on the subjective pole. Ātman is also at times identified as the personal creator and therefore takes the place occupied by Prajāpatī in the Brāhmaṇas. Because of their tendency toward more abstract, nonmythological reflection, the Upaniṣads are not greatly concerned with individual deities. Thus descriptions of goddesses such as those we have seen in the Saṃhitās and to a certain extent in the Brāhmaṇas drop away; only the cosmological and cosmogonic structures remain as topics of concern. This shift in perspective will be reflected in our analysis, which will limit itself to those relevant elements that are important in the Upaniṣads, namely, the waters, the earth, and Vāc.

THE WATERS

Although the waters lose their explicitly feminine identity in the Upaniṣads, they are still affirmed as the basic material matrix of creation. The world is described as being woven "warp and woof" on water (*ap*), and it is said that in the beginning the world was nothing but water.[113] In Aitareya Upaniṣad 1.1.1–2, a personal creator, identified here as Ātman, is said to create the waters:

> In the beginning, Ātman, indeed, only one, existed—no other blinking thing whatsoever. He thought, "Let me now create worlds." He created these worlds: water (*ambhas*), rays of light (*marīci*), death (*mara*), the waters (*ap*). That is the water, beyond heaven; heaven is its foundation. The rays of light are the midregions; death, the earth; what is beneath, the waters.

In this text, there is a clear distinction drawn between *ap* and *ambhas*; the waters (*ap*) are underneath the earth, whereas water (*ambhas*) is celestial, existing above heaven. The waters are also linked with the birth of the primal man, Puruṣa, whom Ātman draws forth from the waters and from whom the cosmos is formed:

> Extracting a person (*puruṣa*) right from the waters, he shaped (him). He heated him. The mouth of the one heated was separated out, like an egg. From the mouth, speech (*vāc*) (was separated out); from speech, fire.[114]

The association of the waters with gross matter reappears in Aitareya Upaniṣad 1.3.2, where Ātman heats (*abhi* √*tap*) the waters and produces from them material form (*mūrti*).

The waters are manifest also in the human order in the form of a component derived from semen.[115] Here, the waters are not primordial matter or the womb-like matrix from which Puruṣa is born, but the male fluid of generation. This identification is echoed in Aitareya Upaniṣad 1.2.4, where it is said that the waters become semen and enter the sexual organ of Puruṣa. The correspondence between cosmic creation and human procreation is described further in Aitareya Upaniṣad 2.4.1–3, where it is stated that a human is produced as an embryo, *garbha*, when semen is poured into a woman, who then bears the *garbha*. The same term, *puruṣa*, is used to describe both the cosmic person and the human person, suggesting a correlation between the two. Furthermore, the term *garbha*, which in earlier texts refers to the cosmic embryo/germ, is also the term used to describe the human embryo. Finally, semen is explicitly connected with both the cosmic waters and human procreation.

EARTH

Like the waters, the earth loses an explicit gender identification in the Upaniṣads, yet the basic cosmogonic and cosmological structures relating to earth endure. As in the Brāhmaṇas, the earth is described in the Upaniṣads as derived from the primordial waters. In Bṛhadāraṇyaka Upaniṣad 1.2.1–2, which also forms part of the Śatapatha Brāhmaṇa,[116] it is stated that the waters (*ap*) are produced while the creator is worshiping. The froth on the waters is then compacted and becomes the earth. Taittirīya Upaniṣad 2.1 asserts that earth comes from water; in Chāndogya Upaniṣad 1.1.2, it is said that the essence of earth is water, and in 7.10.1 it is stated that the earth—along with the atmosphere, sky, gods, men, beasts, birds, and so on—is just water (*ap*) solidified. Thus water is seen as the most abstract level of matter, and earth is a concrete manifestation of the waters.

VĀC

In the Upaniṣads, the creative role of Prajāpati and mind in conjunction with speech remains. In Bṛhadāraṇyaka Upaniṣad 1.2.4–5, which also forms part of the Śatapatha Brāhmaṇa,[117] the interplay of the creator—here represented by death or hunger but in essence a Prajāpati-like figure—and Vāc/speech is described on two levels corresponding to the two stages of creation. Here, Vāc is both the creator's divine consort and the faculty of speech itself:

> He desired, "May a second self of me be produced!" With mind (*manas*), he—death, hunger—copulated with speech (*vāc*). That which was semen, that became the year. . . . He bore him for a time as long as a year.

> After that long a time, he [death] begot him. He [death] opened his mouth to swallow the one born. He [the one born] cried, '*bhāṇ*!' That became speech. He [death] thought, "If, indeed, I threaten him, I will make less food." With that speech (*vāc*), with that self, he created this whole world, whatever exists: The *ṛc*s, the *yajus*es, the *sāman*s, meters, sacrifices, men, cattle.[118]

The creative role of Prajāpati's speech is also affirmed in Maitri Upaniṣad 6.6, where Prajāpati calls forth the three worlds (earth, midregions, and sky) by speaking their names. The link between the faculties of speech and mind also persists in the Upaniṣads. Thus, in the passage above, for example, the creator copulates with Vāc in her capacity as the faculty of speech by means of (his) mind. The connection between the two faculties is also affirmed in Bṛhadāraṇyaka Upaniṣad 1.4.17, where the creator, who is identified as Ātman, is equated with mind, and Vāc/speech is said to be his wife.

Although Vāc's identity as a goddess is not emphasized in the Upaniṣads, it appears that she retains her femaleness as Prajāpati's mate. The bovine symbolism of Vāc also reappears in Bṛhadāraṇyaka Upaniṣad 5.8, where it is said that one should revere Vāc as a cow. The notion that the world manifests itself as a result of the relations between male and female creative elements persists despite the rather abstract character of most of the accounts of creation found in the Upaniṣads and is explicitly articulated in Bṛhadāraṇyaka Upaniṣad 1.4.1–4, where the incipient cosmos is described as the Self (Ātman) alone in the form of a person. Feeling without delight, Ātman desires a second, so he causes himself to fall into two pieces, therefore giving rise to a husband and a wife. These two copulate in different forms, thus spawning different types of creatures.

The penchant for correspondences among the different levels of reality that we have seen in the Brāhmaṇas is also present in the Upaniṣads, and the correlation between speech and the earth persists. In Bṛhadāraṇyaka Upaniṣad 1.5.4, the links among speech/mind/breath are accommodated, and it is stated that this world is speech, the middle world is mind, and that (sky) world is breath. Earth is also said to be the body of speech, and as far as speech extends, so far extends the earth.[119] Thus speech is manifest materially as the physical world.

As in the Brāhmaṇas, Vāc in these texts is the unmanifest activating principle that, through interaction with a creator figure, is projected forth and transformed into the manifest world. It is notable that in at least one passage Vāc is identified with Virāj, who in the Atharva-Veda (see above) is also associated with energy and linked to materiality.[120]

In the Upaniṣads, the cosmological and cosmogonic structures established in the Brāhmaṇas persist. Although the descriptions of the process and nature of creation are not as concretely gender-specific as those accounts found in the Saṃhitās and Brāhmaṇas, the basic symbolism remains the same. The feminine principle is both an activating principle and also the gross, abstract material from which the manifest cosmos is formed.

The Vedic materials are, in general, rather obscure and difficult to interpret with any certainty. Nevertheless, we can conclude our observations by noting that, vague though it may be, some sense of a feminine principle that forms part of both cosmogonic narrative (often in conjunction with a male consort figure) and cosmological speculation begins to emerge and take form in the Vedic literature. Different goddesses embody this feminine principle and represent its diverse manifestations. Thus we find, for example, that certain female divinities, such as the waters or the goddess earth, seem to be allied more with the material pole of creation, whereas others, such as Śacī/Indrāṇī or Vāc, tend to be associated more vigorously with the enlivening, active principle of creation. Yet all of these various expressions of the feminine seem to be interrelated dimensions of a single principle that can be characterized as a kind of material energizing presence, a presence that both propels creation into being and also exists in embodied form as the physical cosmos itself.

CHAPTER TWO

Prakṛti, Māyā, and *Śakti*: The Feminine Principle in Philosophical Discourse

Our investigation began with an examination of Vedic associations of female divinity generally with materiality and energy. We will now turn to look at the formulation of the feminine in philosophical discourse as the principles *prakṛti, māyā,* and *śakti.*

The most elaborate and logically consistent descriptions of the nature and function of *prakṛti, māyā,* and *śakti* as principles are found in the literature of the major "orthodox" (*āstika*) Brahmanical philosophical schools. These descriptions, however, are tied into a larger web of reflections in which they constitute strong but not exclusive threads. In exploring these three principles' many layers of meaning in philosophical discourse, as well as their various connotations and nuances, one must also look at relevant related materials. Thus our investigation will take us into not only philosophical literature but other kinds of literature as well.

Prakṛti

THE TERM *PRAKṚTI* IN EARLY VEDIC, GRAMMATICAL, AND RITUAL CONTEXTS

It is notable that the term *prakṛti*, so important in later Brahmanical thought, does not occur at all in any of the Vedic Saṃhitās and appears to occur only once in the Brāhmaṇas.[1] It is found, however, in the Vedāṅgas, the "limbs" or subsidiary texts of the Vedas, in both grammatical and ritual contexts. In these environments, the term has a technical meaning denoting the basic, uninflected, or unelaborated structure that can then be modified or embellished in different ways in other contexts. In the former case, *prakṛti* means the primary, radical form of a word,[2] whereas in the latter it signifies the paradigmatic sacrifice on which other sacrifices are modeled.[3] The similarity between these two senses of the term *prakṛti* is more than coincidental. Louis Renou has suggested that one can find many parallels between ancient grammatical formulations and those of ritual. He further suggests that the Sanskrit grammatical tradition draws upon notions prevalent in the Vedic ritual tradition and reapplies them with slightly different inflection. With respect to the term *prakṛti*, he notes:

> *Prakṛti* means "base": the word is glossed *mūla*, *yoni* (the commentary of Hiraṇyakeśi-śrautasūtra gives it as an equivalent of *nimitta* or of *kāraṇa*) and designates those rites that, once described, will not be repeated anymore when one will treat other ceremonies. It is with regard to *prakṛti* that *vikṛti* or variety, the "ectype" if one prefers with respect to the "archetype," is posited. . . . The same meaning of "base" exists in the grammarians and the phoneticians: thus "radical" as opposed to *pratyaya*, or rather "original, primitive state" of a word as opposed to its "modified state" which is denoted by the term *vikṛti* and more often *vikāra*. . . . The usage of the term in grammar can be thus understood as a borrowing from ritual language.[4]

The term *prakṛti* in the sense of "uninflected root" is also found in the Mīmāṃsā-Sūtras.[5]

There are two points that should be noted about the use of the term *prakṛti* in these contexts. First, the term seems to have ritual and linguistic significance but no explicitly stated cosmological implications. Second, the term *prakṛti* as it is used in these texts does not have any clear association with materiality. A form that is *prakṛti* is described as foundational in a structural, but not material, sense.[6]

It is not necessarily significant that we can find no evidence in these texts of any metaphysical reflection about *prakṛti* as a cosmic principle of materiality. The focus of the Saṃhitās is mainly mythological, although certain hymns are more philosophically oriented in nature than others; grammatical texts are concerned with language; and the Brāhmaṇas and Mīmāṃsā-Sūtras concern themselves mainly with Vedic ritual and proper performance of the sacrifice (*yajña*), so cosmological speculation articulated in these texts generally focuses on the ritual act. Thus one would not expect to find assertions regarding the nature of material reality in these texts since inquiry into this kind of problem does not fall within their domain. What is significant, however, is the use of the term *prakṛti* to express the fundamental state of the structure, either grammatical or ritual, which is of ultimate concern in these environments. The use of the term to indicate the foundational constituent on which all other related constituents are based and from which they are derived also applies to its use in later contexts.

The term *pradhāna,* which in later texts is often used as a synonym for the term *prakṛti,* has a meaning in grammatical and ritual contexts that is quite different. Renou observes, for example, that the word *pradhāna* indicates the "principle," as opposed to the "subordinate," position of a term. In a compound, *pradhāna* denotes the principal member, the "determined" as opposed to the "determining" agent (for example, *puruṣa,* "man"—as opposed to *rājan,* "king"—

in *rājapuruṣa*, "king's man" or "king's servant"). In ritual contexts, the term designates the essential portions of a given ritual that give it its individual flavor and that vary from sacrifice to sacrifice.[7]

PRAKṚTI AS A MATERIAL PRINCIPLE

The most systematic formulation of the concept of *prakṛti* as a principle of materiality is found in the Sāṃkhya-Kārikā, the central treatise of the school of Brahmanical Hindu philosophy known as classical Sāṃkhya. The Sāṃkhya-Kārikā appears to have been compiled by Īśvarakṛṣṇa around the fourth century C.E. Much of what the treatise expounds, however, including its doctrine of *prakṛti*, is rooted in earlier materials and traditions, including some of the Vedic materials explored in the previous chapter. In fact, the understanding of *prakṛti* as it is expressed in the Sāṃkhya-Kārikā emerges out of the confluence of a variety of mythological, speculative, and philosophical streams of thought. Because of the close relationship between Sāṃkhya's formulation of *prakṛti* as a material principle and the various elements to which this formulation is connected, it is impossible to separate the development of *prakṛti* as a material principle from the historical evolution of Sāṃkhya philosophy in general.

In order to place the understanding of *prakṛti* as it appears in its classical form in proper context, it is helpful to look at the historical development of the term and its meaning in different environments prior to the recording of the Sāṃkhya-Kārikā. We will not examine every occurrence of the term *prakṛti* in the entire history of Indian literature but will rather focus on tracing the emergence of a notion of *prakṛti* as a principle of materiality that is a cosmogonic and cosmological abstraction. We will turn first to those pre-Sāṃkhya texts and passages that relate directly to the Sāṃkhya-Kārikā's later formulation of *prakṛti* as a principle of materiality, focusing particularly on lines of continuity between the Vedic materials that we have looked at and later materials. We will then turn to look at the Sāṃkhya-Kārikā itself. As we shall see, in fact, there is much more narrative and structural similarity between some of the Vedic and epic materials and aspects of *prakṛti* in later philosophical materials than one might suspect.

PRAKṚTI IN VEDIC AND PROTO-SĀṂKHYA CONTEXTS

In his discussion of the history of Sāṃkhya philosophy, Gerald J. Larson distinguishes between two discernible stages of development prior to the emergence of the classical Sāṃkhya expounded in the Sāṃkhya-Kārikā: a period of ancient speculations (including the Vedic hymns and some of the oldest Upaniṣads, e.g., the Bṛhadāraṇyaka, Chāndogya, and Taittirīya, eighth or ninth–ca. fourth centuries B.C.E.), and a period of proto-Sāṃkhya developments (including some of the middle Upaniṣads like the Śvetāśvatara, the *Caraka Saṃhitā,* the Bhagavad-Gītā, and the Mokṣadharma section of the Mahābhārata, ca. fourth century B.C.E. to first century C.E.).[8] In the first period, Sāṃkhya as such is "nowhere to be found," but many motifs and ideas that are later assimilated into Sāṃkhya contexts begin to emerge.[9] In the second period, a definite Sāṃkhya tradition starts to take shape, and many of the technical terms that are associated with later classical Sāṃkhya also appear.[10] Consistent descriptions of the nature and function of *prakṛti* as a material principle only begin to come to the fore in the period of proto-Sāṃkhya. As we move out of the Vedic materials and into post-Vedic texts, we see an increasingly complex and distinctly proto-Sāṃkhyan delineation of *prakṛti,* as well as an increasingly standardized description of its nature and function. Motifs related to the later understanding of *prakṛti* as a material principle, however, can be traced back even to the Vedic Saṃhitās.[11]

As we have already seen, several passages in the Vedic texts postulate the existence of a primordial, undifferentiated matrix of water that forms the material basis of creation, and the similarities between Vedic portrayals of the cosmic waters and later descriptions of *prakṛti* are striking. Both are abstract, cosmic principles of materiality. The motif of evolution that is associated with the function of the waters in creation also comes up in later descriptions of *prakṛti*. In proto-Sāṃkhya and Sāṃkhya materials *prakṛti*, like the waters of Vedic cosmogonies, evolves from its primordial state of non-differentiation to a differentiated state and gives rise to various forms.

Other Vedic cosmogonic motifs and structures also have counterparts in later materials concerning *prakṛti*. In the Saṃhitās and Brāhmaṇas, for example, accounts of cosmogony sometimes describe the evolution or emergence of the waters from heat (*tapas*): thus in Ṛg-Veda 10.190 it is said that heat (*tapas*) generates the cosmic waters in the form of an ocean (*samudra*), and in Śatapatha Brāhmaṇa 6.1.3 Prajāpati performs austerities (*tapas*), and when he becomes heated (√*tap*), the waters are produced from him.[12] The Upaniṣads articulate a similar motif, only they tend to replace the term *tapas* with *tejas*, which can mean heat or fire, or *agni*, which means fire. The Taittirīya Upaniṣad, for example, states that water comes from fire (*agni*).[13] In later classical Sāṃkhya, as we shall see, a similar sequence is expressed in the evolution from *prakṛti* of the elements, where the element water is said to evolve from the element fire (*tejas*). Furthermore, in its capacity as the source of the cosmic waters, heat or fire is the more abstract equivalent of speech (*vāc*), which, as we have also seen, sometimes is described as the waters' source; in fact, the correlation between heat/fire and speech is recognized in the Chāndogya Upaniṣad, where it is stated that the minutest particles of fire (*tejas*) become speech when fire is eaten and that speech consists of fire.[14] The word used here, *tejas*, means not only heat or fire, but also power, and both heat or fire and speech are portrayed in a general way as sources of creative power that produce or evolve into the cosmic waters. This motif of a principle of creative energy or power giving rise to a principle of primordial materiality also has parallels in later Purāṇic literature where, as we shall see, *śakti* gives rise to *prakṛti.*

The heat/fire-to-water sequence is picked up and elaborated in the description of cosmogony found in Chāndogya Upaniṣad 6.2.1–4.

> In the beginning, this (world) was Being (*sat*) only, one only, without a second. . . . It thought, "Let me be many! Let me procreate!" It sent forth (√*sṛj*) fire (*tejas*). That fire thought, "Let me be many! Let me procreate!" It discharged water (*ap*). . . . Those waters thought, "Let me be many! Let me procreate!" They discharged food (*anna*).[15]

The description of Being addressing its desire to create by sending forth fire directly parallels the description of creation in Pañcaviṃśa Brāhmaṇa 7.6.1–3, where Prajāpati addresses his desire to reproduce by producing a thought and sending it forth through speech. Thus we again see the correlation between heat/fire and speech. Yet it is especially notable that the evolutionary sequence in this passage includes a third element, food, for water becomes food (*anna*). The transformation of water into food parallels the transformation of water into earth in many of the Vedic passages explored in the previous chapter, implying a loosely analogous relationship between food and earth.[16] The sequence of evolution from fire to water to food also has parallels in later materials where the elements fire, water, and earth are the last three principles to emerge from *prakṛti.* It is quite likely that the placement of fire, water, and earth as the final three elements in the successive evolution of the elements in proto-Sāṃkhya and later classical Sāṃkhya is directly influenced by the older Vedic schemes, which identify heat or fire as the source of water, and water as the immediate material source of earth and/or the material cosmos in the unfolding of creation.

The basic tripartite division of a single primordial substance into heat/fire, water, and food is also repeated in other Upaniṣadic passages and adumbrates related themes that come up in later proto-Sāṃkhya and Sāṃkhya. Chāndogya Upaniṣad 6.4.1.1–5, for example, establishes correspondences among the three evolutes heat/fire, water, and food and the three colors red, white, and black. Chāndogya Upaniṣad 6.4.6 then generalizes the relationship between the colors and the three evolutes:

> Which red form is in fire (*agni*), that is the form of heat/fire (*tejas*); which (form is) white, that (is the form) of water (*ap*); which (form is) dark, that (is the form) of food (*anna*). . . . They knew that which was as if red, that (was) the form of heat. They knew that which was as if white, that was the form of water. They knew that which was as if dark, that was the form of food.

The correspondences established in this passage have later counterparts in classical Sāṃkhya, where *prakṛti* is described as comprising three *guṇas*, "strands," which are *prakṛti*'s consitutent parts: *sattva*, the *guṇa* of purity; *rajas*, the *guṇa* of activity; and *tamas*, the *guṇa* of lethargy.[17] In Sāṃkhya, white is associated with the *guṇa sattva*, red is associated with *rajas*, and black is associated with *tamas*. The Śvetāśvatara Upaniṣad, which is somewhat later than the Chāndogya Upaniṣad,[18] also refers to the same three colors and portrays them as constituting an "unborn female" (*ajā*), who is described as the foundational principle that produces other constituents like her:

> With the one unborn female (*ajā*), who is red, white, and black, (and) who sends forth (√*sṛj*) many creatures having the same form (as her), there lies the one unborn male taking his pleasure.[19]

The description of this unborn principle sounds like Renou's description of *prakṛti* in ritual and grammatical literature as denoting an "archetype" from which the "ectypes" are derived (above). Furthermore, the portrayal of a unique female principle consisting of the colors red, white, and black (the colors of the *guṇas*) and sending forth creatures having the same form as herself also parallels later descriptions of *prakṛti* that identify *prakṛti* as an uncreated female principle of materiality from which other material forms evolve.

The Śvetāśvatara Upaniṣad passage quoted above mentions an unborn male who lies with the female, "taking his pleasure," and these two unborn principles are also described as "two birds, bound companions" who "clasp the same tree."[20] The pairing of male/female consorts is, as we have seen, not uncommon in the Vedic texts. But the impersonal nature of this description and the designation of the two as "unborn" set this passage apart from the others that we have explored in the previous chapter, for the two take on a character that is more abstract than the male/female pairs we have seen portrayed in other contexts. This pairing resonates with an equally impersonal pairing described in another Upaniṣad, the Maitri. Here, *prakṛti* is portrayed as the object of enjoyment consisting of three *guṇas* and is contrasted with the person (*puruṣa*) who enjoys her:

> The person abides inside matter (*pradhāna*). That very one is an enjoyer; thus he enjoys/eats (√*bhuj*) the food derived from nature (*prākṛta anna*). This self consisting of the elements, indeed, is his food. Its maker is matter (*pradhāna*). Therefore, that which is to be enjoyed consists of three qualities (*guṇas*), and the enjoyer is the person who abides inside. . . . Therefore, the person is the enjoyer, nature (*prakṛti*) is what is to be enjoyed. Standing in it, he thus enjoys. . . . The enjoyer of it (*prakṛti*) is without qualities (*nirguṇa*).[21]

It is difficult to discern whether the term *guṇa* in this passage is being used in a generic sense to mean "quality" in general or whether it is meant to refer specifically to the technical designation of the three *guṇas* as the three "strands" or constituent aspects of *prakṛti* (*sattva, rajas,* and *tamas*). In any case, *puruṣa,* the enjoyer of *prakṛti,* is said to be without qualities or "strands" (*nirguṇa*), whereas *prakṛti* consists of three qualities or "strands" that are not named. The pairing of the unborn male with the unborn female and the pairing of *puruṣa* and *prakṛti* in these passages hint at the standard pairing in later classical Sāṃkhya of *puruṣa,* the principle of pure consciousness, with *prakṛti,* the principle of materiality consisting of its three *guṇas* (*sattva, rajas,* and *tamas*) from which *puruṣa* always remains distinct. It is also notable that this last passage plays upon the relationship between *prakṛti* and food (*anna*). The "enjoyer" is said to eat or enjoy (√*bhuj*) food derived from *prakṛti,* but is also said to eat or enjoy *prakṛti* itself. The doubling of food and *prakṛti* adumbrates some kind of analogous relationship between the two.

Śvetāśvatara Upaniṣad 4.9–10 contains another reference that is relevant to our investigation. This passage equates *prakṛti* with the principle of *māyā* and describes God as the possessor of this *māyā:*

> Sacred hymns, sacrifices, sacrificial rituals, ordinances, the past, the future, and what the Vedas say, all this is created by the possessor of *māyā* (*māyin*) from this, and in it the other is confined by *māyā.*[22]
>
> Know thus that *prakṛti* is *māyā;* the Great Lord (Maheśvara) then is the possessor of *māyā* (*māyin*). Verily, all this world is pervaded by beings (*bhūta*) that are parts of Him.

We will examine the concept of *māyā* more closely at a later point in this chapter. Suffice it to say for now that *māyā* in the Upaniṣads is often conceived in conjunction with *prakṛti.* In the passage above, *prakṛti/māyā* is not independent from God but is, rather, under God's control. This is also implied in 6.2:

> (He) by whom this whole (world) is eternally covered, the knower, the time-maker, the possessor of the *guṇas* who is the all-knower, controlled by that one, this work (*karman,* = the world) revolves, (which) is thought (to be) earth, water, fire, air, and ether.

This passage also enumerates the five principles that classical Sāṃkhya later lists as the five gross elements: earth, water, fire, air, and ether. Elsewhere, *māyā* is again mentioned, this time in relation to the term *pradhāna.*[23]

> What is perishable is *pradhāna.* What is immortal and imperishable is Hara. One god (*deva*) rules both the perishable (*pradhāna*) and the self (*ātman*). From meditation on him, from uniting (with him), and from (realizing his) true being still more, there is finally cessation from all *māyā.*

Here, the term *pradhāna* seems to have the force of the meaning that we would also associate with the term *prakṛti;* that is, it seems to mean the material, manifest cosmos. *Māyā* in this passage is often interpreted to mean illusion, and the relationship between *pradhāna* and *māyā* is not explicitly articulated. Yet there seems to be an important connection between the two principles. This becomes clearer when one explores the context in which this material is found. Immediately prior to this passage, Brahman is described as having three aspects: the knowing, omnipotent one (God, the supreme Self), the unknowing, impotent enjoyer (the self, *ātman*), and that which is connected with the enjoyer (the world, or *prakṛti/pradhāna*). All three are described as unborn (*aja*):

> That (which is) joined together is perishable and imperishable, manifest and unmanifest. The Lord (Īśa) supports it all. And without the Lord, the self is bound because of its nature as an enjoyer. Knowing God (*deva*), (it) is released from all bonds. The two unborn ones (are the) knowing (Lord) and the unknowing

> (self), the powerful and the impotent. That female one is also unborn, who is united with the enjoyer and objects of enjoyment.[24]

Without God (Īśa), the self (*ātman*) is bound because it is an enjoyer; by knowing God, it is released from all bonds. What are these bonds (*pāśa*)? Since the self is bound by being an enjoyer, and the object of enjoyment is a feminine entity, presumably *prakṛti*, the fetters must be those created by the involvement of the self with that entity. By knowing God, there is release from these fetters. The force of this passage is essentially the same as that of the immediately following passage, 1.10 cited above, which states that through meditation on God, there is cessation from *māyā*. Some kind of parallel between involvement with *prakṛti*/*pradhāna* on the one hand and *māyā* on the other is therefore indicated.

The relationship between *prakṛti* and *māyā* in these texts is important. As we shall see, although these two principles will be differentiated in later philosophical literature, there is not always a clear-cut distinction between them in these earlier contexts. They are sometimes explicitly equated, as in Śvetāśvatara Upaniṣad 4.10 above, but this is not always the case. We will look at this problem more closely at a later point in this chapter.

THE MARRIAGE OF VEDIC AND PROTO-SĀṂKHYA MATERIALS IN THE MAHĀBHĀRATA

What is perhaps most interesting for our investigation is to explore some of the ways in which the concept of a fundamental material principle presented along discernible proto-Sāṃkhya lines develops in post-Vedic literature with respect to the Vedic elements that we have already explored. Although many post-Vedic texts do not concern themselves at all with Vedic narratives, others do. This is most clearly the case in the Mahābhārata, especially in the

Mokṣadharma portion of the Śānti-Parvan and the Bhagavad-Gītā, but elsewhere as well. Because of its composite nature and the diversity of its contents, the Mahābhārata includes Vedic, post-Vedic philosophical, and non-Vedic mythological material, and it often attempts to weave diverse strands of thought into a single cloth. This is in fact what happens with respect to reflections regarding the nature of materiality. Thus we find that assertions about a material principle in terms and categories that fit a discernible proto-Sāṃkhya mold exist side by side with assertions that seem contradictory or attempt to combine these categories with those of the older Vedic literature.

The proto-Sāṃkhya materials in the Mahābhārata, like those found in other proto-Sāṃkhya environments, posit a material principle that has a variety of names. This principle is sometimes referred to as *prakṛti* but also quite often is called *avyakta* ("the unmanifest"), *pradhāna* ("the originator"), *sattva* ("purity"), and other names as well. The term *prakṛti* itself frequently is used to denote an eightfold entity consisting of a material principle designated as *prakṛti* plus seven other principles that evolve out of it: *mahat* ("the great principle," a synonym of *buddhi* or intellect), *ahaṃkāra,* ("egoity"), and the five gross elements ether, wind or air, fire, water, and earth. In later classical Sāṃkhya, the five gross elements are the last of several evolutes to evolve from *prakṛti* and come forth in this precise order, but this is not always the case in the Mahābhārata, as we shall see. Several passages in the epic also mention sixteen *vikāra*s or secondary modifications of *prakṛti*: *manas* or "mind," hearing, touching, seeing, tasting, smelling, speaking, grasping, walking, excreting, procreating, sound, contact, form, taste, and smell. In later classical Sāṃkhya, these last fifteen principles are said to be the five sense capacities (*buddhīndriya*), action capacities (*karmendriya*), and subtle elements (*tanmātra*). The eight portions of *prakṛti* along with the sixteen secondary modifications are sometimes designated as twenty-four essential principles of material reality called *tattva*s, but different passages in the epic propose different numbers of *tattvas*.[25] Some passages count *puruṣa*, "consciousness," as the unmanifest part of *prakṛti*, but others include *puruṣa* in the list of *tattvas* as a twenty-fifth principle. The list of twenty-five *tattvas* that we find in some passages of the Mahābhārata corresponds to the twenty-five *tattvas* of later classical Sāṃkhya. *Prakṛti* and *puruṣa* are sometimes paired in the epic, and where this occurs, the text often refers to them with the terms *kṣetra*, "field," and *kṣetrajña*, "knower of the field." As we shall see, some passages in the epic even postulate a twenty-sixth principle, a supreme Absolute, which is the ultimate source of all the others.[26]

In many of the sections of the Mahābhārata where we find proto-Sāṃkhya materials related to the understanding of *prakṛti* as a material principle, these materials are woven together with corresponding Vedic materials. The Bhīṣma-Parvan of the Mahābhārata, for example, asserts the supremacy of the earth as a primordial material principle, echoing the Vedic theme of the earth as supreme mother and material matrix of creation. Thus we find in Bhīṣma-Parvan 5.20–21:[27]

> Everything is born from the earth and everything disappears into the earth. The earth is the foundation of (all) creatures, (and) the earth alone is (their) final resort. He that has the earth has the entire world with its inanimate and animate population.

This praise of earth as the totality of creation appears entirely without reference to proto-Sāṃkhya categories. Then, a bit further, in section 6.3–5,[28] earth is described in relation to the four other gross elements of proto-Sāṃkhya description—water, wind, fire, and space—and their qualities, sound, touch, form, taste, and smell, five of the secondary modifications of *prakṛti*:

> O great king (Dhṛtarāṣṭra), all things present in the world have been said by the wise to be equal to the five

> elements—earth (*bhūmi*), water (*ap*), wind (*vāyu*), fire (*agni*), and space (*ākāśa*)—on account of accumulation. (That is,) they all possess the qualities of the superior (element). Earth is the foremost (*pradhānatas*) of them. Sound (*śabda*), touch (*sparśa*), form (*rūpa*), taste (*rasa*), and scent (*gandha*)—these are said by seers (*ṛṣis*) acquainted with the truth to be the qualities of earth.

The importance of the earth is now explained and justified using a schema that contains elements clearly related to the categories of proto-Sāṃkhya. Earth is foremost because it contains all five of the possible qualities mentioned, qualities that correspond to the five subtle elements (*tanmātras*) recognized both elsewhere in the epic itself and in later classical Sāṃkhya.[29]

The combination in the epic of proto-Sāṃkhya principles with older Vedic elements is especially notable with respect to reflections regarding the evolution of the cosmos from its primordial material state. The water cosmology that we have seen throughout the Vedic texts persists in the Mahābhārata, but there is now an attempt to recast it and integrate it with proto-Sāṃkhya materials regarding cosmology and cosmogony, which describe the evolution from *prakṛti* of the other twenty-three material *tattvas* and tend to count the five gross elements—ether, wind or air, fire, water, and earth—as the last of the evolutes. The Vedic understanding of the waters as the primordial matrix present at the beginning of creation is merged with the placement of the waters toward the end of the unfolding of creation in the proto-Sāṃkhya system. This is especially evident in the Mokṣadharma section of the Śānti-Parvan, where proto-Sāṃkhya categories play the greatest role.

In the Mokṣadharma, cosmogony is also often discussed in conjunction with the opposite process, dissolution. As the cosmos emanates forth, so it will be dissolved in a process that reverses the order of emanation. Each principle flows forth from the one that precedes it and will dissolve back into that same principle. Since much of the material regarding the role of the waters is found in passages describing dissolution, not creation, we will explore these passages as well, always bearing in mind that this process mirrors that of cosmogony.

There are several passages in the Mokṣadharma where the gross material universe is described as emerging out of the primordial waters. In 12.176.2–16,[30] for example, which is included in the Mokṣadharma, water is said to be the foundation of all that exists. In this passage, however, the five gross elements (space, wind, fire, water, and earth) are now introduced into the narrative:

> Bhṛgu said: Mānasa produced the varied creation of beings by means of his mind (*manas*). First off, he created water (*jala*) for the stimulation (*saṃdhukṣaṇa*) of creatures. Water is that which is the breath of all creatures, by means of which beings grow, and deprived of which all perish. The whole universe is pervaded by it [water]. The earth, mountains, clouds, and all other things that have form should all be known again as related to water as (that which forms when) the waters (*ap*) become solid (√*stambh*).
> Bharadvāja said: How did the waters (*salila*) spring up? And how (did) fire and wind (arise)? And how was the earth created? I have great doubts about these points.
> Bhṛgu said: Formerly, in the Brahmakalpa, oh holy one, when the Brahmanical seers (*brahmarṣi*) were gathered together, doubt about the creation of the world arose in these great souls. Taking up contemplation, remaining silent and immovable, abandoning food, consuming (only) air, the twice-born ones ruled (*ati* √*ṣṭhā*) for a thousand celestial years. A righteous voice (*vāṇī*), the divine Sarasvatī, arose there from out of the firmament (and) reached the ears of them all: "Formerly, there was only infinite space (*ākāśa*), completely tranquil, soundless, motionless, and immovable. Without moon,

sun, or wind, it was as if asleep. Then the waters (*salila*) sprang into existence. . . . Then from the pressure of the waters (*salila*) arose wind (*marut*). . . . Then in that friction of wind and water, blazing heat (*tejas*) possessed of great might arose. . . . Joined together with the wind, fire (*agni*) drew space and water together. That fire, from combining with the wind, became solidified. While falling from space, its liquid part (*sneha*) became hard and became the earth."

The order in which the gross elements are cited as appearing is different from that of the standard order of evolution — ether, wind or air, fire, water, and earth—asserted elsewhere in the text and in later classical Sāṃkhya. This passage places the appearance of water before that of wind (*marut/vayu*) and fire. Although space (*ākāśa*) comes first, the succession given in this passage gives primacy to water, for space is simply the backdrop against which the drama of creation unfolds. Thus this narrative effectively integrates older Vedic cosmogonic elements with proto-Sāṃkhya elements by retaining the primacy of the waters in the process of emanation but including the waters in the list of elements that is found in proto-Sāṃkhya and in later classical Sāṃkhya. The Brāhmaṇa motif concerning the creative role of thought is also picked up in this passage, for the creator Mānasa, the equivalent of Prajāpati in the Brāhmaṇas, creates the waters with his mind. There are also faint echoes in this passage of the creative relationship between thought and speech established in the Brāhmaṇas, for the seers' contemplations stimulate the appearance on the scene of a celestial voice that, while not directly involved in cosmogony, recounts a cosmogonic narrative. Furthermore, the voice is likened to Sarasvatī, who in the Brāhmaṇas is equated with the goddess of speech, Vāc.

The primacy of water as the material foundation of the gross, manifest universe is again reconciled with proto-Sāṃkhya motifs in 12.195.1–2.[31] In this passage, however, there are two distinct stages of cosmic evolution. In the first stage, subtle principles, such as wind and light, emerge. The end of this stage is marked by the appearance of water. In the second stage, gross creation, the universe itself, flows forth.

> Manu said: From the imperishable (*akṣara*) sprang space (*kha*); from space came wind (*vāyu*); from wind came light (*jyotis*); from light came water (*jala*); from water sprang the world; and from the world, that which moves in it. These, along with (their) bodies, go first to water; and from water, heat, wind, and space (are also gone to).

This passage adheres to the more standard order of the gross elements' manifestation that we find in proto-Sāṃkhya and classical Sāṃkhya but affirms the important place of water as the source of the material cosmos. At the time of dissolution the order of emanation is reversed, and the entire cosmos withdraws back into the principle or principles from which it originally came. Thus in this passage, the entire universe not only springs from water but disappears back into it when creation is dissolved.

The place of water in the dissolution of the universe against a backdrop of proto-Sāṃkhya categories occurs again in 12.224.74–225.9.[32] Here again, there are two distinct stages of dissolution. In the first stage, all of gross creation is absorbed back first into earth and then into the waters, which alone remain. In the second stage, more subtle principles are dissolved:

> I will now convey the dissolution of the world at the beginning of the night, when the day is gone, in which way the supreme Self (Adhyātma), Īśvara, makes this all extremely subtle. As suns burn in the sky, in that way fire burns with seven flames. Then the whole world, filled with flames, blazes forth.
>
> Vyāsa said: All things on the earth, (both) mobile and immobile, first disappear and merge into the earth.[33]

> After all mobile and immobile things are dissolved, then earth, having no timber or grass, looks like a tortoise shell. Water takes up odor (*gandha*), the quality of earth. When odor is taken up, it [the earth] is fit for dissolution. The waters (*ap*) then abide. Billowy and producing great noise, having filled this all, they both remain still and move about. Then, oh dear one, light (*jyotis*) takes up the qualities of water. And when the qualities of water are taken up, then (the waters) come to rest in light. When the flames of fire conceal the sun standing in the middle, the sky, filled with flames, blazes forth. When wind (*vāyu*) takes up form (*rūpa*), the quality of light, then light disappears. The great wind moves violently. . . . When space (*ākāśa*) swallows up touch (*sparśa*), the quality of wind, then wind disappears. . . . When space takes up sound (*śabda*). . . .

The process of dissolution ends when all existent creatures are withdrawn into Brahman. In all of these passages, the place of water as the immediate source of the cosmos is neatly absorbed into the identifiably proto-Sāṃkhyan schema of the evolution of gross elements that is found in this portion of the epic and that is assimilated into later classical Sāṃkhya. It is evident that the Mokṣadharma self-consciously attempts to weave Vedic and proto-Sāṃkhya motifs and patterns together.

The dissolution of the known world into water is one stage of dissolution, that of the gross world, but the introduction of proto-Sāṃkhya elements into the cosmological system requires a higher stage of emanation and/or dissolution in which those aspects of creation that are not included in the schema of gross elements are also created or dissolved. Thus many of the narratives in the Mokṣadharma stressing dissolution include another level culminating in the complete absorption of all elements, both gross and subtle, manifest and unmanifest, into a single, ultimate, nonmaterial principle that is the most subtle of all. This principle is usually identified as Brahman or Puruṣa. The schemes presented in these passages do not appear to recognize any ultimate autonomous principle of materiality, for all of material creation is ultimately reabsorbed. In 12.224–225 cited above, for example, after the material cosmos dissolves into water, there is a further stage of dissolution that results in complete absorption of everything into Brahman. A similar pattern is presented in 12.326.30,[34] where everything ultimately dissolves first into *prakṛti* and then into *puruṣa.* Elsewhere the distinction between the two phases of dissolution collapses, and the waters take the place of undifferentiated Brahman. In 12.329.3,[35] for example:

> At the time of dissolution at the end of four thousand *yugas*, when all creatures, mobile and immobile, disappear into the unmanifest [*prakṛti*], when light, earth, and wind disappear, when there is intense darkness, when the world is nothing but an expanse of water, when (the world) is overcome with darkness (*tamas*), when the one possessing consciousness (*saṃjñaka*) stands without second, when it is neither day nor night, when there is neither existence (*sat*) nor nonexistence (*asat*), when neither manifest (*vyakta*) nor unmanifest (*avyakta*) exists, at the time of that state . . . imperishable Hari, who is Puruṣa,[36] appeared from that eternal darkness (*tamas*).

In this passage, the waters become identified with the ultimate, unmanifest, undifferentiated source of the manifest, differentiated cosmos, a description that also applies to the principle of materiality (*avyakta,* and so forth) of proto-Sāṃkhya. But the waters are also said to exist prior to the appearance of the unmanifest (= *prakṛti*) and are said to be the matrix from which Puruṣa, who is here identified as Hari (Viṣṇu), appears. In other passages of the Mokṣadharma, that which transcends both *prakṛti* and *puruṣa* and is their source is undifferentiated Brahman. The description of the waters presented here is reminiscent of Ṛg-Veda 129.1–3, where the primordial waters are said to be present at the dawn of creation, before the distinction between existence (*sat*) and nonexistence (*asat*), when darkness is hidden by darkness.[37]

Elsewhere the identification of water as an ultimate principle of materiality is asserted even outside of any context concerning the processes of creation or dissolution. Thus in 12.180.22,[38] two principles are described, here identified as Brahman and physical form, which is derived from water:

> All this is composed of water alone. Water (*ap*) is the form of all embodied creatures. There (in that water) is the mental Self, Brahman, the maker of all (abiding) in all things.

In this passage, water seems to be an all-pervading material principle and, along with Brahman, the second existent—a description that would also fit the *prakṛti* and *puruṣa* of classical Sāṃkhya, as we shall see.

In all of these passages cited above, even when the waters are not identified with some ultimate principle, their function is nevertheless quite similar to that of the ultimate principle of materiality—*avyakta, prakṛti, pradhāna, sattva,* and so forth—described in the epic's proto-Sāṃkhya speculation. When the waters are presented as the material matrix of gross, manifest (*vyakta*) creation, their role as foundation or substratum echoes that of the primordial, subtle, unmanifest (*avyakta*) material matrix described in other contexts.

Although the identification of the two ultimate principles, *puruṣa* and *prakṛti,* with gender categories in later classical Sāṃkhya is dubitable, we find several assertions in the Mokṣadharma associating primordial materiality with femaleness. In 12.292.27,[39] for example, *prakṛti* is referred to as *devī,* which may be an adjective meaning "divine" or a noun meaning "goddess." In 12.293.12ff.,[40] the relationship between male and female is compared with that of *puruṣa* and *prakṛti* (here in the sense of ultimate principle of materiality) who are described as the imperishable (*akṣara*) and the perishable (*kṣara*):

> Janaka said: Oh Bhagavān, the relation (*saṃbandha*) of those two, the imperishable (*akṣara*) and the perishable (*kṣara*), is regarded as that between male and female. The relation is said to be the same. Here, a female cannot conceive an embryo without a male, just as a male cannot create form without a female. Because of their union with one another, and because of the attachment of each to the attributes of the other, form arises.

Elsewhere, the terms *kṣetra* and *kṣetrajña*, which are used to describe the two ultimate principles of proto-Sāṃkhya reflection, are associated with human women and men:

> By nature (*prakṛti*), women are like *kṣetra*, and men are characteristically *kṣetrajña*.[41]

Thus there is evidence that in the Mokṣadharma the principle of materiality is associated with female gender.

The Bhagavad-Gītā, which forms part of the Bhīṣma-Parvan or sixth book of the Mahābhārata, also seems to identify the source of material creation with feminine attributes. Bhagavad-Gītā 14.3, for example, describes the female sexual organ (*yoni*) of God (Bhagavān), which is called the great *brahman* (*mahat brahman*), in which God places the seed that is the origin of all beings. As the source of creation, the *mahat brahman* here functions like *prakṛti*, although the two are not explicitly equated.[42]

In the Bhagavad-Gītā generally, the identity of *prakṛti* as the term used to designate an abstract, ultimate principle of materiality is more firmly established than in the Mokṣadharma. The precise nature of this principle is nevertheless still too slippery to grasp with any confidence. Surendranath Dasgupta identifies in the Gītā two senses of the term, which he sees as designating (1) a primary and ultimate category and (2) an aspect of God's being. He also asserts that the two are not necessarily incommensurable, for *prakṛti* as an ultimate principle may simply be the hypostatization of God's nature.[43] The text itself identifies two different levels of meaning of the term:

> This [*buddhi, ahaṃkāra, manas,* and the five gross elements] is the lower (*prakṛti*), but know here my other, higher *prakṛti* consisting of souls (*jīvas*), by which this universe is sustained, O Mighty-Armed One.[44]

Both lower and higher forms of the created universe are aspects of God.

The relation between God and *prakṛti* in this passage echoes the similar relation between God and *prakṛti* that we saw in the Śvetāśvatara Upaniṣad, where God (Maheśvara) is described as possessing *prakṛti/māyā*.[45] Like this Upaniṣad, too, the Gītā also establishes some kind of connection between the terms *prakṛti* and *māyā,* although it is not clear in this case precisely what kind of connection is implied. Thus in 4.6:

> Although unborn, having an imperishable self, although being Lord of Creatures, having taken control of my own *prakṛti,* I come into being by my own *māyā.*

The nature of the relationship between *prakṛti* and *māyā* in this passage remains a puzzle, although both are designated as belonging to God and both are cited in relation to the process of God's coming into being. Elsewhere (7.14), the identity of the two seems to be implied when *māyā* is described as consisting of *guṇas,* which are normally cited in the Gītā as attributes of *prakṛti:*

> This my *māyā* is indeed divine, consisting of *guṇas,* difficult to penetrate; those who take refuge in me only, they transcend this *māyā.*

We will discuss further the meaning and importance of the relationship between *prakṛti* and *māyā* at a later point in this chapter.

PRAKṚTI IN CLASSICAL SĀṂKHYA

A number of the diverse threads of reflection that we have seen scattered throughout ancient and proto-Sāṃkhya materials are brought together in the normative system of classical Sāṃkhya expounded in Īśvarakṛṣṇa's Sāṃkhya-Kārikā.

The Sāṃkhya-Kārikā posits two ultimate and opposing ontological principles, *puruṣa* and *prakṛti.* There are a multitude of different *puruṣas,* but there is only one *prakṛti.* Both are uncreated and eternal. *Puruṣa* is the principle of consciousness; it is inactive and incapable of creative activity. *Prakṛti* is the principle of materiality and is the basis for all activity and creation. *Prakṛti* is the original "ground" or "stuff" from which all other products are derived and, as previously mentioned, is composed of three basic *guṇas* or "strands," namely, *sattva,* the principle of purity, *rajas,* the principle of activity, and *tamas,* the principle of lethargy. As in proto-Sāṃkhya, these three *guṇas* or strands together constitute the basic tendencies inherent within *prakṛti.* All three are necessary components of the manifest world, which arises through their mutual interaction. Yet because of their different characters, they are continually in tension with one another.[46]

When the *guṇas* are in equilibrium, *prakṛti* is said to be in an unmanifest (*avyakta*) state and is also called *mūlaprakṛti* or *pradhāna.* When the *guṇas* are stirred, *prakṛti* becomes manifest. The process of evolution brings about the manifest (*vyakta*) world consisting of twenty-three essential principles or *tattvas* that evolve out of *mūlaprakṛti* in an established order: first *buddhi* ("intellect"; also called *mahat*), then *ahaṃkāra* ("egoity") followed by *manas* ("mind"), then five *buddhīndriyas* ("sense capacities": hearing, touching, seeing, tasting, smelling), five *karmendriyas* ("organs of action" or "action capacities": speaking, grasping, walking, excreting, procreating), five *tanmātras* ("subtle elements": sound, contact, form, taste, smell), and five *mahābhūtas* ("gross elements": ether, air, fire, water, earth).[47] These twenty-three principles plus *prakṛti* and *puruṣa* together constitute the twenty-five *tattvas*, the same twenty-five that are enumerated in some of the proto-Sāṃkhya materials of the Mahābhārata. The process of emergence or "evolution" of the entities or *tattvas* that are derived from *prakṛti* is determined by the respective dominance of each of the three *guṇas*. The first, for example, *buddhi* or intellect, is characterized by a predominance of *sattva*. The *tanmātras* or subtle elements, which provide the essence of the gross physical world, are characterized by a predominance of *tamas*.[48]

In its unmanifest (*avyakta*) state, *prakṛti* is the cause of the manifest cosmos, the singular, ultimate source of all material forms. Though imperceptible, it can be inferred from the existence of its effects, the above-listed twenty-three *tattvas* that constitute the basis of the phenomenal world.[49] The initial impulse toward manifestation is produced by the stirring up of the *guṇas*. The cosmos itself is the final effect of *prakṛti's* evolution; it results from a transformation of primordial materiality into a manifest, differentiated state and is preexistent in latent form in *mūlaprakṛti*. This doctrine of causation upholds the preexistence of the effect in the cause and is known in Indian philosophy as *satkāryavāda*. Although the created cosmos, the effect, is inherent in *prakṛti*, the cause, and results from transformation of the cause, the production of the world does not exhaust *mūlaprakṛti*, which continues to exist eternally in its *avyakta* state.

Mūlaprakṛti is capable of transformation because it possesses the power or *śakti* of manifestation (*pravṛtti*) by means of which it is able to evolve and produce its effect. According to Sāṃkhya-Kārikā 15 and 16, the unmanifest (*avyakta*) is called the cause (*kāraṇa*) of the manifest world in part because of this power (*śakti*):

> Because of the measuring out of specific things (in the world); because of regular order (in the world); and *because of (its) power (śakti) of manifestation (pravṛtti);* because of the distinction between (the) cause and (its) effect; because of the undividedness of the diverse world; *the unmanifest (avyakta) is the cause.* And it is set into motion from the interaction of the three *guṇas*, which are modified like water (*salila*), due to the particular nature abiding in each of the respective *guṇas*.[50]

The manifest cosmos made up of manifold entities consisting of different combinations of the *guṇas* emerges from *mūlaprakṛti* when it transforms from its primordial state to its manifest form by means of its *śakti.* Thus in the Sāṃkhya-Kārikā, the term *śakti* is used to designate the capacity of *prakṛti* to unfold and is an aspect of *prakṛti* itself. It is perhaps significant that the three *guṇas* of *prakṛti,* which are modified when the process of transformation is set in motion, are in this capacity compared to water (*salila*). As we have seen, the term *salila* and other such terms are used in the Vedic literature and in the Mahābhārata to designate the primordial waters that form the foundation of the created universe and that are manipulated or modified in some way at the beginning of the creative process. Like the three *guṇas*, the waters form the basis of the material world. It is therefore possible that the comparison between the *guṇas* of *prakṛti* and water in this passage implies a comparison between the role of the *guṇas* in the Sāṃkhya-Kārikā's explanation of cosmogony and the role of the waters in some of the various cosmogonies that we have looked at.

Although *puruṣa* is left out of the scheme of manifestation, its presence is nevertheless a vital component, for it is only in the presence of *puruṣa,* the principle of pure consciousness, that *prakṛti* can evolve. *Puruṣa* is the inactive, indifferent spectator or witness that is completely distinct from anything having to do with *prakṛti.*[51] Because the two are always in proximity with one another, an interplay between them occurs that is necessary in order for *prakṛti* to evolve. *Puruṣa* is the catalyst of *prakṛti's* evolution. Furthermore, each appears to acquire the characteristics of the other even though they remain completely distinct.[52] Each is reflected in the other.

There is little discussion among scholars regarding the gender identity of *prakṛti* in the classical literature. Although *prakṛti* is a feminine noun in Sanskrit, there is no clear assertion in the Sāṃkhya-Kārikā that *prakṛti* is conceived as an unequivocally feminine principle. However, the function of *prakṛti* as the source of the material world adumbrates a maternal function, and in one place *prakṛti* is compared to a dancing girl (*nartakī*).[53] It is also important to note that the two levels of *prakṛti*—the primordial or "root" level (*mūlaprakṛti*) indicated by designations that include nonfeminine Sanskrit terms (*pradhāna, avyakta*), and a concrete level indicated more distinctly by the more or less equivalent feminine term (*prakṛti*)—are reminiscent of the two levels of the waters that we have seen in the Vedas, the waters as both abstract materiality (*ambhas, samudra, salila*) and as the feminine source of the manifest world (*ap*). The similarity between these two schemes again indicates that there may be some genuine but incompletely articulated connection between the Vedic waters and the *prakṛti* of Sāṃkhya.

Māyā

The significance of the concept of *māyā* in Brahmanical literature is in many ways closely related to that of *prakṛti*. We have already noted in the previous chapter the significance of the term *māyā* in the Vedic Saṃhitās with respect to its connection with Virāj. We have also seen that in the Upaniṣads and the Bhagavad-Gītā, *māyā* tends to be equated or at least associated with *prakṛti*. Although a detailed study of the significance of the term in the history of Indian religion and philosophy is well beyond the scope of this investigation, it will be helpful to explore a bit more deeply some of the various connotations of *māyā* and its relationship not only to *prakṛti* but also to *śakti*.

MĀYĀ IN VEDIC AND EARLY POST-VEDIC CONTEXTS

Jan Gonda argues that the term *māyā* possesses a central meaning that underlies all uses of the term in Vedic and post-Vedic texts and can be defined as "incomprehensible wisdom and power enabling its possessor, or being able itself, to create, devise, contrive, effect, or do something."[54] This definition is helpful for understanding the general sense of the term but is perhaps not adequately context-specific. If we look at the earliest uses of the term in the Saṃhitās, *māyā* seems to have several meanings, including (1) ethically neutral power possessed by the gods (*devas*) or demons (*asuras*), (2) a special ability of a god to create or assume different forms, (3) marvelous skill or capacity of achieving the marvelous, (4) divine ability or wisdom, (5) achievement made possible by supranormal or superhuman skill and ability, (6) ability of the gods to interfere in worldly events, and (7) cunning, design, or trickery.[55] In the Vedas, *māyā* is associated particularly with the *asuras*.

Teun Goudriaan draws upon Gonda's definition of *māyā*, but he offers a more thorough examination of the various dimensions of *māyā* in a variety of different genres of literature, focusing on the nonphilosophical, primarily mythological significance of the term. Goudriaan asserts that the term *māyā* in the Vedic Saṃhitās stands for a neutral force used for the creation of a real, material form, human or nonhuman, and by means of which the creator of that form demonstrates his incomprehensible power.[56] The god or demon who applies *māyā* does so in two ways: (1) by causing some new form to originate, or (2) by applying his creative power to himself so that he appears in a new and different form, a disguise that is not perceived as such by mortals. Thus, *māyā* is, among other things, a power or ability associated with both creation and transformation. The term *māyā* is used to describe three different aspects of these two processes: (1) it is the power that is used to create a new appearance; (2) it is the creation of that appearance as an abstract performance; and (3) it is the result of the process, the form that is created. There are no clear distinctions made among the power, its manifestation, and the result of the process.[57] These different meanings of the term in the mythological literature of the Saṃhitās are then reapplied philosophically in the Upaniṣads and the Bhagavad-Gītā, but the different levels of meaning are not clearly distinguished.

The implication of Goudriaan's observations is important for our understanding of the relationship between *prakṛti* and *māyā* in the early texts. If *māyā* refers to all three processes—the power of creation or transformation, the act of creation or transformation, and the resulting material form—then *prakṛti,* which is the principle of materiality, can be seen as one dimension of *māyā,* that is, as the material form resulting from either creation by God or God's transformation of himself into either abstract or concrete form. Thus the equation between the two principles in Śvetāśvatara Upaniṣad 4.10 and the seeming equation between them in Bhagavad-Gītā 7.14 make perfect sense. Yet the apparent distinction between them in Bhagavad-Gītā 4.6 ("Having taken control of my own *prakṛti,* I come into being by my own *māyā*") also makes sense; in this passage, *prakṛti* probably means the third aspect of *māyā,* material form resulting from a process of creation/transformation, whereas the term *māyā* is used to denote the power of transformation or the act itself by means of which the created form comes about. The various levels of meaning of the term also provide an important link between *prakṛti* and *śakti,* for they can both be subsumed under the different layers of meaning of the early use of the term *māyā.* Goudriaan himself notes that as power *māyā* can be compared to or equated with *śakti*, whereas as material form it can be identified with *prakṛti*.[58] *Śakti* and *prakṛti* represent successive stages in the process of manifestation. This interpretation of the relationship between the two notions is quite different from that of Sāṃkhya-Kārikā 15 and 16, where *prakṛti* is the ultimate cause of creation and the term *śakti* describes *prakṛti*'s ability to manifest.

The association of *māyā* with trickery or delusion of some kind is also present in the Vedic literature. In the Saṃhitās, the word is often used to denote the wiles of different beings.[59] This sense of the term *māyā* also appears in the Upaniṣads. In the Praśna Upaniṣad, one of the older Upaniṣads, the term *māyā* appears once and is associated with crookedness (*jihma*) and falsehood (*anṛta*).

> Those who possess austerity (*tapas*) and continence (*brahmacārya*), and in whom the truth is established, they indeed possess that world of Brahman (Brahmaloka). To them belongs the pure world of Brahman, in which there is no crookedness (*jihma*) no falsehood (*anṛta*), and no *māyā*.[60]

The passage ascribes a negative connotation to the term *māyā* and asserts that only those who are free from it will attain the world of Brahman. The precise meaning of the term in this passage, however, is not clear, although it is associated with wrong knowledge or wrong behavior and leads away from a desirable goal.

MĀYĀ IN ADVAITA VEDĀNTA

As *māyā* has so many connotations in the Vedas, a clear distinction between the meaning of the terms *prakṛti* and *māyā* arises only in later philosophical literature, where the connotations of the word *māyā* with illusion or delusion—connotations that are present from the earliest occurrences of the term in Vedic literature through the Upaniṣads, as we have seen—rise to the fore. This happens in later centuries when clearly defined, rival philosophical schools form. As Sāṃkhya concerns itself with the nature of ultimate reality, which it presents as consisting of two independent and incommensurate principles, there is another school of thought in Brahmanical Hinduism, the school of Advaita Vedānta, that focuses on similar concerns. Advaita Vedānta takes the Upaniṣads as its starting point and builds upon Upaniṣadic reflections to arrive at an ontology that is somewhat different from that of Sāṃkhya-Yoga. Although we will not embark upon a detailed discussion of Advaita Vedānta, it is important to understand some of its essential tenets and to note the significance and importance of the term *māyā* in this school of philosophy.

According to Śaṃkara, the prime exponent of the school of Advaita Vedānta, there is only one principle that is truly real, not two principles, as we have seen to be the view held by Sāṃkhya. As in the Upaniṣads, on which all schools of Vedānta are ultimately based, this principle is designated as Brahman or Ātman. Basing his arguments on the Upaniṣads, Śaṃkara proposes that there are two distinct levels of Brahman.

> Brahman is understood to have two forms: one is possessed of the conditioning factors that characterize the diverse elements of the world, which represent the modifications of name and form, and the other is free from all conditioning factors and is opposed to the earlier one.[61]

On the highest level, Brahman is described as pure being or truth (*sat* or *satya*), pure consciousness (*cit* or *caitanya*), and pure bliss (*ānanda*) but is also said to be devoid of all particular qualities or attributes (*nirguṇa*).[62] This conception of Brahman is very much out of Upaniṣadic thought. In the Upaniṣads, Brahman is said to be beyond comprehension and is described by negation as being "not this, not that" (*neti, neti*). In Advaita Vedānta as well, Brahman is said to be beyond rational comprehension and is described with negative language. Śaṃkara quotes passages from the Upaniṣads to illustrate the nature of Brahman, arguing that Brahman is an infinite impersonal principle that is formless, changeless, indivisible, and without any limitation or qualifier whatsoever:

> "It is without parts, without action, tranquil, without imperfection, spotless, the supreme bridge of immortality, like fire that has burned out its fuel" (Śvetāśvatara Upaniṣad 6.19). It is "not this, not that" (Bṛhadāraṇyaka Upaniṣad 2.3.6); "It is neither gross nor minute" (Bṛhadāraṇyaka Upaniṣad 3.8.8).[63]

There is also a second, lower level of Brahman that is said to be possessed of attributes (*saguṇa*). On this level, Brahman is conceived to be personal and is designated as God (Īśvara). Ultimately, however, this aspect of Brahman is not ontologically distinct from the higher, formless level of Brahman, which alone is truly real. Brahman with attributes is Brahman as interpreted by the human mind, which has a limited and hence ignorant perspective.[64]

The world arises from out of Brahman. Śaṃkara tells us that Brahman fashions the world out of a sense of play (*līlā*) and with no other motive whatsoever:

> Just as in the world the activities of some king or king's minister whose desires are fulfilled become a form of play (*līlā*), without any aim and without any motive, in the manner of sports and pastimes, or as exhalation, inhalation, and so forth occur spontaneously, without aim and without any external motive, so also the activity of God (Īśvara) is only a form of play (*līlā*) arising spontaneously, irrespective of any other motive. Although the fashioning of the sphere of this world appears to us to be a very difficult task, nevertheless for God it is just play, because his power (*śakti*) is unlimited.[65]

Although this process of fashioning the world takes place, cosmogony in the conventional sense never actually occurs. Since Nirguṇa Brahman is the only ultimately real principle, the world, like the lower level of Brahman, cannot be said to be truly real, for it has no independent existence apart from Brahman. Although the created world is real from a practical, phenomenal perspective, existing independent of our thoughts and thus present to us in name and form, it is ultimately unreal from a metaphysical perspective. The illusion of the true reality of the world is superimposed, as the image of a snake may be superimposed on a piece of rope, or as a single moon may appear as double.[66] In fact, the universe is ultimately not in any way distinct from Brahman.

> Just as the spaces within pots, water jars, and so forth are not different from cosmic space, or just as water in a mirage, and so forth is not different from salty soil, and so forth, because they appear and then disappear by nature and are not clearly discernible, in this way it is to be seen that this diverse world of enjoyers, things enjoyed, and so forth has no existence apart from Brahman.[67]

That by means of which the appearance of the world is brought about is termed *māyā*, which is a kind of creative potency or *śakti* inherent within Brahman. For Śaṃkara, *māyā* is applied on two levels. First, *māyā* is the power by means of which Nirguṇa Brahman becomes Saguṇa Brahman or Īśvara. In this regard, it is said that Brahman takes on form by means of his *māyā* for the sake of his worshipers, that is, so that Brahman may become accessible to them.[68] Second, *māyā* is also the power through which Īśvara then brings into being the phenomenal-empirical realm. In other words, it is the power by means of which the delusory sphere of relative, conditioned reality is projected from out of Brahman.[69] Thus *māyā* is both creative, in the sense that it brings into being the relative world, and delusive, in the sense that what *māyā* creates is essentially a kind of delusion. The relative world, which is the product of *māyā*, is unreal, and the belief in its reality is a product of ignorance. Even the existence of the lower level of Brahman, his *saguṇa* form as Īśvara, is not truly real. Thus, *māyā* also impedes a true understanding of Brahman.

Because of its role as the concealer of the true nature of reality, *māya* is also called ignorance, *avidyā*, and is opposed to knowledge, *vidyā*. Whereas *avidyā* represents ignorance of the true nature of Brahman and leads to entrapment in the continual round of birth and rebirth, *vidyā* represents the spiritual realization of Nirguṇa Brahman and leads to liberation. *Avidyā* appears to be the epistemological equivalent of the term *māyā*, which applies more to the level of ontology. The precise relationship between these two terms in Śaṃkara's work, however, is not clear.[70]

In his discussion of *māyā*, Śaṃkara often argues against the basic tenets of Sāṃkhya and claims that what may appear in the Upaniṣads as evidence that would support Sāṃkhya's description of *prakṛti* actually has to do with *māyā*. He takes the term *avyakta*, for example, to refer primarily to *māyā*, not *prakṛti*. His discussion of the Śvetāśvatara Upaniṣad's equation of *prakṛti* and *māyā* is quite interesting in this regard:

> That seed-power (*bījaśakti*, = Brahman's ability to create) consists of ignorance (*avidyā*); it is denoted by the word "unmanifest" (*avyakta*), has the highest Lord as its substratum, (and) is of the nature of *māyā*. . . . Sometimes it is called *māyā* (as in) "Know thus that *prakṛti* is *māyā*; the Great Lord (Maheśvara) then is the possessor of *māyā* (*māyin*)" (Śvetāśvatara Upaniṣad 4.10). That *māyā* is surely the unmanifest (*avyakta*), for it cannot be defined either as real or as not real.[71]

Śaṃkara understands the passage as giving priority to *māyā*, and he imbeds this discussion of *māyā* in the context of a long refutation of the position that the term *avyakta* denotes the *pradhāna/prakṛti* of Sāṃkhya.[72] Since for Śaṃkara the Upaniṣads articulate the nature of *māyā* as the unmanifest source of the universe, *māyā* takes pride of place over *prakṛti*. Śaṃkara again addresses the relationship between *prakṛti/pradhāna* and *māyā* in his discussion of Śvetāśvatara Upaniṣad 4.5, the above-discussed passage that refers to the unborn female *(ajā)* who is red, white, and black.[73] Śaṃkara, however, interprets *ajā* as denoting *māyā* and asserts that the three colors refer not to the *guṇas* but to the three elements fire, water, and earth, the last of which he understands to be meant by the term "food" (*anna*).[74] Furthermore, he argues that in this passage, the term *ajā* does not mean "unborn female" but "she-goat," and that what is meant by this passage is a metaphor.

> Just as in the world, there may by chance be some she-goat (*ajā*) that is red, white, and black in color with many kids that are of the same form, and some he-goat might lie with her taking his pleasure while some other might leave her after enjoying her, similarly this source of all beings [= *māyā*] consisting of fire, water, and food/earth (*anna*) and having three colors generates many animate and inanimate products that have the same form as her, is enjoyed by the ignorant knower of the body (*kṣetrajña*), and is abandoned by the wise.[75]

In such ways, Śaṃkara attempts to undermine the claims of Sāṃkhya and its doctrine of *prakṛti* by appealing to the authority of the Upaniṣads.

If we compare the assertions of Advaita Vedānta and those of Sāṃkhya, it is clear that there are some important similarities as well as essential differences. Nirguṇa Brahman is very much like the *puruṣa* of Sāṃkhya philosophy. Both are defined as pure consciousness and transcend the kinds of qualifications that are applied to the phenomenal world. It is important to note, however, that despite their similarities, there is at least one important difference between Brahman and *puruṣa*, namely, that there is only one Brahman but many *puruṣas*. Similarly, *māyā* is, like *prakṛti*, the basis for the manifestation of the phenomenal material world. Yet there is also an important distinction between *māyā* and *prakṛti*: *māyā* ultimately cannot be said to be real. For Śaṃkara, *māyā* is neither real, nor unreal, nor both real and unreal, nor neither real nor unreal. *Māyā* is indescribable (*anirvacanīya*). But if we must describe it in some way, we can say that, unlike *prakṛti*, *māyā* has no true existence but is a kind of illusion or delusion that is projected forth. In Advaita Vedānta, everything is ultimately based on a single, uniquely real principle, Brahman. Sāṃkhya, on the other hand, is essentially dualist, for *prakṛti* and *puruṣa* are both fully real and at the same time completely distinct.

In the history of the texts of Vedānta, the clear delineation of *māyā* as a kind of illusion or delusion appears quite late. We have already seen that its meaning in the Upaniṣads is equivocal. In the fundamental text of the school of Vedānta, the Brahma- or Vedānta-Sūtras, which date from about the second century B.C.E.,[76] the term *māyā* appears only once and is associated with the incomplete manifestation of the attributes of waking reality in the dream state.[77] The connection of the term with the notion of illusion in later Advaita Vedānta literature, most especially the works of Śaṃkara approximately one thousand years later, shows clearly the influence of Śūnyavāda Buddhism, the texts of which date from the first centuries of the Common Era and expound a similar doctrine of *māyā*.[78] It is notable also that the mother of the Buddha in early Buddhist accounts of the life of Gautama the Buddha is called Mahāmāyā ("great *māyā*"), indicating a connection in this literature of the term *māyā* with maternal femininity. As we shall see, the terms *māyā* and *mahāmāyā* become important in the Purāṇas, where they are often used to designate the supreme goddess equated with certain cosmogonic principles.

It is not at all clear whether or not the comprehension of *māyā* as predominantly a principle of delusion is very important in the passages of the Upaniṣads and Gītā cited above, where *māyā* is associated with *prakṛti.* It is quite possible that the sense of the term as indicating something illusory is *not* its primary force in such contexts, and that it is used more in the sense of the capacity for God to create, the act of creating, and the creation that results. Thus, in Bhagavad-Gītā 4.6 cited above, "taking control of my own *prakṛti,* I come into being by my own *māyā,*" the sense of the term *māyā* may be more that of a kind of neutral ability or power of manifestation possessed by God than a power of illusion. Thus *māyā* is in one sense *prakṛti,* but it is also *śakti,* a concept to which we will now turn.

Śakti

An exploration of the origins and development of the concept of a cosmological principle of power or *śakti* is rather complex for three primary reasons. First, the concept itself incorporates several distinct elements. Second, the lines of development are not very clear. And finally, the systematic articulation of *śakti* as an important cosmogonic and cosmological notion emerges quite late and does so primarily outside of the mainstream Vedic-Brahmanical tradition, namely, in the scriptures of the Tantric and Śākta traditions. This corpus is not only expansive, but also quite diverse, and thus it frustrates attempts to locate unifying principles.

Despite such difficulties, however, it is possible to sketch a broad outline of the lines of development of the *śakti* idea. In doing so, we will focus particular attention on three primary areas: (1) the idea of a female figure as a consort and/or aspect of a male divinity described particularly as manifesting his ability to create; (2) the development of the idea of a cosmogonic power that is possessed by a single, supreme god (Deva/Īśvara) and embodies his ability to create the world but is not necessarily identified as female, and (3) the notion of an abstract, all-pervasive power inherent within creation. Speech (*vāc*) and the role that speech plays in creation help connect all of these different notions. We will then explore how these different ideas are brought together to give rise to the notion of a supreme female divinity who represents the *śakti* of her divine male consort and embodies his ability to create the manifest world.

As it is not possible to highlight every occurrence of the term *śakti* in the history of Indian literature, we will instead focus on paradigmatic interpretive fields of the term, that is, the different genres of conceptualization of the term.

VEDIC ROOTS

Although the term *śakti* appears in Vedic literature, it does not have any great theological, cosmological, or metaphysical significance in this context. In the Ṛg-Veda, there appear to be two distinct meanings of the term: *śakti* denotes either "ability, power, capacity," or "help, service." The use of the term to designate different kinds of ability is also found throughout the Vedic Saṃhitās and Brāhmaṇas.[79]

More interesting for our discussion are the Vedic mythological structures that seem to represent the foundation from which later conceptions regarding the notion of *śakti* emerge. As discussed in chapter one, the association between certain Vedic goddesses and a principle of energy can be found in seed form in the Vedic literature. The first clear articulation of the cosmogonic result of sexual union of a god with his female consort appears in the Brāhmaṇas. Of primary importance in this regard are the goddesses Indrāṇī/Śacī and Vāc. Both divinities are associated with a male consort figure with whom they unite, leading to creation of the manifest world.[80] Furthermore, both are conceived to represent a creative capacity or ability of the god with whom they are associated—Indrāṇī as Indra's "might" or *śacī* and Vāc as Prajāpati's creative speech. Thus we find in the Brāhmaṇas an understanding of the union of a god with his consort as the initial impulse that sets the stage for the emanation and manifestation of the cosmos.

Discussion of this kind of mythological cosmogonic union seems to be absent from the Upaniṣads. However, its influence can be discerned in the Śvetāśvatara Upaniṣad, where a similar concept is described in the more speculative language characteristic of Upaniṣadic inquiry. Thus in Śvetāśvatara Upaniṣad 4.1, there is one supreme god who is described as bringing about the manifestation of the diverse world by applying his power or *śakti*:

> He (who is) one, without color (*avarṇa*), places many colors in his hidden purpose by means of the manifold application of his power (*śakti*); and into whom, in the beginning and at the end, this all is gathered, he (who is) divine/God (*deva*)—may he endow us with a clear intellect (*buddhi*).

In this passage, the means by which this single, supreme divinity creates is the application of his capacity or *śakti* in manifold ways.[81] This description of God creating by means of the application of his *śakti* parallels the descriptions in the Brāhmaṇas where Prajāpati creates through union with Vāc.[82] We should also add the coupling of Indra/Indrāṇi to that of Prajāpati/Vāc as the mythological precursors of this Upaniṣad's more abstract description.

The term *śakti* is used elsewhere in this Upaniṣad as well to denote God's power and is described as belonging to him. Thus we find in 1.3:

> Those who followed after meditation and yoga saw the self-power of God (*devātmaśakti*) hidden by his own qualities (*svaguṇa*). He who is one rules over all these causes connected to time and the Self.

The self-power of God (*devātmaśakti*) mentioned in Śvetāśvatara Upaniṣad 1.3 is not further elaborated. The text then continues by describing the relationship between God and creation:

> (We understand) him (to be a wheel) with one felly, threefold, having sixteen ends, fifty spokes, twenty counterspokes and six sets of eights, whose one rope is manifold, which has three different paths, whose one delusion (*moha*) (arises) from two causes.
> We understand him to be a river of five streams, having five sources, mighty and crooked, whose waves are the five vital breaths, whose original source is fivefold perception, having five whirlpools, an impetuous flood of five forms of suffering divided into fifty kinds (and) having five branches.
> In this vast wheel of Brahman that enlivens all things (and) stands in all things, the soul (*haṃsa*) flutters about thinking that the self and the inciter (*preritṛ*) are different. Then, when favored by him, he (the soul) attains immortality.[83]

What are these different portions of God? Both Robert E. Hume and S. Radhakrishnan take these different elements to refer to the various categories enumerated in Sāṃkhya. Thus, the threefold form may refer to the three *guṇas* of *prakṛti*; the sixteen ends may be the five gross elements, the five sense capacities, the five action capacities, and the mind; and so forth.[84] The relationship between the *śakti* of God and the material world with which he is identified is not clear. It is possible, however, that the qualities or *guṇas* mentioned earlier in 1.3 may refer to the three *guṇas* of *prakṛti* implied in 1.4 by the phrase "threefold" (*trivṛtam*). Therefore, God's self-power or *śakti* mentioned in 1.3 could refer to the ability of the *guṇas* to unfold. This interpretation would understand the significance of the term *śakti* in this passage in a way that would be consonant with its meaning in Sāṃkhya-Kārikā 15 and 16, where the term *śakti* designates the ability of *prakṛti* to manifest.[85]

The other principal Upaniṣads do not mention *śakti* at all. Thus it seems that the sole Upaniṣadic articulation of the term understands it to refer not to any kind of general ability or power but specifically to the power of the one supreme God himself. This represents a transformation from the use of the term in the earlier Vedic texts and indicates a new emphasis on the use of the term *śakti* specifically to denote divine power.[86]

It appears, then, that there are two main contributions of the Vedic literature with respect to later construction of a metaphysics of the term *śakti*: (1) the coupling of a male god (Indra, Prajāpati) with a female divinity (Indrāṇī/Śacī, Vāc) who is construed as representing some creative or cosmogonic capacity of that god; and (2) the notion found in the Śvetāśvatara Upaniṣad of a single, absolute divinity possessed of a unique power described as his *śakti*.

ŚAKTI IN PHILOSOPHICAL LITERATURE

As in the Vedas, the term *śakti* in the early Indian philosophical literature does not seem to have any great cosmological or metaphysical significance. There is nonetheless a line of speculation that can be traced from Vaiśeṣika through Mīmāṃsā that develops a notion of an unseen potency (*adṛṣṭa*, *apūrva*) that by about the sixth or seventh century comes to be identified in Mīmāṃsaka literature with the term *śakti*.[87]

The Vaiśeṣika-Sūtras of Kaṇāda, the foundational *sūtras* of the school of Vaiśeṣika philosophy, probably date no later than the first century of the Common Era.[88] Although the first sūtra asserts that the object of inquiry is the nature of *dharma* (law, order, or duty), the text is more generally preoccupied with questions concerning the nature of the material world. The chief feature of the Vaiśeṣika-Sūtras is the description and analysis of the different categories (*padārtha*) of material reality, namely, substance (*dravya*), quality (*guṇa*), action (*karma*), class (*sāmānya*), particularity (*viśeṣa*), and inherence (*samavāya*), knowledge of which is said to produce the supreme good and the understanding of which is said to be conducive to *dharma*.[89]

The fifth book of the Vaiśeṣika-Sūtras discusses among other things the nature of an unseen power, called the *adṛṣṭa*, which brings about the consequences of actions and is responsible for all inexplicable phenomena. The circulation of water in trees, for example, is said to be caused by the *adṛṣṭa*, as are a variety of other processes and effects.[90] It appears that this unseen force is the cause and support of all forms of life including human life, for without it, according to one passage, there can be no conjunction of the soul with the body, hence no birth or rebirth.[91] This *adṛṣṭa* on which life processes depend is generated and supported by human action. The performance of deeds condoned in the Veda by dharmic injunction, such as ablutions, fasts, or sacrifices, results in unseen (*adṛṣṭa*) and desirable fruits.[92] One sūtra states that the performance of such actions, both those that can be seen to be good or useful and those that are less obviously so but are nonetheless prescribed in the Vedas, is favorable because it produces *adṛṣṭa*.[93] Thus the very support of the known world, the *adṛṣṭa*, is the unseen force that is generated by the performance of Vedic injunctions.

It appears clear, then, that in the Vaiśeṣika-Sūtras this *adṛṣṭa* is a force inherent within the material world. But to what extent is it a cosmogonic force? Sūtra 5.2.13 states that the initial (*ādya*) movement of fire, air, atoms, and the mind is caused by the *adṛṣṭa*. In his commentary, the *Upaskāra*, Śaṃkara Miśra (fifteenth century) interprets the term *ādya* to refer to the beginning of creation. It is in fact the case that beginning in approximately the sixth century, Nyāya-Vaiśeṣika philosophers did postulate the *adṛṣṭa* as a clearly cosmogonic power that impels creation into existence and is responsible for its dissolution.[94] Whether or not this is the force of the term in the Vaiśeṣika-Sūtras, however, is difficult to determine.

The school of Pūrva-Mīmāṃsā, which is particularly concerned with the upholding of *dharma* and Vedic injunctions, postulates a force similar to the *adṛṣṭa* called *apūrva*, which is a subtle, invisible power that produces beneficent results from the performance of the Vedic sacrifice. Kumārila Bhaṭṭa (sixth or seventh century), one of the main exponents of Pūrva-Mīmāṃsā, explicitly describes the *apūrva* as a kind of *śakti*. He argues that the *apūrva* is only a particular kind of *śakti* inherent in either the means or the ends of the sacrificial act itself.

> The *apūrva* is only the *śakti*, either of the process—the sacrifice and so forth—aiming for a result, or of the [desired] result itself, cattle and so forth. It is not different from this.[95]

Kumārila also expounds a more general understanding of *śakti* as the power inherent in all objects that determines the relationship between an individual cause and its particular, appropriate effect. Why, he asks in his polemic against the Buddhists, should it be the case that a conjunction of threads produces cloth and not a jar? He argues that there must be some inherent power or *śakti* that determines what effect will come from what cause.[96] Furthermore, Kumārila subsumes linguistic categories that are developed by the grammarians and that, as we shall see, emphasize the role of *śakti* in connection with the semantic capability of words. Kumārila adheres to the position that each word has a fixed power of denotation, a *śakti*, that links it to its meaning or meanings.[97] Prabhākara (sixth or seventh century), another Mimāṃsaka and a rival to Kumārila, appears to share the latter's understanding of *śakti* as embodying the power inherent in the relationship between any cause and its effect but goes even further, proposing the existence of *śakti* as an independent category of material reality (*padārtha*).[98]

Thus we find that in these lines of speculation there is the notion of some unseen potency—*adṛṣta*, *apūrva*, or *śakti*—which inheres in the natural (and also verbal) world as well as the sacrificial order and provides a link between cause and effect on a variety of levels. It is important to note, however, that Mīmāṃsā has no doctrine of creation. Thus in the Mīmāṃsā texts, reflections regarding this unseen potency are never applied to cosmogony; the link between cause and effect is described only in terms of the manifest world, not in terms of the mechanisms of creation and manifestation of the universe.

The term *śakti* appears in an important passage in the Yoga-Sūtras, but in this context *śakti* does not relate to either cosmogony or cosmology but rather to that which transcends both. The term *śakti* is used to describe the power of consciousness (*citiśakti*) that is beyond the *guṇas*:

> Isolation (*kaivalya*) or the power of consciousness (*citiśakti*) standing in itself arises when the *guṇas* return to their original state, devoid of the objects of consciousness (*puruṣārtha*).[99]

In other words, *citiśakti* is *puruṣa*, pure consciousness. In this context, *śakti* has nothing at all to do with the creation but rather represents the ability of consciousness to stand apart from the evolution of the *guṇas*. Finally, the term *śakti* is also found in the Brāhma-Sūtras, where it is mentioned at least twice, in 2.2.9 and 2.3.38. In the former instance, it is stated that the *pradhāna* (*prakṛti*) of Sāṃkhya cannot be the principle of causation because it has no power of intelligence (*jñaśakti*). In 2.3.38, it is said (according to Śaṃkara's interpretation of this sūtra) that intellect (*buddhi*) cannot be an active agent because if it were, there would be a reversal of *śakti* (*śaktiviparyaya*). Neither passage seems to understand the term as referring specifically to cosmological or cosmogonic phenomena. It is true that Śaṃkara, probably drawing on the similarity between the use of the term *māyā* in Upaniṣadic thought and in the Bhagavad-Gītā and the conception of *śakti* in not only the Śvetāśvatara Upaniṣad but also the Tantric and Śākta thought of the period in which he lived, elevates the concept by describing *māyā* as the divine, creative power (*śakti*) of the Absolute Brahman; his understanding, however, appears rather late.[100]

The notion of *śakti* as a general force inherent in creation begins to develop in the philosophical materials of the classical period. It is important to note, however, that in these philosophical systems, this force is never construed in mythological or gender-specific terms and is never interpreted theistically.

ŚAKTI IN GRAMMATICAL LITERATURE

Along with the Vedic and philosophical traditions, there is yet another stream of reflection that contributed to the rise of the notion of *śakti*, namely, the grammatical tradition. This line of thought develops and elaborates the Brāhmaṇas' notion of speech (*vāc*) as a supreme creative principle and combines it with the notion of a cosmogonic and cosmological energy (*śakti*) of God that impels creation into manifestation, resulting in a new synthesis of these two strands of speculation.

In the grammatical tradition, the term *śakti* can be used to refer to the "power" of a case or the relation that is conveyed by a case and thus signifies the semantic significance of the inflection of words in any given phrase or sentence. The *śakti* of a word determines its ability to convey meaning in the context in which it is found. The term *śakti* is also used to refer to the capacity of a word generally to possess and convey signification. Thus *śakti* is that which determines the ability of a word to have meaning.[101]

The elevation of the notion of *śakti* in a context of language theory is most remarkable in the work of Bhartṛhari (ca. fifth century), one of the most famous of the grammatical theoreticians. In his *Vākyapadīya*, Bhartṛhari carries his speculations far beyond the confines of concrete expressions of language and attempts to understand and interpret language on a metalevel. For Bhartṛhari, the Absolute, Brahman, is conceived of as a principle of language and is called Śabdatattva or Śabdabrahman. Śabdabrahman is not only ultimate reality; it is also both the efficient and the material cause of the universe. Creation is described as a kind of manifestation or emanation of the world from the Ultimate:

> The imperishable Brahman, having no beginning nor end, whose essence is the Word (*śabda*), evolves/comes forth (*vi* √*vṛt)* by appearing in objects, from which (then) arises the production of the world.[102]

Although Śabdabrahman is a monistic principle, it possesses various powers or *śakti*s. These are its attributes and are not ontologically distinct from it.

> It [Śabdabrahman] is described as singular, but it becomes divided into parts on the basis of (its) *śakti*s, from which it is not different. Although it is not different from the *śakti*s, it appears different.[103]

Śabdabrahman is beyond creation but becomes capable of creation through the activation of its various *śakti*s. The most important of these is the power of time or *kālaśakti*, for it is this *śakti* that is responsible for creation:

> Relying on the *kālaśakti*, (the other *śakti*s) are the sources of the six transformations, birth and so forth.[104]

At the beginning of creation, Śabdabrahman appears as different forms that are manifest in an order determined by the *kālaśakti*. The process of world-evolution set in motion by the *kālaśakti* of Śabdabrahman takes place along two lines: evolution of form or speech and matter or meaning. At the level of the Absolute, these two are identical. The difference between name and meaning that we experience on the phenomenal-empirical plane is not present at the highest level but is a distinction that becomes discernible only when the cosmic process begins.[105]

To describe the relation between the Absolute level of reality and the relative world, Bhartṛhari posits an unfolding of Śabdabrahman in terms of three main levels that represent successive stages of differentiation between name and meaning. These are articulated quite simply in a single verse of the text.

> (The tradition of grammar) is the supreme and wonderful abode of *vaikharī, madhyamā,* and *paśyantī,* the threefold word (*vāc*) that has many channels through which it unfolds.[106]

Paśyantī, madhyamā, and *vaikharī* represent increasingly differentiated levels of word or speech (*vāc*). *Paśyantī* is the purest aspect of *vāc* and is identical with Śabdabrahman. At this level, there is inherent within the word the power (*śakti*) to unfold in succession, but this power is held in restraint. The expressive potential of *paśyantī* is then fully realized in the level of speech called *vaikharī vāc,* which is the level of ordinary speech. Between these two is a middle level, *madhyamā vāc,* which is the subtle level of speech perceived internally by the mind.[107] Considering the passages cited above, it would appear that the *paśyantī* level of word or speech assumes the more differentiated levels of *madhyamā* and *vaikharī* through the agency of the *kālaśakti.*[108]

In the *Vākyapadīya,* the understanding of speech as a creative force is joined with the notion of *śakti* as a cosmogonic power of the Absolute. Creation comes about through the successive unfolding of increasingly differentiated levels of speech, an unfolding that is prompted by the supreme power or *śakti* of the Absolute here conceived in terms of speech and described as Śabdabrahman. Thus the Brāhmaṇa tradition of portraying speech, *vāc,* as a cosmogonic force is fully developed in the *Vākyapadīya* and explicitly connected with the notion of a divine, cosmogonic *śakti* that is an inherent aspect of the Absolute. Whereas *vāc* is often described as a goddess in the Brāhmaṇa literature, however, this is not the case in Bhartṛhari's philosophy of language.

ŚAKTI IN TANTRIC LITERATURE

The different strands of thought described above that pertain to the understanding and use of the term *śakti* in diverse textual environments represent different yet related notions. In Tantra, these diverse conceptual threads are then woven together along with others. It is in Tantric treatises arising outside the Vedic-Brahmanical tradition that the most fully and systematically articulated conception of *śakti* as a cosmogonic and cosmological capacity identified as an omnipresent and omnipotent goddess develops. It is beyond the scope of this study to present an elaborate description of Tantric texts or doctrines. There are in fact many excellent studies already available that address such issues in detail, and there is currently a marked increase in scholarly output in this area.[109] Rather, we will give a brief summary of the essential elements of Tantric thought that are directly relevant to the present investigation and represent the most distinctive features of the Tantric understanding of *śakti.* As the portrayal of *śakti* in Tantrism has a great deal in common with the portrayal also found in Purāṇic literature, this issue will be addressed in greater length in the next chapter.

The chronology and history of early Tantric literature are obscure. Scholars not only argue about dates, but they even disagree on what exactly the terms "Tantra," "Tantrism," "Tantric literature," and so forth designate. It is difficult to distinguish clearly between Tantric elements and Tantrism as a fully developed ritual and doctrinal system. Furthermore, there are certainly many Tantric elements that existed prior to the first appearances of such elements in texts.[110] Although texts identifying themselves as "Tantras" began to appear only in approximately the ninth century, the seeds of the "Tantric tradition" were clearly sown prior to this period. Thus the boundaries of the tradition are unclear. To add to the confusion, Tantric elements appear not only in the Hindu tradition, but also in Buddhist and Jain environments as well. In order to circumvent terminological traps, then, it is perhaps best to speak of a kind of orientation or tendency that can, for the sake of convenience, be termed "Tantric" and to limit our discussion to texts that are Hindu in emphasis.

In Tantra, some of the various strands that we have seen to be present in the mainstream Vedic-Brahmanical tradition are woven together with others that probably sprang originally from various non-Vedic, popular traditions. The former elements include, among others, the tendency found in the Brāhmaṇas and Upaniṣads to correlate different levels of reality, namely, the cosmic, natural, human, and sacrificial orders.[111] Cosmic processes are not only macrocosmic but reverberate on the microcosmic plane and are reproduced on all levels down to the structure of human physiology. Speculation regarding the term *śakti* and the notion of speech as a cosmogonic and cosmological principle is thus subsumed and absorbed into Tantric categories in terms of both micro- and macrocosmic structures. We will focus on reflections regarding the macrocosm.

One of the most distinguishing features of Tantrism—and its main contribution to our discussion—is the elevation of non-Vedic goddesses to supreme status in Tantric mythology. The tendency to revere specific female divinities as supreme, especially when the goddesses in question are non-Vedic in origin and endowed with qualities that stress their powerful nature, is most likely primarily an autochthonous tendency. In the history of Tantrism, it appears that a preoccupation with the divine power of the Absolute coupled with an emphasis on female symbolism led to written expression of already existing traditions of worship of various goddesses and an elevation of them such that, depending on the individual tradition, various different goddesses became identified as unique, all-powerful mother goddesses.[112] This applies to Śākta tendencies as well, which, although not equivalent to Tantrism, also elevate the stature of specific goddesses and form with Tantrism "two intersecting but not coinciding circles."[113]

What is most important to us about the Tantric orientation is the way in which it interprets cosmogony and cosmology. Many forms of Tantra propose the existence of a divine power or *śakti* that is described as supreme in both cosmogonic and cosmological contexts and is clearly identified as feminine. Such an orientation can be discerned in all kinds of literature—including, as we shall see, the Purāṇas—but is most clearly elaborated in the Tantra, Āgama, and Saṃhitā scriptures of the sectarian Śākta, Śaiva, and Vaiṣṇava schools.

In Tantra generally the Absolute, although singular in essence at the highest level, is understood to be essentially polarized into female and male aspects. The female pole is that of energy, *śakti.* The male aspect of God cannot act alone but only through his energy, his *śakti,* with whom he is inseparably united and who is hypostatized as a goddess. Thus the supreme Śakti, without whom God would be incapable of action, is that aspect of the Godhead that is ultimately responsible for the creation or manifestation of the cosmos. She is especially identified as the fountainhead from which spring other female forms that unite on all levels with complementary male forms. The created world ultimately arises through such coupling.[114] In Śaiva and some Śākta traditions, Śiva is identified as the supreme god, and the goddess associated with him—Pārvatī, Durgā, and so forth—is Śaiva and is subordinate to him. This is not always the case, however. In Vaiṣṇava Tantrism, the supreme is conceived to be Viṣṇu or one of his incarnations and the goddess associated with him is Vaiṣṇava (Lakṣmī, for example). In Śākta Tantrism, the goddess who is identified as Śakti is usually elevated above the male aspect of the Godhead. The distinction between male and female that occurs in manifest creation is ultimately rooted in gender polarities inherent within the Absolute.

In some Tantric schools, the understanding of a supreme feminine principle who is *śakti* is coupled with reflections regarding the nature of speech, *vāc*, often discussed in terms of Śabdabrahman, and the unfolding of creation in cosmogony is embodied in and expressed as the unfolding of language. As we have seen above, a tendency to elevate speech to the status of a goddess is already present in the Vedas. In the Brāhmaṇas, Vāc as a goddess and/or a faculty of speech is the instrumental agent through which Prajāpati, the creator, creates. A similar structure is described in the Upaniṣads, where God creates by applying his power or *śakti*. Much later, Bhartṛhari understands speech to be a cosmic phenomenon that penetrates the different levels of creation but is ultimately unified through the *kālaśakti*, the power through which speech unfolds. In Tantric materials, these tendencies are united with the impulse to conceive of the *śakti* of God as a female divinity, who then sometimes comes to be identified with Śabdabrahman or with the goddess Vāc as the creative, female energy of God that when activated gives rise to the cosmos. In this regard, some Tantric schemes add a fourth, higher level of speech above *paśyantī*, often called *parā vāc* but sometimes identified in other ways as well. Such representations of a cosmic *śakti* identified with a cosmic principle of speech are found in various different schools of Tantra.

In Pāñcarātra, for example, a Tantric Vaiṣṇava school, we find such a homologization of the female consort of Brahman, who in this system is identified as Viṣṇu-Nārāyaṇa, with Śabdabrahman. According to the Lakṣmī Tantra, one of the central treatises of Pāñcarātra, the goddess Śrī or Lakṣmī is Nārāyaṇa's consort and his inherent *śakti*, who dwells eternally with him:

> Viṣṇu-Nārāyaṇa is flawless, not governed (by anyone), blameless, eternal, the possessor of Śrī, and the eternal

> supreme Self (Paramātman). . . . (He is) ever existent, the highest, and the supreme syllable "OM." I [Śrī or Lakṣmī] am his most excellent, eternal *śakti*, and I possess his attributes.[115]

It is said that as Viṣṇu-Nārāyaṇa's *śakti* Lakṣmī has two main aspects, namely, *bhūtiśakti*, "being-power" or material creation, and *kriyāśakti*, "doing-power" or Viṣṇu-Nārāyaṇa's creative ability. *Kriyāśakti* is also named consciousness (*cit*),[116] and the nature of Lakṣmī as consciousness is stressed throughout the text. As Brahman, Viṣṇu-Nārāyaṇa is essentially changeless and perfectly tranquil, but his *śakti* is not, and it is she who is the immediate, active cause of creation.

The materials that we find in the Lakṣmī Tantra concerning cosmogony are quite variegated and complex. According to one perspective, however, Lakṣmī is described as possessing a creative urge (*sisṛkṣā*).[117] When this urge is activated, she comes forth and is manifest as Śabdabrahman:

> I, Śrī, am his [Viṣṇu-Nārāyaṇa's] supreme *śakti*, not different from him, the support and *śakti* of all, omniscient and facing in all directions. Through me the universe becomes visible, as a mountain (is visible) inside a mirror. My inherent nature (*svarūpa*) is characterized by pure, blissful awareness (*bodha*). . . . Evolving that portion of myself that represents awareness (*bodha*), becoming Śabdabrahman, I evolve through the course of my portions (*kalā*).[118]

Creation is then described in terms of the evolution of speech as it is described in Bhartṛhari's system. When the urge to create is stirred, this creative *śakti*, which at this point resides in a peaceful (*śānta*) state as Śabdabrahman, begins to evolve forth. This evolution is expressed in terms of successive changes of form from *śānta* first to *paśyantī*, then *madhyamā*, and finally *vaikharī*. This sequence is described both in terms of cosmogonic evolution and in terms of the manifestation of speech, and these four successive evolutions are said to constitute the four forms of the goddess herself.[119]

A similar conceptualization of creation is found in the texts of nondualistic Kashmir Śaivism. In this system, Brahman is identified as Śiva and is said to be united eternally with his feminine side, which is his *śakti.* This primal *śakti* is equated with *vāc,* speech, and is conceived to be a goddess. At the highest level, she is called *parā vāc* and is identified with supreme consciousness (*parā saṃvid*). She is Śiva's creative energy and the immediate source of creation.

> This universe . . . abides without difference in one, supreme, divine, Bhairava-consciousness (*bhairava-saṃvid*) in the form of awareness (*bodha*). . . . The entire manifestation lies clearly there at rest. All this (universe) . . . resides in that consciousness itself in its own form, which is predominantly *śakti* characterized by the particular creative pulsation (*spanda*) of Bhairava.[120]

As the mechanisms of creation unfold, the supreme *śakti,* who is consciousness, expands and becomes manifest on different levels, bringing about and penetrating the creation of which she is the ultimate source. This expansion is described in terms of the evolution of *śakti* as *parā vāc* from a supreme state to lower states in successive stages, from *parā,* first to *paśyantī,* then to *madhyamā,* and finally to *vaikharī.*[121] In this system, too, as in Pañcarātra, this sequence is understood both in terms of the unfolding of the cosmos and in terms of the manifestation of speech.[122]

Thus the various lines of reflection present in the different textual genres that we have looked at meet in the Tantric materials, which weave together different threads of thought found in diverse environments.

As we have seen, the association with female divinity of a principle of materiality and a principle of energy or power that are cosmological and/or cosmogonic in nature is present from the earliest layer of the Vedic texts. In the

Vedas, materiality and power are not clearly distinguished. Thus we find that goddesses like Vāc or Virāj tend to embody both principles. In the post-Vedic period up to the end of the classical period (ca. sixth century), various schools of thought appear in which elaborate and detailed reflections regarding each of these principles arise. The understanding of an ultimate principle of materiality is most elaborately defined within the confines of Sāṃkhya philosophy, culminating in the system enumerated in the Sāṃkhya-Kārikā. In these lines of thought, materiality is called *prakṛti* (or, sometimes, *pradhāna, avyakta,* and so forth) and, in the normative formulation, is not clearly described as female, although the function that it serves as the source of the manifest world may be seen as female in character and parallels the role played in other scriptures by divinities or elements that are explicitly described as female (water and earth, for example).

During the same period and beyond, a separate line of thought develops in which an abstract principle of cosmogonic and cosmological power or energy is described. This stream of thought is fed by two sources: (1) the old Vedic notion of a female figure as a consort and/or aspect of a male divinity, particularly described as his ability to create; and (2) Upaniṣadic and philosophical assertions regarding either an abstract cosmological force or a cosmogonic power possessed by God and embodying God's ability to create the world. This principle of power or energy is usually called *śakti* and is described in various ways. The notion of a supreme *śakti* that is clearly feminine and is described as a goddess is articulated most explicitly in the literature of various Tantric schools, which begin to emerge in approximately the ninth century. In addition, a third principle called *māyā,* which is related to both *prakṛti* and *śakti,* is also developed in various environments during the classical period.

In the Purāṇas, these strands all come together, and *prakṛti, śakti,* and *māyā* come to be seen as related aspects of creation. In many Purāṇas, they are explicitly identified with a supreme goddess who is the female pole of the Godhead, Brahman, and the consort of the supreme male God. In Purāṇas or Purāṇic passages where the Great Goddess herself is identified as Brahman, the same pattern persists. It is to the exploration of this phenomenon that we will now turn.

CHAPTER THREE

The Feminine Principle in Purāṇic Cosmogony and Cosmology

Introduction to the Goddess Materials in the Epics and Purāṇas

There is yet another important genre of Brahmanical literature that arises in the post-Vedic period. This genre represents a new narrative tendency that diverges from the tradition of Vedic narrative and includes the two great epics (*itihāsas*) of India, the Mahābhārata and the Rāmāyaṇa, and the vast mythological compilations called Purāṇas. The epic and Purāṇic texts incorporate some of the older Vedic mythological material but recast it by combining it with philosophical materials, as we have seen to be the case in the Mahābhārata, and non-Vedic mythological elements. In these texts, there is also increasing importance placed on devotion (*bhakti*) to a supreme divinity as a proper human endeavor. As devotion begins to take center stage, there is a corresponding increase in concern with delineating the natures and actions of different deities.

The influence on the Brahmanical tradition of popular devotional cults centering on different autochthonous Indian goddesses becomes increasingly evident in this literature. From approximately the beginning of the Common

Era on, non-Vedic goddesses are incorporated into the mainstream tradition and thus begin to be recognized as legitimate members of the "orthodox" Brahmanical pantheon. In the Mahābhārata, for example, the non-Vedic goddess Durgā appears frequently in the text and is associated with both Śiva and Kṛṣṇa. Whereas the tendency to elevate goddesses to high status seems to be part of the indigenous impulse of India, this impulse begins to find expression in the Brahmanical literature at a fairly early date.

One of the ways in which the autochthonous Indian goddesses are incorporated into the epic and Purāṇic tradition is through the identification of these different goddesses with those of the established Vedic pantheon. In the Mahābhārata, for example, Umā is equated with the Vedic goddess Sarasvatī; in the Harivaṃśa, which is a supplement to the Mahābhārata, Durgā is equated with both Sarasvatī and Sāvitrī.[1] The identification of non-Vedic elements with those that are Vedic is seen throughout the post-Vedic narrative texts and functions as a legitimizing mechanism whereby non-Vedic elements are introduced into the discourse without threatening the authority of the earlier Vedic tradition.

The conflation of Vedic and non-Vedic identities in the goddess-related materials found in this literature is indicative of a larger pattern of representing different goddesses as partial manifestations of a single female deity or principle that transcends all individual goddesses and is their source. As early as the fifth or sixth century of the Common Era,[2] there begins to appear the notion of a single Great Goddess, Devī or Mahādevī, of whom all individual goddesses are discrete manifestations. Her identity is usually expressed in one of two ways: either a particular goddess, such as Durgā, is lauded as the supreme female divinity of whom all other goddesses are partial manifestations, or else the existence of a single female reality is affirmed as the unique source of all goddesses—and often nondivine female beings, such as human women, as well—who are described as her portions.[3]

The Devī-Māhātmya

The theology of the Goddess is crystallized in a text of approximately the sixth century called the Devī-Māhātmya, which forms part of the Mārkaṇḍeya Purāṇa (ca. 300–600 C.E.).[4] This text extols the Great Goddess who is the source of all creation. Since she has manifold forms, she is given many epithets. Included among these are three that implicate her in cosmogony as they are related to or borrowed from philosophical materials concerning creation: *mahāmāyā*, "great *māyā*," *prakṛti*, and *śakti*.[5] Thus the Devī-Māhātmya introduces categories from philosophy and equates them with the Goddess, although not in any systematic way.

In the Devī-Māhātmya, the Great Goddess is represented in ways that portray her as Brahman, although such an identification is not made explicitly in the text. On the one hand, she is described as the ultimate, highest reality, a description that is often applied in other texts to whichever god is considered to be Brahman. She is higher than Brahmā, Viṣṇu, or Śiva. When she reveals herself, it is said that it only appears as if she is born, but in fact she is eternal.[6] She is therefore never really born, and she never really dies. But she also has a form, for she is embodied as the Devī, the Goddess, and is portrayed as a great slayer of demons and protectress of the gods.

There are two important myths in the text that describe the manifestation of the Goddess. According to one account, two demons (*asuras*), Madhu and Kaiṭabha, are born from Viṣṇu's ear while Viṣṇu lies asleep on the primordial ocean at the end of the *kalpa*. They attempt to kill Brahmā, who is seated on the lotus growing from Viṣṇu's navel. Frightened, Brahmā tries to waken Viṣṇu, who does not respond. He is under the influence of the Goddess in her form as *yoganidrā*, yoga-sleep. Brahmā invokes the Goddess by extolling her and asks her to leave Viṣṇu so that he may rise and help fight the demons. The Goddess complies; Viṣṇu awakens and saves Brahmā. Invoked by Brahmā, Devī manifests herself.[7] Another account details the manifestation of the Goddess from the collective energies of the gods. The *asura* Mahiṣa defeats the gods in battle and usurps them. The gods become angry and emit great heat-energy, *tejas*, which is produced from their anger. All their emitted *tejas* becomes unified and transforms into the Goddess.[8] It might be significant that the term *tejas* is used in this context. As we have seen in the previous chapter, the Upaniṣads tend to portray *tejas* as the source of the primordial waters, which function as the matrix from which the created world issues forth. In the Devī-Māhātmya, the Goddess has similar attributes and functions. She is also said to abide in the form of earth (*mahī*) and to fill up the universe in the form of water (*ap*), echoing some of the Vedic motifs that we have explored, and she is described as the cause of all the worlds.[9]

Although there are no passages describing the mechanisms of cosmogony per se in the Devī-Māhātmya, nevertheless the Goddess is described as instrumental in creation. She plays three different cosmogonic roles. First, she is the supreme creator who wills creation and sends the cosmos forth. Thus she is the efficient cause of creation. As the immediate source of the universe, she is Mūlaprakṛti, primordial Prakṛti.[10] Thus she is the material cause, the basic matter from which the cosmos is formed. And, finally, she is creation itself. According to the text, the world is her form, and the entire universe with all its parts is ultimately identified with the Goddess.[11]

In the Devī-Māhātmya, Devī is also called Śakti and Mahāmāyā. As Śakti, she is the power that makes possible not only the creation but also the maintenance and destruction of the universe.[12] She transcends the universe and controls its rhythms. Yet she is also immanent, for it is said that she abides in all beings in the form of *śakti* and is described as the *śakti* of all that is.[13] Coburn observes that in the Devī-Māhātmya, *śakti* is something that the Devī *is* as well as something that each individual deity *has*.[14] As this universal-abiding Śakti, she is present everywhere and in everything. The Goddess is also extolled as Mahāmāyā and is described as both creative and deluding:

> Indeed, this venerable goddess Mahāmāyā, having forcibly seized the minds of even those who are knowledgeable, delivers them over to delusion. This entire movable and immovable world is created by her.[15]

As Coburn has also noted, in this text the principle of *māyā* is sometimes equated with the principle of *prakṛti*, an equation that we have seen made before in the Upaniṣads and Bhagavad-Gītā.[16] Thus the Goddess is called Mahāmāyā, for example, and as such is designated "the *prakṛti* of all, manifesting the triad of *guṇas*."[17] As Mahāmāyā/Prakṛti also, the Goddess is a singular and universal phenomenon.

Many scholars have noted the importance of the Devī-Māhātmya in establishing the identity of a Great Goddess. Coburn, for example, remarks that the Devī-Māhātmya is "not the earliest literary fragment attesting to the existence of devotion to a goddess figure, but it is surely the earliest in which the object of worship is conceptualized as Goddess, with a capital G."[18] We certainly do not wish to dispute the text's centrality in this regard. It is important, nonetheless, to look at the Devī-Māhātmya in the general context of the Brahmanical tradition, and especially the Purāṇas, for the Devī-Māhātmya does not exist in a vacuum. The formulation of the Great Goddess in this text is already somewhat influenced by Vedic-Brahmanical themes and narrative structures of the type that we have seen, and the identification of the Goddess as *śakti*, *māyā*, and *prakṛti* in this text must be understood in relation to these larger patterns. In terms of the ways in which it depicts the essential identity of the Goddess, the Devī-Māhātmya is not anomalous; it is the earliest and among the most forceful expressions of a theology of a Great Goddess, but this theology is adopted and adapted to at least some degree by later texts, both Śākta and non-Śākta.

Cosmogony and Goddesses in the Purāṇas

In several of the Purāṇas that postdate the Devī-Māhātmya, the tendency toward the conflation of non-Vedic and Vedic elements and the introduction of the notion of a single Great Goddess combined with the incorporation of philosophical categories into mythological narratives contributes to a recasting of cosmogonic accounts that absorbs different goddesses into the mechanisms of creation and equates them with the cosmogonic principles *śakti, prakṛti,* and *māyā* or *mahāmāyā.* Even where the accounts of cosmogony themselves do not explicitly identify specific structures as feminine, passages elsewhere in the text often refer to these principles and identify them with a female divinity. In order to understand how such notions develop and are articulated, it is necessary to place them within the context of certain observations about post-Vedic cosmogonies in general and Purāṇic cosmogonies in particular.

The accounts of creation in post-Vedic texts do not abandon either the essential structures or the basic themes found in Vedic cosmogonies. Like their predecessors, post-Vedic creation narratives maintain two distinct phases of creation. Holdrege has noted that the account of cosmogony given in the Manu-Smṛti (ca. second century B.C.E.–C.E.) presents a basic, two-stage pattern that marks a transition from Vedic to later post-Vedic cosmogonies. It borrows themes from earlier Vedic cosmogonies but reworks them, and the newer account provides a core narrative upon which later cosmogonies then elaborate:[19]

> This was covered with darkness, undiscerned, without any distinctive marks, incomprehensible by reason, un-

> knowable, as if completely asleep. Then the divine Self-born (Svayambhū), unmanifest, making this—the gross elements and so on—manifest, appeared with energy set into motion, dispersing the darkness. He who is to be perceived nonsensuously, subtle, unmanifest, eternal, consisting of all creatures, and inconceivable, he alone appeared of his own accord. In the beginning, desiring to give rise to various kinds of beings from his own body, meditating (*abhi* √*dhyai*), he created the waters alone and placed his seed in them. That (seed) became a golden egg (*haima aṇḍa*) having splendor equal to the sun. In that (egg), he himself was born as Brahmā, the grandfather of the whole world. The waters are called *nārāḥ*, (for) the waters, indeed, are the offspring of Nara. Since they were his first abode (*ayana*), he is thus named Nārāyaṇa. From that which was the unmanifest, eternal cause, which is both real and unreal, was produced that Puruṣa, who is celebrated in this world as Brahmā. He, the divine one, having remained in that egg for a full year, by himself alone, divided that egg in two with his own thought. From those two halves he fashioned heaven and earth, between them the midregions, the eight points of the horizon, and the eternal abode of the waters.

In the first stage, the unmanifest, divine source of creation appears as the self-existent Nārāyaṇa who brings forth the waters and plants his seed in them. The seed becomes a golden egg (*haima aṇḍa*). In the second stage, Nārāyaṇa then enters the egg and is born from it as Brahmā (Puruṣa), the progenitor of the worlds, who then fashions creation. This account retains many of the themes found in early cosmogonies: a two-stage creative process similar to that noted by Kuiper with respect to Vedic cosmogonies, and themes such as the primordial waters, the cosmic egg, and so forth. Similar accounts of creation are given in Harivaṃśa 1.23–27 and in the Matsya Purāṇa, one of the earliest Purāṇas (ca. 200–400 C.E.).[20] Most of the Purāṇic cosmogonies, however, while adopting this basic two-phase scheme are much more elaborate.[21]

It is difficult to make too many broad generalizations regarding the Purāṇas because of the volume of literature that is recognized as belonging to this category and because of the variety of perspectives that are represented within it. The Brahmanical tradition recognizes eighteen major (Mahā-) and eighteen minor (Upa-) Purāṇas, although there is some disagreement over exactly which Purāṇas belong in which category.[22] Many of the Purāṇas can be classified according to their sectarian perspectives. Viṣṇu and Śiva are the primary deities celebrated in the Mahā-Purāṇas, and many of these are clearly Vaiṣṇava or Śaiva, promoting one or the other god as the highest deity of the Hindu pantheon and subordinating all other divinities to the one receiving prime favor. Thus, for example, the Viṣṇu Purāṇa (ca. 300–500 C.E.)[23] celebrates Viṣṇu as the supreme divinity and sees Śiva as merely an aspect of Viṣṇu, whereas the Liṅga Purāṇa (ca. 700–1000 C.E.) adopts the opposite perspective. Four of the Upa-Purāṇas and portions of different Mahā-Purāṇas are essentially Śākta in orientation and elevate the Goddess to the highest position in the divine hierarchy. Several Purāṇas, such as the Kūrma (ca. 550–800 C.E.), are cross-sectarian, and others, such as the Mārkaṇḍeya, cannot be classified as having any clear sectarian interests.

Certain generalizations regarding the Purāṇas are made within the tradition itself. They are characterized as a class of text that treats five different kinds of subjects: creation of the cosmos (*sarga* or *prākṛta sarga*), re-creation of the cosmos after dissolution (*pratisarga* or *visarga*), genealogies of kings and sages (*vaṃśa*), Manu-intervals (*manvantara*), and accounts of the dynasties of great kings and sages (*vaṃśānucarita*). Since these five types of subjects are considered to be the essential contents of the Purāṇas, they are called the *pañcalakṣana* or "five characteristics." In truth, these five items constitute very little of what is actually contained in the Purāṇas as a whole. All of the major Purāṇas, nevertheless, contain materials regarding creation.

The Purāṇic accounts of the two stages of cosmogony, primary creation (*sarga* or *prākṛta sarga)* and secondary creation (*pratisarga* or *visarga*), are understood in relation to endlessly repeating cyles of time within which the universe is continually created, dissolved, and re-created. Each cycle of four ages or *yugas* is called a *mahāyuga* and comprises four increasingly unstable *yugas* called Sat or Kṛta (1,728,000 years), Dvāpara (1,296,000 years), Tretā (864,000 years), and Kali (432,000 years).[24] At the end of every *mahāyuga*, the earth is submerged under water. One thousand of these *mahāyuga* cycles constitute a *kalpa*, which is a single day in the life of Brahmā the creator. At the end of each *kalpa*, Brahmā goes to sleep and a minor dissolution occurs; when he reawakens, he ushers in a new cycle of secondary creation. At the end of Brahmā's lifetime, which consists of one hundred years of Brahmā days and nights, there is a major dissolution, after which a new primary creation takes place. The entire cycle of creations and dissolutions continues eternally.

To best understand the place of the feminine principle in the process of creation, one must distinguish among not only different levels of cosmogony but also the different interpretive inflections that diverse Purāṇas give to their accounts. In the remainder of this chapter we will explore the role and function of the feminine principle in the different Purāṇas' versions of cosmogony according to the essential patterns that are found throughout the various Purāṇic accounts. Beginning with the most basic patterns pertaining to both primary and secondary creation, we will then investigate how the feminine principle is incorporated into this pattern such that the idea of a Great Goddess emerges.

Our analysis will be organized thematically according to the degree to which the Goddess is integrated into cosmogonic speculation, but within these broad thematic categories we will generally proceed historically. It is well known by scholars studying the Purāṇas that the dating of these texts is fraught with difficulties. As C. Mackenzie Brown notes, because of the fluid nature of the Purāṇas and the way in which they mix new and old materials, they are something of a text-historian's nightmare, and he asserts that the dating of individual Purāṇas and the various parts of these Purāṇas "has become something of a game, a game which some scholars, perhaps not unwisely, refuse to play."[25] While not wishing to enter too deeply into the fray, we will nevertheless attempt to respect the relative chronology of the texts as dictated by scholarly consensus to the extent that this is possible.

First, we will explore various explanations of primary creation in many of the Purāṇas—for example, the Mārkaṇḍeya, Viṣṇu, and Brahmāṇḍa (ca. 400–600 C.E.)[26] Purāṇas—which adopt either Sāṃkhya categories or those of the Upaniṣads and Advaita Vedānta philosophy, subsuming these categories under a theistic perspective. The supreme divinity, Viṣṇu or Śiva, is both Nirguṇa (without qualities) and Saguṇa (with qualities) Brahman. On the *nirguṇa* level, the favored deity is usually described as transcending and incorporating both *puruṣa* and *prakṛti*. As Saguṇa Brahman, he is also often identified as Puruṣa, an appellation that is used more as a proper name than as a designation of an impersonal principle. When *prakṛti* is disturbed, the twenty-three remaining *tattvas* begin to evolve, and the process of creation begins. Other accounts, such as some of those found in the Bhāgavata Purāṇa (ca. 800–1000 C.E.), emphasize the uniqueness of God, either Viṣṇu or Śiva identified as Brahman, and describe primary creation as a result of Brahman's primordial impulse to create. This impulse is usually called *śakti* or the power of *māyā* possessed by Brahman. These two different explanations are often conflated such that *prakṛti* becomes identified in some way with Brahman's *māyā* or *śakti*. Several of the Purāṇic cosmogonies simply lay out these mechanisms of creation without explicitly introducing the feminine element.

We will then turn to the standard accounts of secondary creation set forth in most of the Purāṇas. Secondary creation begins after the *tattvas* are gathered together in the form of a cosmic egg that resides in the primordial waters and contains the universe in incipient form. Brahmā the creator is born from the egg and fashions the three worlds; following this, he then proceeds to create animate and inanimate beings. Thus there are two stages of secondary creation. In the first phase, the account of the formation of the different worlds, the old Vedic theme of the waters as the cosmic womb reappears. In the second phase, the feminine principle is introduced as necessary for the creation of individual beings, especially humans, to continue evolving. At a certain point, the whole process comes to a standstill, for Brahmā's progeny, which he has created by himself up to this point, have no interest in furthering creation. The body of Brahmā then splits into female and male portions. The sexual interaction of female and male leads to the production of more prolific beings. Thus the introduction of the female element at this point reinvigorates the entire process of creation.

Third, we will investigate the accounts narrated in sectarian Vaiṣṇava and Śaiva contexts, such as those found in the Garuḍa (ca. 850–1000 C.E.)[27] and Liṅga Purāṇas, in which the feminine principle is absorbed explicitly into the mechanisms of creation on the primary level and is identified with certain cosmogonic and cosmological structures that are borrowed from philosophical discourse. Generally, the power (*śakti* or *māyā*) of whichever god is identified as Brahman—according to the sectarian perspective of the text or passage—is described as the catalyst of creation and is homologized with the female divinity or divinities associated with the supreme male deity. Sāṃkhya categories are also used, and *prakṛti*, which is often seen as evolved from *śakti* in some way, is identified as another aspect of the same goddess or goddesses. When the feminine principle is explicitly represented in the *sarga,* accounts of the *pratisarga* sometimes incorporate it by identifying certain principles on the lower levels of creation with the higher feminine principle. Although the structure is essentially the same in most of the accounts that are explored in this section, we will consider the accounts given in Vaiṣṇava and Śaiva contexts separately since they differ with respect to the identities of the divinities involved.

Finally, we will turn to look at the Devī-Bhāgavata Purāṇa (ca. 1000–1200 C.E.), which is a Śākta Purāṇa.[28] The same basic themes regarding the incorporation of the feminine on the levels of both primary and secondary creation persist in this text yet, in following the path laid out by the Devī-Māhātmya, the Devī-Bhāgavata identifies the highest divinity and ultimate reality not as Viṣṇu or Śiva but as the Great Goddess.[29] She is identified as Brahman, both without qualities (*nirguṇa*) and with qualities (*saguṇa*), but she is also consistently described as *śakti, māyā,* and *prakṛti.* Thus although in this text the Great Goddess takes the place of Viṣṇu or Śiva in the non-Śākta Purāṇas as Brahman, we find the same basic structures with respect to the cosmogonic process.

*Primary Creation (*Sarga*): Basic Cosmogony*

SĀṂKHYA-TYPE ACCOUNTS OF COSMOGONY

In her book *Cosmogonies Purāṇiques,* Madeleine Biardeau identifies a basic pattern of primary creation that is found in several Purāṇas, including the Vāyu (ca. 300–500 C.E.), Viṣṇu, Mārkaṇḍeya, Brahmāṇḍa, Agni (ca. 800–900 C.E.), Padma (ca. 850–950 C.E.), and Brahma Purāṇas, among others.[30] This pattern adopts the basic themes of earlier orthodox cosmogonies but identifies mythic elements with philosophical constructs such that categories borrowed from Sāṃkhya are recast in a theistic framework. According to these accounts, two entities that are considered to be distinct yet inseparable are present at the dawn of creation. They are complementary elements and, Biardeau maintains, cannot be conceived apart from one another.[31] These two entities are essentially the *pradhāna/prakṛti* and *puruṣa* of Sāṃkhya, although they have numerous epithets.[32]

In these accounts, as in Sāṃkhya, *pradhāna/prakṛti* is the subtle, unmanifest, material principle of creation from which the cosmos evolves. With some slight variation, the process of cosmogony described in these passages parallels that described in the Sāṃkhya-Kārikā and other Sāṃkhya philosophical texts: the *guṇa*s of *pradhāna/prakṛti* are disturbed, giving rise to intellect, which is generally called *mahat* (not *buddhi*) in the Purāṇas, which in turn gives rise to *ahaṃkāra*. Usually a threefold *ahaṃkāra—vaikārika, taijasa,* and *bhūtādi*—is posited based on the three *guṇas—sattva, rajas,* and *tamas*—of *pradhāna/prakṛti.* From the triple *ahaṃkāra,* the remaining *tattva*s evolve.[33] The principal gods are also produced at this stage of creation.

In relation to Vedic cosmogonies, as well as the account given in Manu-Smṛti, *prakṛti* replaces the primordial waters in these Purāṇic cosmogonies as the unmanifest, subtle material matrix from which creation evolves. Just as the waters appear as primal soup or subtle matter in the first stage of Vedic cosmogonies, in the Purāṇas *prakṛti* appears in this capacity at the dawn of primary creation. Thus in these accounts *prakṛti* plays a role parallel to that of the undifferentiated primordial waters in the Vedic accounts.

Puruṣa is the witness of creation and is often identified with the *saguṇa* form of the supreme divinity, usually Viṣṇu in this group of Purāṇas. Whereas the process of evolution in Sāṃkhya philosophy is catalyzed by the presence of *pradhāna/prakṛti* before the passive *puruṣa*—a theme that appears to be adopted by certain Purāṇic accounts[34]—other types of explanations are also given. Many Purāṇas present Puruṣa as an active agent and identify him as the lord of creation who himself willfully sets in motion the whole cosmogonic process. According to the Brahma Purāṇa (ca. 1200–1400 C.E.), for example, Puruṣa, who is also called Brahmā, Nārāyaṇa, and the self-born (Svayambhū), engages himself in the act of creation and evolves the universe out of *pradhāna*:

> *Pradhāna* is the eternal, unmanifest cause that is of the nature of existence (*sat*) and nonexistence (*asat*). The lord (Īśvara), Puruṣa, produced the universe. . . . Then the self-born lord (Bhagavān) wished to create varieties of beings from it (*pradhāna)*. He produced waters alone at the beginning.[35]

In other accounts, both *pradhāna/prakṛti* and *puruṣa* are portrayed as more passive principles, and the supreme divinity presiding over both activates the process. In these accounts, *puruṣa* tends to be portrayed more as an impersonal principle than as a personal form of the supreme deity. Thus, for example, Viṣṇu Purāṇa 2.29–30 contains an account in which Hari (Viṣṇu), who is Brahman, enters *prakṛti* and *puruṣa,* which are forms of him, and thus stimulates the evolution of the *tattvas.*

> When the time of creation (*sarga*) had arrived, having entered into *pradhāna* and *puruṣa,* the perishable and imperishable (*vyayāvyaya*), by means of his own desire, Hari agitated them. Just as odor (*gandha*) is produced, agitating the mind merely by its presence and not from any operation of the mind itself, thus the supreme lord (Parameśvara) (produced the world).

One passage in the Mārkaṇḍeya Purāṇa asserts similarly that the supreme lord enters into *puruṣa* and *prakṛti* and agitates them with his supreme power (*para yoga*).[36] In Agni Purāṇa 17.2, likewise, Viṣṇu enters both *prakṛti* and *puruṣa* and agitates them in order to begin creation. In all these cases, *prakṛti* is the material cause of creation but is never the efficient cause or willing agent of creation. Whenever an efficient cause is designated, some outside agent is said to act upon *prakṛti* in some way to cause the *tattvas* to evolve. *Prakṛti* is rather the subtle matrix that is the ultimate material source of the manifest universe.

While many of these accounts integrate theological and narrative material with philosophical material by equating *puruṣa* with the supreme divinity—Viṣṇu in this group of texts, who is male in his manifest (*saguṇa*) form—the principle of *pradhāna/prakṛti* is not as well integrated. Most of the epithets used to designate the material principle are impersonal and are devoid of explicit mythological or theological connotations. Nevertheless, there appears to be some tendency in these texts to identify *pradhāna/prakṛti* as feminine. The Viṣṇu Purāṇa, for example, describes *pradhāna/prakṛti* as the womb of the world (*jagadyoni*), and the Mārkaṇḍeya Purāṇa describes Brahmā as the lord or husband (*pati*) of *prakṛti*.[37]

After the *tattvas* evolve out of *pradhāna/prakṛti*, they are gathered together in a single mass, forming a cosmic egg in which the potential universe is contained in seed form.

RECONCILIATION OF COMPETING PHILOSOPHICAL SYSTEMS IN ACCOUNTS OF PRIMARY CREATION

While this basic cosmogonic pattern is found with slight variation in several of the Purāṇas, other accounts of creation elaborate upon this system still further. In some Purāṇic cosmogonies, there is a tendency toward conflation of philosophical ideas that attempts to reconcile competing philosophical systems. Thus while the categories of Sāṃkhya are usually retained, those of the Upaniṣads and Advaita Vedānta philosophy are grafted onto the foundational system. One of the most obvious indications of this kind of synthesizing of categories is the tendency to introduce the notion of an essential power, *śakti* or *māyā*, of the god that is responsible for creation and to equate it or at least in some way associate it with *pradhāna/prakṛti*. When the term *māyā* is used in the cosmogonic context of these texts, its meaning tends to resonate with the meanings of the term prominent in the Vedic literature and Bhagavad-Gītā indicating the creative capacity of Brahman. The use of the term *māyā* to indicate "illusion" or "delusion," however, a meaning of the term that is emphasized in Advaita Vedānta, also appears in the Purāṇas in cosmogonic contexts. Nevertheless, as illusion or delusion, *māyā* is also essentially creative, for, according to Vedānta, it is on account of Brahman's power (*śakti*) of *māyā* that the world is said to appear as real, that is, to be created in a provisional sense.

The best examples of the conflation of systems are found in the descriptions of creation in the Bhāgavata Purāṇa. In this text, Viṣṇu is lauded as the highest divinity, especially in his form as Kṛṣṇa. As supreme lord, he is called Brahman or Bhagavān. Daniel Sheridan has noted that the Bhāgavata Purāṇa is essentially nondualist in orientation and adopts the basic metaphysical position of Advaita Vedānta.[38] The world is thus seen as ultimately indistinct from Brahman. Because of its nondualist emphasis, the text tends to downplay the Sāṃkhya cosmogonic scheme, which is essentially dualist. Rather, the tendency of the Upaniṣads and Advaita Vedānta to view the manifestation of the world as a function of God's power—a power that is ultimately identical with God—and the terminology associated with such views are adopted by the text and adapted to its sectarian perspective. The term used to designate this creative power is either *māyā* or *śakti.* Thus, for example, we are told that Viṣṇu/Kṛṣṇa creates all beings out of the five elements by means of his *māyā* or, in a similar vein, that he creates all beings by means of his own *śakti.*[39] The essentially dualistic framework of Sāṃkhya along with its categories are then subsumed under the Bhāgavata Purāṇa's monistic perspective, resulting in a tendency to identify *pradhāna/prakṛti* with *māyā,* a tendency that we have also seen in the Upaniṣads and Bhagavad-Gītā as well as the Devī-Māhātmya.

In the first book, for example, we find the following description of creation:

> Although he is without qualities (*aguṇa*), he, the lord Bhagavān alone, created this (universe) in the beginning through his own *māyā*, which has both real and unreal form and consists of the three *guṇas*. Having entered into these three *guṇas*, which have come forth by means of it [*māyā*], he who is manifest by means of consciousness (*vijñāna*) appears as if possessed of the three *guṇas*.[40]

In this passage, the term *māyā* seems to designate both Viṣṇu's power to create and the material principle from which creation flows. *Māyā* is described as both an aspect of Bhagavān that is beyond creation and, when activated, as the immediate source of creation that assumes the role of *pradhāna/prakṛti*. The identification between *māyā* and *prakṛti* is evident from the description of *māyā* as consisting of three *guṇas*, a description that is usually applied to *prakṛti*.[41] In the third book, a similar kind of equation occurs, only here the term *śakti* also enters into play. The *śakti* of Bhagavān, which lies dormant, is identified with *māyā*.

> In the beginning, Bhagavān alone was here. . . . [A]ll his powers (*śakti*) were asleep, (although) his consciousness (*dṛś*) was awake. This energy (*śakti*) of that all-seeing one, of the nature of both existence (*sat*) and nonexistence (*asat*), (and) called *māyā*, is that by means of which the lord produced this world, oh eminent one. When this *māyā* consisting of the *guṇas* was disturbed by the force of time, Viṣṇu, who is possessed of virility/energy (*vīryavat*), placed in it (his) semen/energy (*vīrya*) as Puruṣa in the form of the Self (Ātman). From that unmanifest (*avyakta*) arose the *tattva* intellect (*mahat*).[42]

Both *śakti* and *māyā* designate the creative power of Bhagavān.[43] They also denote the same reality that is designated by the term *prakṛti* in other contexts and to indicate the unmanifest cause of creation consisting of the *guṇas*.

The description of Bhagavān placing his *vīrya* in *māyā* is similar to the description of Svayambhū planting his seed in the waters in the Manu-Smṛti's, Harivaṃśa's, and Matsya Purāṇa's cosmogonies. Thus the role of *māyā* in this passage, like that of the waters in the other passages, is to be the maternal womb receiving the masculine seed of creation. Also, as in the other accounts, this kind of primordial insemination sets in motion the process of creation that results in the formation of the cosmic egg. The Bhāgavata Purāṇa's account, however, is more elaborate than the earlier accounts and goes on to describe the evolution of the various *tattvas*.[44] The use of the term *vīrya* in this passage is also quite interesting. Although *vīrya* can mean semen, it also means power or energy, and in Pāñcarātra, a Tantric Vaiṣṇava movement, it has a technical meaning as one of the six qualitites of Viṣṇu. As we shall see, the description given in this account of Bhagavān placing his *vīrya* in *māyā* parallels another given in a roughly contemporanous Vaiṣṇava Purāṇa, the Garuḍa, which is influenced by Pāñcarātra.

In the Bhāgavata Purāṇa, the understanding of cosmogony as a result of the activation of God's power is conflated with Sāṃkhya's understanding of creation as a result of the activation of *pradhāna/prakṛti* before *puruṣa*. Because of the influence of Advaita Vedānta on this text, however, creation is not always deemed to be truly real since only Bhagavān is real in an absolute sense. Thus *māyā* as the creative power of the Godhead is also described as a power of delusion on account of which there appears existence, despite the nonexistence of the world as an independent reality.[45] This dual understanding of *māyā* as both a creative capacity and a power of delusion, since the creation that *māyā* ushers in is not fully real, persists throughout the Purāṇas wherever the influence of Advaita Vedānta is present.

The Kūrma Purāṇa also contains an account of cosmogony that combines Sāṃkhya categories with those of

Vedānta. In this text, however, the essential metaphysical orientation is not thoroughly nondualist but adopts a more moderate perspective. At the beginning of creation, unmanifest Brahman gives rise to three principles: time (*kāla*), *pradhāna/prakṛti*, and *puruṣa*. These three principles are described as inherent in Brahman and are both identical to and different from him.[46] *Prakṛti* gives birth to the entire universe beginning with *mahat*, which is identified with both *ahaṃkāra* and Ātman. *Puruṣa* is described as superior to *prakṛti* and devoid of creative proclivities; it becomes involved in creation, however, because of ignorance, which is produced from the union of *prakṛti* and time.[47]

This description of the basic cosmogonic framework is immediately followed by another that is similar but uses categories strictly from Vedānta, eliminating the Sāṃkhya elements from the account of creation altogether. Brahman describes himself as the unmanifest, eternal source of the universe who is the master of his own *māyā*.

> There is no stationary or moving being in the world (who) is eternal, except for me alone, the highest lord, unmanifest, having the form of space. United with time, I, that god, consisting of *māyā* (and) possessing *māyā*, send forth (√*sṛj*) and withdraw (*saṃ* √*hṛ*) this whole world.[48]

The supreme Brahman who creates, preserves, and destroys the worlds is said to be the possessor of *māyā*, which is nothing but his power (*śakti*). The term *māyā* designates Brahman's creative power but also denotes the power of delusion. In the latter case, it is said that Brahman dispels *māyā* with the help of his highest power (*para śakti*), which is knowledge (*vidyā*).

> I [Brahman] alone am the destroyer, creator (and) maintainer (of creation). I am the possessor of *māyā*. *Māyā*, which deludes the world, is my power (*śakti*).

> And that (power) which is, indeed, my highest power (*parāśakti*), is called knowledge (*vidyā*). Seated in the hearts of yogins, I dispel *māyā* with it (*vidyā*).[49]

In this passage, *māyā* and *vidyā* are understood as opposing capacities or *śaktis* of Brahman; whereas *māyā* tends to delude, *vidyā* illuminates. Although *māyā* and *vidyā* are the most important of Brahman's powers, there are others as well. Brahman is said to be the root of all *śaktis*, which he brings forth. Three of these *śaktis* are evolved and assume forms as the creator (Brahmā), preserver (Nārāyaṇa), and destroyer (Rudra) of creation.[50]

Creation is described yet again a bit further on in the text in an account that simply mixes the Sāṃkhya-type of system and the Vedānta-type of system together. The lord of creation (Īśvara) describes himself as the supreme Brahman, inherent in all phenomena and the originator of *māyā* (*māyātattvapravarttaka*). The cosmogonic process is set into motion by his *śakti*, which is described specifically as his power of action (*kriyāśakti*):

> Residing within all beings, I set this whole world into motion. This is my power of action (*kriyāśakti*). It is that by which this universe, following after my own nature, is stirred. . . . I have no beginning, middle, or end; I am the originator of *māyā*. At the beginning of creation (*sarga*), I agitate both *pradhāna* and *puruṣa*. From these two, which are joined together, the universe arises in succession, in the order beginning with *mahat*. . . . I am Bhagavān, the lord (Īśa), my own light, eternal, the supreme Self (Paramātman), the supreme Brahman; there is nothing other than me.[51]

When his *śakti* is activated, Brahman agitates *pradhāna* and *puruṣa*, who are united; and from these two principles the entire universe, beginning with the *tattva mahat*, evolves. This is the scheme of evolution according to Sāṃkhya. Yet the text also states that Brahman alone exists ("there is nothing other than me") and is associated with *māyā.* Thus Sāṃkhya and Vedānta categories are mixed together.

In these texts, the terms *māyā* and *śakti* are used in such a way that they create a link between the creator and his creation. *Māyā* and *śakti* are associated both with the efficient cause of creation, Brahman himself, and the material cause, *prakṛti,* even though the precise nature of the relationships among these different elements is not always systematically articulated.

Secondary Creation (Pratisarga)[52]

CREATION OF THE WORLDS

After the different *prākṛta* creations are evolved, they are assembled into a cosmic egg. Brahman abides within the egg, which floats on the primordial waters, and infuses it with life. After a time, the egg hatches, and Brahman is reborn as Brahmā the creator. Brahmā then takes the egg and divides it, forming the three worlds.[53] When the account of creation describes not the successive stages of primary and secondary creation but rather focuses on a *pratisarga* following a minor dissolution, it is frequently said that Brahmā emerges from a lotus that comes out of the navel of Viṣṇu-Nārāyaṇa, who is sleeping on the serpent Śeṣa in the primordial waters. Viṣṇu or Brahmā, who is often described as a manifestation of Viṣṇu, takes the form of a boar and dives under the waters to rescue the earth, which is submerged beneath them. Brahmā then fashions the different worlds.[54]

A fairly elaborate account of the creation of the worlds in the *pratisarga* is given in the Viṣṇu Purāṇa. At the end of the *kalpa,* Viṣṇu-Nārāyaṇa, who is Brahman, lies asleep in the midst of the primordial waters. Concluding that the earth is lying within the waters, he creates a second self in the shape of a boar in order to rescue it and plunges into the waters.

> When the world was nothing but ocean, the lord of beings (Prajāpati, = Nārāyaṇa), understanding through reflection that the earth was situated within the waters, wished to raise her up. He made another form of himself, just as (he had done) formerly in the beginnings of (other) *kalpas*, first as a fish and then a tortoise. Thus he took the form of a boar.[55]

The goddess earth, seeing him beneath the surface of the primordial ocean, praises him. Nārāyaṇa in the form of a boar, pleased with the earth's flattering words, grabs her with his tusks and lifts her up. He then proceeds to create the different worlds.[56]

Some accounts of the *pratisarga* do not follow this schema precisely but vary it somewhat according to the perspective of the text. The Bhāgavata Purāṇa's account of this stage of creation, for example, adapts it to emphasize the dependence of creation on Bhagavān. The whole universe is described as submerged in water, and Nārāyaṇa lies asleep on Śeṣa in the midst of the primordial waters, having deposited all subtle bodies in himself. While he sleeps, he keeps his *śakti* in the shape of time (*kāla*) active. At the appropriate time, the worlds in the form of subtle matter emerge out of his navel and become a lotus. Viṣṇu himself enters the lotus and is reborn from it as Brahmā. Looking around him, Brahmā sees only the lotus in the midst of the waters; he dives into it, seeking the ground from which the lotus has sprung. Brahmā fails to find the earth. Instead, Viṣṇu-Nārāyaṇa instructs Brahmā to practice austerities (*tapas*) and to concentrate on and offer worship to him. Brahmā does this and sees the cosmos existing in potential form resting in Viṣṇu-Nārāyaṇa. He then enters the corolla of the lotus and divides it into three portions, thus fashioning the three worlds.[57]

There are a number of different Vedic themes that are adopted by the Purāṇas in the description of creation at this level, and the place, role, and identification of certain elements with feminine principles or deities persist. The theme of the female waters, *ap,* as the maternal womb that contains the primordial embryo/germ or egg—a theme that is found not only in the Vedas but in the accounts of creation in the Manu-Smṛti and Harivaṃśa as well—continues to appear. The rescue of the earth from beneath the primordial waters, a theme that is first found in the Yajur-Veda, also persists, as does the understanding of the earth as a goddess.

Creation of Progeny

After Brahmā creates the worlds, he decides to create different species of beings. Through contemplation, he fashions five classes of secondary creations, called the *vaikṛta* creations, which include insentient and immobile creatures, animals, divine beings, and humans.[58] These five *vaikṛta* creations are juxtaposed with three other creations, namely, *mahat,* the *tanmātras,* and the *vaikārika* creations—probably the *buddhīndriyas* (hearing, touching, seeing, tasting, smelling) and *karmendriyas* (speaking, grasping, walking, excreting, procreating), both of which are said to emerge from the *vaikārika* form of *ahaṃkāra*—which are deemed *prākṛta.* Dissatisfied, he fashions another creation, called *kaumāra,* which is both *prākṛta* and *vaikṛta.* This *kaumāra* creation appears to consist of Brahmā's mind-born (*mānasa*) sons.[59] Other passages describe Brahmā's attempts to create different kinds of beings—*asuras, devas, pitṛs,* and humans—from his own body. On every occasion, he abandons the body with which each class of beings is made and takes up a new one with which to create the next class of beings.[60] Other creatures such as animals, *yakṣas, rākṣasas,* and so on are produced from his body in a similar manner.

The creations that Brahmā fashions are barren. Thus Brahmā finds that the process he has toiled to set in motion is in danger of coming to an abrupt end, and he seeks other means by which his creation can be furthered.

Brahmā divides his own body into two portions, one of which becomes male and the other of which becomes female. The Brahma Purāṇa, for example, states:

> Then the beings produced (by Brahmā) did not multiply. Dividing his own body in two, he became a man with one half and a woman with (the other) half. He [the man] begot of her [the woman] various kinds of beings.[61]

In some accounts, the male portion becomes Manu, and the female portion is named Śatarūpā, "she who has one hundred forms."[62] In several Purāṇas, including the Viṣṇu Purāṇa, the origin of Manu and Śatarūpā is cast in a slightly different context. Brahmā sees that his mind-born sons are more interested in meditation that procreation. Realizing that his self-generated progeny will not reproduce, Brahmā becomes angry. Out of his anger emerges Rudra, who is half male and half female.

> They [Brahmā's mind-born sons] (were) without attachment to the world, undesirous of progeny, filled with knowledge, without passion or envy. There arose in Brahmā a great anger toward those ones who were indifferent to the creation of the world, (an anger that was) capable of burning up the three worlds. Oh sage, then everything, the whole triad of worlds, became exceedingly bright from the garland of flames rising up from his, Brahmā's, anger. From his frowning forehead inflamed with anger sprang forth Rudra in a form that was half female and half male (*ardhanarīnara*), fierce, bulky, (and) radiant as the midday sun.[63]

Brahmā commands Rudra to divide himself, which Rudra does; the male half divides into several parts, as does the female half. Usually, the male portions are numbered at eleven and become the eleven Rudras, although variable accounts appear. Inspired by Rudra's division of himself along the lines of gender, Brahmā then creates (usually from himself) according to this model a man, Manu, who is often described as another form of Brahmā himself, and a woman, Śatarūpā.[64] They create sons and daughters through copulation. Brahmā then gives their daughters to his non-fruitful, agamically generated progeny, who in turn produce their own children.

Another variation appears in the Matsya Purāṇa. Seeing that his mind-born sons are not reproducing, Brahmā seeks another avenue by which to carry on his work of creation. He invokes the goddess Sāvitrī (Gāyatrī), who is called by many names, including the name Śatarūpā. She appears in the form of a woman from half of Brahmā's body. Brahmā falls in love with her, much to the distress of his mind-born sons, who consider her to be Brahmā's daughter and thus find his love for her to be incestuous.[65]

> Having seen her, the lord trembled greatly, struck by the arrow of desire. And the lord of beings (Prajāpati, = Brahmā) said, "Oh, what a beautiful form! Oh, what a beautiful form!" Then (the mind-born sons,) headed by Vāsiṣṭha, cried out, "(She is our) sister!" Brahmā did not notice anything, except for the sight of her face. He said over and over, "Oh, what a beautiful form!"[66]

Brahmā marries her, and they beget progeny, beginning with Manu.[67]

The introduction of the woman Śatarūpā in the process of creation catalyzes a shift from the use of asexual modes of production to the use of a sexual mode of reproduction through male/female copulation. The Padma Purāṇa, for example, explicitly asserts that in ancient times, creation had been effected by volition (*saṃkalpa*), sight (*darśana*), and touch (*sparśa*); but after Prācetasa Dakṣa, one of the mind-born sons of Brahmā who marries the first-born daughter of Manu and Śatarūpā, creation is effected by coitus (*maithuna*).[68] Similarly, the Brahma Purāṇa states that the beings created during the time of Nārāyaṇa's creation as well as Manu's were not born of the womb (*ayonija*), but Śatarūpā delivered her progeny righteously (*dharmeṇa*).[69] In another passage, a slightly different version of the story is given, and Dakṣa is born of Māriṣā, the mother of the lunar race. Dakṣa creates women, and it is only after this that procreation by means of coitus begins; prior to this, it is said that beings are born of volition, sight, and touch, as is also stated in the Padma Purāṇa.[70] The introduction of Śatarūpā also catalyzes a shift from a barren creation to a fruitful one. Just as in the Brāhmaṇas mind needs speech and Prajāpati needs Vāc, in the Purāṇas Brahmā and Manu need Śatarūpā if creation is going to succeed.

The role of Śatarūpā in the production of beings in the *pratisarga* is similar to that of *prakṛti* in the *sarga* as the source of the *tattvas*. Just as the interaction of *prakṛti* with *puruṣa* stirs up the *guṇas* of *prakṛti* and induces the evolution of the *tattvas*, which results in the formation of the *prākṛta* creations, the interaction of Manu and Śatarūpā spurs on the creation of fruitful progeny beginning in Śatarūpā's womb and insures the survival of the *vaikṛta* creations. The resemblance between *prakṛti* and Śatarūpā is noted in the Brahmāṇḍa Purāṇa, which makes an explicit connection between them. Śatarūpā is described both as created from *prakṛti* and as being herself *prakṛti*:

> From half of the body of the one who was pleased with himself [Brahmā] a woman issued forth. . . . That sensual woman was indeed created from *prakṛti*, (and) she was beautiful. She was called Śatarūpā (and) she was called thus again and again. . . . After dividing his own body in two, he [Brahmā] became a man by one half. That woman Śatarūpā arose by his (other) half. She was Prakṛti, the mother (*dhātrī*) of living beings.[71]

The Vāyu Purāṇa makes a similar equation but identifies *prakṛti* not with Śatarūpā but with the female side of Rudra, who has split into male and female halves at the behest of Brahmā. This goddess divides herself into black and white forms. She has individual manifestations as different goddesses—Lakṣmī, Sarasvatī, Umā, Gaurī, and so forth—but she is also simply called Devī, implying that she is not just a goddess but is *the* Goddess.[72] This passage thus advocates a doctrine of a Great Goddess who has many forms and is identified with a cosmogonic principle, but it has absorbed such ideas into the explanation of secondary, not primary, creation. The tendency to designate the female half of Rudra as Prakṛti or as the Great Goddess, as we shall see, is dominant in the Śaiva Purāṇas.

The identity of Śatarūpā and the goddess who is Rudra's female half with the principle *prakṛti* also indicates that in these contexts *prakṛti* is conceived to be female. The understanding of *prakṛti* as essentially feminine in gender is further borne out structurally, if we examine the diverse roles and manifestations of the male creative principle at different levels of creation and the interaction of diverse pairs of elements. Viṣṇu-Nārāyaṇa takes the form of Puruṣa and is born in and from the cosmic egg as the creator Brahmā. Brahmā then re-creates himself as Manu. Correspondingly, Prakṛti is paired with Puruṣa; in relation to Brahmā and the egg, she is replaced by the primordial, womb-like waters, whose role is clearly feminine. Finally, she is reborn as Śatarūpā and is paired with Manu. Thus on all levels, there are corresponding couplings. On at least one level, the final level, the pair is explicitly said to be a male/female couple. The gender identifications of Manu and Śatarūpā combined with the correlations of the different pairings on different levels and the various feminine associations with both *prakṛti* and the waters imply that *prakṛti* is understood to be female. *Prakṛti,* the waters, and Śatarūpā are all different manifestations of the feminine cosmogonic principle, even though gender identity is not always explicit.

The Explicit Introduction of the Feminine Element in Creation: Prakṛti/Śakti as the Consort of God

REFERENCES OUTSIDE OF ACCOUNTS OF COSMOGONY

In the Mahā-Purāṇas, there is a tendency to equate the creative power of God, designated by the term *śakti* or *māyā*, and/or the material foundation of creation, *pradhāna/prakṛti*, with the goddess associated with the deity recognized in the text as supreme—either Viṣṇu or Śiva—outside of any cosmogonic context, even where such an equation does not occur within the accounts of creation themselves. In many of the Purāṇas, this conflation of philosophical categories and mythological elements with respect to the feminine principle is not always carried out consistently throughout the texts but is mentioned nevertheless in different places. Thus, for example, the Brahma Purāṇa describes the goddess Satī, the consort of Śiva, as *prakṛti* and as the cause of the worlds,[73] even though this equation does not appear within the account of creation contained in the text. In the Bhāgavata Purāṇa, Lakṣmī is called Mahālakṣmī, "great Lakṣmi," and is explicitly equated with both the principle *prakṛti* and Viṣṇu's *māyā*, sometimes described as *māyāśakti*, "the power of *māyā*."

> You [Viṣṇu] are the lord of all, the ultimate cause of the world. She [Mahālakṣmī] is subtle *prakṛti* as well as the power of *māyā* (*māyāśakti*). . . . This goddess is the manifestation of the *guṇas* (*guṇavyakti*). . . . [T]he almighty goddess represents name and form (*nāmarūpa*).[74]

The appearance of such references indicates an attempt, however incomplete, to integrate more fully the philosophical cosmogonic and cosmological categories adopted by the Purāṇas with their essentially mythological orientation. As the Purāṇas equate the *puruṣa* of Sāṃkhya or the Brahman of Upaniṣadic and Vedānta thought with the deity who is lauded as supreme in the particular text, it would follow that the complementary principle—*pradhāna/prakṛti* or *śakti/māyā*—would be equated with the female consort of that deity. This impulse comes to fruition in several Purāṇas where such identifications are made explicit within the narration of cosmogony itself.

Integration of The Feminine Principle in Accounts of Cosmogony: Sarga *and* Pratisarga

The full integration of the feminine principle in the story of creation appears in several of the Purāṇas and indicates a more complete reconciliation of mythological and philosophical categories. In these texts, the direct source of creation—*prakṛti, śakti,* or *māyā*—is equated with the goddess appropriate to the sectarian perspective of the text, who is often celebrated as the supreme female divinity and the immediate cause of creation. She is also often identified more specifically as the source of all other goddesses and female forms within creation as well. The clear integration of the feminine principle into the mechanisms of creation and the identification of different goddesses with philosophical principles are inseparably connected to a theology of a Great Goddess who even in the non-Śākta Purāṇas is conceived to be as praiseworthy as the god with whom she is associated.

In several Vaiṣṇava and Śaiva Purāṇas, respectively, Viṣṇu and Śiva are extolled as supreme and are equated with the principles *puruṣa* and/or Brahman. The consorts of these deities, however, are equally elevated and represent the complementary principles. As *prakṛti,* the Goddess is the material cause of creation. As *śakti* or *māyā,* she is usually associated both with the material cause *prakṛti,* with which she is frequently identified, and with the efficient cause, the creator himself who possesses and wields the power that is equated with the Goddess. In Śākta contexts, the Goddess is both the supreme Brahman who wills creation into being and the material cause, *prakṛti*, which is the immediate source of the universe.

As part of the tendency to view different individual female forms as diverse manifestations of a single, supreme feminine principle identified as a Great Goddess (Mahādevī), some of these Purāṇas also explicitly identify the goddesses active on the level of secondary creation (*pratisarga*) as manifestations of the feminine principle that is the source of primary creation (*sarga*). Some of the links that were implicit in other Purāṇas are now made explicit. In order to demonstrate these associations with the greatest clarity, we will treat together the accounts of *sarga* and *pratisarga* in each individual text. We will not include the accounts of secondary creation that do not differ significantly from the standard account given above.

As different sectarian perspectives influence the way in which cosmogony is narrated, one must consider Vaiṣṇava, Śaiva, and Śākta texts separately. The Kūrma Purāṇa, which is cross-sectarian, will be taken up in both the Vaiṣṇava and the Śaiva sections. We will begin our analysis by exploring different cosmogonies that celebrate the ultimate supremacy of Viṣṇu or his incarnation as Kṛṣṇa in five different Purāṇas: the Kūrma, Varāha, Garuḍa, Nārada, and Brahmavaivarta Purāṇas. In the first two instances, different levels of the Goddess's identity are articulated but are not clearly placed in any kind of cosmogonic sequence. The last three texts, however, tend to place different principles and aspects of the Goddess more clearly in a cosmogonic framework.

VAIṢṆAVA PURĀṆAS AND VAIṢṆAVA SECTIONS OF CROSS-SECTARIAN PURĀṆAS

The Kūrma Purāṇa is one of the earliest Purāṇas to clearly incorporate a goddess into descriptions of cosmogony. Lakṣmī, Viṣṇu's spouse, is described as the power by which Viṣṇu creates, the power by which he deludes his creation, and the material principle that serves as the immediate source of creation. These three functions correspond to those of *śakti*, *māyā*, and *prakṛti*, all of which are equated with Lakṣmī.

The text asserts that when the gods ask Viṣṇu about the identity of Lakṣmī, he responds by identifying her as his highest power (*paramā śakti*). This power is both creative and delusive. She is also described as the supreme *prakṛti* that is the immediate source of the entire creation as well as the supreme *māyā* of Viṣṇu-Nārāyaṇa.

> She [Lakṣmī] is that supreme power (*paramā śakti*) wholly consisting of/absorbed in me (*manmayi*), of the nature of Brahman, my beloved, endless *māyā* by which this universe is deluded. Through her, I delude, swallow up, and recreate the whole world. . . . [D]epending on parts of her, the twice-born (and) the gods—Brahmā, Śiva (Īśāna), and so forth—have become possessed of power (*śaktimat*). She is my entire power (*sarvaśakti*). She is the source of the entire universe, *prakṛti* possessing three *guṇas*.[75]

In response, Lakṣmī then reaffirms her identity as Viṣṇu's supreme *māyā*, asserting that there is ultimately no difference between herself and Viṣṇu.[76] Such an assertion of equality between the supreme male and his consort is quite common in the Purāṇas, as we shall see, but in Vaiṣṇava and Śaiva contexts, it is always the male who is supreme. This is borne out in the fact that although it is said that ultimately there is no distinction at all between Śakti and the possessor of Śakti (*śaktimat*, = Viṣṇu/Kṛṣṇa or Śiva), nevertheless it is the male who possesses the Goddess. Śakti is never described as the possessor of her consort.

The identity of Lakṣmī with the creative/delusive power of Viṣṇu and with *prakṛti* is clearly indicated in the account of creation that follows shortly thereafter. This theory of creation does not follow the usual pattern but rather reflects another explanation of cosmogony that often appears in the Purāṇas alongside the Sāṃkhya-type theory and in which Brahman produces Brahmā, Viṣṇu, and Śiva—the creator, preserver, and destroyer of the worlds—at the beginning of the cycle. Brahmā then proceeds to create the worlds. In the Kūrma Purāṇa's account, Viṣṇu-Nārāyaṇa awakens from his slumber and ponders creation. Grace (*prasāda*) descends upon him, from which is born Brahmā, the creator. Then Rudra is born from his anger. Following this, the goddess Lakṣmī appears.

> Then came the goddess Śrī (Lakṣmī). . . . Nārāyaṇī, Mahāmāyā, imperishable Mūlaprakṛti sat by my side filling this (all) with her own majesty. Seeing her, the venerable Brahmā, lord of the worlds, said to me, "Oh Mādhava, employ this beautiful one for the delusion of all beings, by means of whom this great creation of mine might prosper."[77]

These narrative elements are included in the text alongside the exposition of a Sāṃkhya-type description of creation that does not explicitly identify *prakṛti* with Lakṣmī.[78]

The identity of Lakṣmī as a cosmogonic principle in this section of the Kūrma Purāṇa is described on two levels. First, Lakṣmī is Viṣṇu's *śakti*, called *māyā*, which is an inherent part of Viṣṇu and is his creative and delusive power. Second, Lakṣmī is identified as Mūlaprakṛti, which is separate from Viṣṇu. In this context, these different aspects of the Goddess are not clearly placed in any cosmogonic sequence.

A rather late section of the Varāha Purāṇa (ca. 750–1500 C.E.)[79] also contains an account of a Great Goddess who is the source of creation. In this text, Viṣṇu-Nārāyaṇa is extolled as the supreme deity. Brahmā arises from him, and Rudra (Śiva) arises from Brahmā. While Śiva is sporting with Gaurī (Pārvatī) and the *gaṇas* on Mount Kailāsa, Brahmā comes to him to ask for help in a confrontation with a demon. Brahmā looks at Śiva and, at the same time, calls to his mind (√*smṛ*) Nārāyaṇa. The three become unified and gaze at one another, and from the unified gazes (*dṛṣṭi*) of the three gods, a girl having a divine form (*kumārī divyarūpinī*) arises. This account echoes the account found in the Devī-Māhātmya where the Goddess is born from the unified energies (*tejas*) of the gods. Here too, the divine maiden represents the unified energies (*śakti*) of the three male divinities. The gods name her Trikalā, "three digits," and ask her to assume three different forms. She thus becomes threefold, assuming a white, red, and black form.[80] These three forms are correlated with the three primary male deities:

> The bright body with beautiful hips is Brahmī, and creation comes forth from her auspiciously as ordained by Brahmā's creative role. The beautiful, red-colored, middle body is the goddess Vaiṣṇavī, who bears conch and disc. She is known as Kalā. She protects the whole universe and is called Viṣṇumāyā. The black-colored body, the goddess Raudrī, bears a trident and has a terrible face. She destroys the universe.[81]

The three colors of this goddess's different forms are those that are associated with the *guṇas* of *prakṛti*. Thus this goddess embodying the unified *śaktis* of the three primary gods of creation is implicitly, although not explicitly, identified with *prakṛti*. This implicit identification is further indicated by her correlation with material creation itself. She is called Sṛṣṭi, "creation," and her three different forms are described as her different aspects. It is said that the entire world of movable and immovable objects is pervaded by her and that she is the origin of everything, the source of all gods and demons, all *yakṣas*, *gandharvas*, *rākṣasas*, animals, and plants.[82] Thus she is represented as being the foundation of all existing things. The identity of the goddess of creation with *prakṛti* is also implied in a later passage in which her three forms are correlated with those of the supreme Self (Paramātman), who is also said to acquire three forms.

> This highest goddess Sṛṣṭi, when white, is of sattvic nature and abides in Brahmā. The very same one, when red, is of rajasic nature and is called Vaiṣṇavī. The very same one, when black, is of tamasic nature and is called the goddess Raudrī. Just as the same supreme Self (Paramātman), although one, manifests itself as threefold [as Brahmā, Viṣṇu, Śiva], so this power (*śakti*), although one, becomes threefold on account of particular functions.[83]

This passage explicitly correlates the three different manifestations of the goddess of creation, Sṛṣṭi, with not only the three colors associated with the *guṇas* of *prakṛti*, but also with the diverse qualities of the *guṇas*. Thus the identification of this goddess with *prakṛti* is again made implicitly through association. Elsewhere in the text, the equation is made explicitly but only with respect to one of her three forms, the *śakti* of Viṣṇu called Vaiṣṇavī, who is lauded as the highest *śakti* and is identified as great delusion (Mahāmāyā), the mother of the universe, Yogamāyā, Prakṛti, and Pradhāna.[84] Given the Vaiṣṇava orientation of the text, it is to be expected that the female form associated with Viṣṇu would be given supremacy over the forms associated with the other gods.

The goddess Sṛṣṭi continues to play a significant role on the level of secondary creation as well. After her three forms are evolved, each disappears to pursue the practice of austerities. Brahmā begins his process of creation, but he reaches a block and cannot progress.

> Now for a long time, the lord of beings (Prajāpati, = Brahmā) undertook to produce progeny. While the strength of him who was engaged in producing (*sṛjat*) multiplied, his—Brahmā's—mind-born progeny did not multiply. Then he thought, "What is this? My progeny aren't multiplying." Then the god Brahmā with his heart engaged in yoga, reflecting, brought to mind (√*budh*) the maiden on that very holy white mountain.

> She was performing austerities (*tapas*), her sins being burned up by austerities.[85]

Seeking a solution to his problem, Brahmā seeks out this white-bodied form of Sṛṣṭi, the form with which he is associated. When he finds her, he propitiates her and tells her that she may seek a boon. She in turn asks that Brahmā make her present everywhere, a request to which Brahmā complies. Sṛṣṭi then dissolves herself in Brahmā, and his creation begins to grow once again.[86] A similar account is given in another passage where Brahmā, wishing to create different beings, enters into deep contemplation but cannot figure out what he should do. Frustrated, he becomes angry, and Rudra is born from this anger. Brahmā gives Rudra Gaurī as his wife and asks Rudra to create. Rudra, however, cannot seem to perform.

> He himself, Brahmā, the lord of beings, (was) filled with the greatest joy, having gotten that handsome woman for Rudra, whose body was without bounds. When it was time for creation, Brahmā told him, "Oh, Rudra! Produce progeny!" Thus he commanded him again and again. (Rudra replied,) "I can't!" and he, the one possessing great strength, dove into the water.[87]

Rudra goes off to do *tapas* in hopes that he will be able to perform more effectively afterwards. Brahmā, however, is impatient; while Rudra is gone, Brahmā takes Gaurī and lodges her in his body. This leads to the creation of mind-born sons. Brahmā then gives Gaurī to his son Dakṣa to be Dakṣa's daughter.[88]

In the materials concerning the goddess Sṛṣṭi, there is a correlation between the function and identity of the feminine principle in primary creation and her role in secondary creation. As *śakti/prakṛti,* the three-bodied goddess Sṛṣṭi is the initial impulse that brings forth creation as well as the power that is responsible for the maintenance and destruction of the universe. Her creative role is repeated in the *pratisarga,* where she serves as the power with which Brahmā is able to further his creation. As in the Kūrma Purāṇa, these different aspects of the Goddess are not clearly placed in any cosmogonic sequence.

In other Purāṇas, the identity of certain cosmogonic principles that function in primary creation as female is more clearly integrated into the Sāṃkhya-type cosmogony. In these contexts, the sequence of events in creation and the levels of the Goddess are often, but not always, more clearly correlated. In the Garuḍa Purāṇa, for example, Lakṣmī, Viṣṇu's spouse, is explicitly identified with *prakṛti/māyā* and is incorporated into the account of primary creation on three levels: (1) Lakṣmī as the female form of Viṣṇu and an integral, inseparable part of him; (2) Lakṣmī as *prakṛti/māyā,* the material foundation of the universe that is different from Viṣṇu; and (3) Lakṣmī as a Great Goddess who is the source of the goddesses Śrī, Bhū, and Durgā. These three different levels of Lakṣmī's identity are incorporated into a description of the process of creation that involves three stages: (1) the initial impulse toward creation that is represented by the activation of Viṣṇu's creative energy; (2) the depositing of this energy in *prakṛti/māyā,* which stirs up the three *guṇas*; and (3) the commencement of the evolution of the *tattvas* from the activated *guṇas*.

It is important to note that the term used in this account for Viṣṇu's creative energy is not *śakti* but *vīrya.* As noted in the discussion of the Bhāgavata Purāṇa, the use of the term *vīrya* is consistent with the tenets of Pāñcarātra, a Tantric Vaiṣṇava movement that seems to have influenced this text. Pāñcarātra and schools and sects based on Pāñcarātra recognize six qualities or *guṇas* of Viṣṇu-Nārāyaṇa, who is recognized in this system as Brahman. The fifth of these *guṇas* is *vīrya,* which is described as the ability of Brahman to remain changeless in spite of being the cause of creation.[89] In the Garuḍa Purāṇa, *vīrya* represents the creative power of Brahman and plays the same role in the context in which this cosmogonic account is found, the Brahma-Kāṇḍa of the

Garuḍa Purāṇa's second part (Uttara-Khaṇḍa), as does *śakti* in some of the other accounts we have seen. It is noteworthy, however, that although Lakṣmī is identified as *prakṛti/māyā* in the Garuḍa Purāṇa's version of cosmogony, she does not seem to be explicitly identified as Viṣṇu's *vīrya.* In fact, *vīrya* can also mean semen, and in this context the principle of creative energy is allied more with the power of male virility than with female creative potential.

In the text Kṛṣṇa describes to Garuḍa the process by which Viṣṇu places his energy (*vīrya*) in *māyā,* which is described as consisting of three *guṇas.* Garuḍa asks whether Viṣṇu's energy is the same as or different from Viṣṇu. Kṛṣṇa responds by telling him that the energy that Viṣṇu deposits in *māyā* is of the same nature as Viṣṇu, but that, being material (*prākṛta*), it is also a separate entity. Viṣṇu's energy is thus both part of him and part of material creation, which is different from him.[90] Kṛṣṇa continues:

> Lord Vāsudeva is of the nature of energy (*vīryasvarūpin*) in all places and in all times. If he were not possessed of all things, oh lord of birds, then he would not be both Īśvara and Puruṣa.
>
> He has two forms, one a female form and the other a male form, along with (other) unthinkable and thinkable powers. The two forms [male and female] are both possessed of power, oh lord of birds, and are to be thought of as being not different, indeed, the same (*samyak*).[91]

Viṣṇu, here called Vāsudeva, is described as having two forms, male and female, both of which are possessed of power (*vīryavat*). Although the identity of the female form described here is not made clear, the text declares that the form of Śrī (Lakṣmī) is reflected in the form of Hari (Viṣṇu), thus implying that the female form of Viṣṇu is Lakṣmī.[92] It is also stated that Viṣṇu can never be without Lakṣmī in any space or time, nor she without him, for the two are inseparable.[93]

This passage then goes on to describe the mechanisms by which the universe is created when Viṣṇu deposits his *vīrya* in Lakṣmī. Here the term *vīrya* is associated more strongly with semen, and the placing of *vīrya* in Lakṣmī has sexual overtones. Kṛṣṇa states that although the demons say that Lakṣmī is his power of illusion (*indrajāla*), this is wrong. Rather, what they really mean is the thing called *māyā*, which is simply the subtle form of *prakṛti*.[94] The identification of Lakṣmī with the principle *māyā/prakṛti* is again implied at the end of the chapter where a passage that parallels the one describing Viṣṇu depositing his energy/semen in Lakṣmī now states that Viṣṇu deposits it in *māyā*.

> Lord Hari, who is called Puruṣa and is possessed of energy (*vīryavat*), deposited that energy (*vīrya*) in *māyā* and produced the three *guṇas*.[95]

Although the precise nature of the relationships among Lakṣmī, *prakṛti* and *māyā* is not explicitly articulated in this passage, parallel phrasing establishes an identity between Lakṣmī and *prakṛti/māyā* as the receptacle of Viṣṇu's *vīrya*. Lakṣmī is both the female form of Viṣṇu that is inseparable from him and is also equated—on a lower level—with the material source of creation, *prakṛti/māyā*, which is separate from Viṣṇu.

Whereas these two levels of identity represent the abstract forms of Lakṣmī, her nature as subtle cosmogonic and cosmological principles, yet a third level of identification is postulated that represents her personal form as a goddess, a form that is manifest as different individual goddesses:

> When the lord created the three *guṇas* of *prakṛti*, there sprang up Lakṣmī in her three forms, Śrī, Bhū, and Durgā. Śrī was characterized by *sattva*, Bhū by *rajas*, and Durgā by *tamas*. Thus say the wise.
> O lord of birds, one should not recognize any difference, on account of their mutual relation, among the forms, nor the *guṇas*, (nor) Durgā, Bhū, and Śrī.[96]

On this level, Lakṣmī is the Great Goddess of whom the three principal goddesses—Bhū, Śrī, and Durgā—are the individual manifestations and represent the three *guṇas* of *prakṛti*. The supreme lord Viṣṇu, here identified as Puruṣa, also assumes corresponding forms as Brahmā the creator, a second form of Viṣṇu who acts as the preserver, and Śiva the destroyer, each of whom is associated with the corresponding *guṇa*—*rajas* for Brahmā, *sattva* for Viṣṇu, and *tamas* for Rudra. The supreme form of Viṣṇu enters the *guṇas* and activates them, causing the evolution of the first *tattva*, *mahat*.[97] The process of creation continues when Viṣṇu and Lakṣmī enter *mahat* together and disturb it, giving rise to egoity, *ahaṃkāra*; they then enter *ahaṃkāra* together, disturbing it as well. Viṣṇu then evolves the *buddhīndriyas* (hearing, touching, seeing, tasting, smelling) and *karmendriyas* (speaking, grasping, walking, excreting, procreating) out of *ahaṃkāra*, and the creation of different principles and beings ensues.[98]

Lakṣmī continues to function on the lower levels of creation as well. When Viṣṇu goes to sleep during the period of dissolution, Lakṣmī serves as the bed of water on which he reclines. The waters are nothing but Lakṣmī herself. Although she is identified with the waters, however, Lakṣmī is also said to pervade them in the form of darkness (*tamas*) and to sleep on them with Hari, to whom she sings praises.

> Viṣṇu slept for a thousand years. . . . And Lakṣmī (was) in the form of water (*udakarūpa*), (which took) the shape of a bed. . . . She also was in the form of darkness (*tamas*). There was nothing else present whatsoever. . . . In the embryo-like waters, Lakṣmī sang praises to Hari. In that way, assuming the forms of Lakṣmī and the earth, *prakṛti* slept with Hari . . . (and) praised Hari in the embryo-like waters.[99]

In this text an explicit connection is made between *prakṛti* and the primordial waters, a connection that we have seen made implicitly in other contexts. *Prakṛti* takes the form of

Lakṣmī, who, in turn, takes the form of the cosmic waters. All three are manifestations of the feminine principle on different levels of creation.

The levels of the Goddess's identity and the corresponding stages of creation as described in the Garuḍa Purāṇa can be schematized as follows:

Stages of Manifestation

The Goddess	*Creation*
Lakṣmī as the female aspect of Viṣṇu, an integral part of him	The initial impulse toward creation that is represented by the activation of Viṣṇu's creative power (*vīrya*)
Lakṣmī as *prakṛti/māyā*, the material foundation of the cosmos that is different from from Viṣṇu	The depositing of creative power (*vīrya*) in *prakṛti*, which stirs up the *guṇas* of *prakṛti*
Lakṣmī as the Great Goddess who is the source of Śrī, Bhū, and Durgā	The commencement of the evolution of the *tattvas* from the activated *guṇas*
Lakṣmī as the primordial waters	Dissolution between primary creation (*sarga*) and secondary creation (*pratisarga*)

The Nārada Purāṇa (ca. 850–1000 C.E.) also explicitly features goddesses in descriptions of the mechanisms of creation and identifies them with cosmogonic principles. Unlike the account given in the Garuḍa Purāṇa, however, the account given here accepts the basic metaphysical propositions of Advaita Vedānta. It incorporates the notion of *prakṛti* as the material basis of creation but places *prakṛti* at a lower level of cosmogony than the power of *māyā*, which is an inherent aspect of the supreme divinity, Viṣṇu.

At the dawn of creation, Mahāviṣṇu alone is said to exist as Brahman. His supreme *śakti* stimulates the process of creation. This *śakti* is described as both existent and nonexistent in nature (*bhāvābhāvasvarūpa*), and is both knowledge (*vidyā*) and ignorance (*avidyā*).[100] These categories *vidyā* and *avidyā* are borrowed from Advaita Vedānta philosophy according to which, as we have seen, knowledge or *vidyā* constitutes the understanding of Nirguṇa Brahman, Brahman without qualities. Ignorance or *avidyā* is the absence of this true understanding. *Avidyā* on the level of epistemology is correlated with *māyā* on the level of ontology. In this passage of the Nārada Purāṇa, *avidyā* is declared to be the false belief that the world is other than Viṣṇu; *vidyā* is the correct understanding of the unity of everything in Viṣṇu, who is supreme Brahman. The universe only appears to be different from Viṣṇu/Brahman because of *avidyā*:

> When the universe is understood to be different from Mahāviṣṇu, then ignorance (*avidyā*), the cause of suffering (*duḥkha*), is attained. Oh Nārada, when the conditions "knower," "to-be-known," and so on disappear, this comprehension of the oneness of everything is called knowledge (*vidyā*). Thus the *māyā* of Mahāviṣṇu, if seen as distinct from him, is the giver of birth and rebirth (*saṃsāra*), but if realized with the comprehension of nondifference from him, it is the destroyer of the round of birth and rebirth.[101]

This two-faceted *śakti*, which is also referred to as Viṣṇu's *māyā*, leads to birth and rebirth (*saṃsāra*) only if its manifestation as *avidyā* is activated. If it is realized with the awareness of its nondifference from Viṣṇu, however, such that Viṣṇu is seen as being the same as his *śakti/māyā*, it leads to the end of the cycle of continual rebirths. Thus it has the potential to be creative or destructive, either perpetuating creation or causing its cessation.

As a creative energy, the *śakti* of Viṣṇu is described as the source of the entire universe of mobile and immobile beings, which it also pervades, and is equated with various female divinities. The influence of Advaita Vedānta, which stresses the all-pervasiveness of Brahman, is again apparent:

> The entire universe of mobile and immobile beings is produced from Viṣṇu's *śakti,* from which all these things, whether they move or not, are different. . . . [J]ust as Lord Hari pervades the entire universe, so also does his *śakti,* oh sage, just as the burning capacity (*dāhaśakti*) resides in charcoal, pervading its own substratum.[102]

The text then declares that this *śakti* of Viṣṇu is called Umā, Lakṣmī, Bhāratī, Girijā, Ambikā, Durgā, and so on, explicitly identifying the cosmogonic power of Brahman with diverse goddesses. The side of Viṣṇu's potency, then, that creates and sustains the world is clearly female. This *śakti* is also described as *vidyā, avidyā, māyā,* and supreme *prakṛti,* all of which seem to be the various aspects of Viṣṇu's *śakti.*[103] The identification of the *śakti* or *māyā* of Viṣṇu with *prakṛti* is made explicit once again a bit further on in the text:

> His *śakti* is the great *māyā,* the trustworthy upholder of the world. Because of its being the primary material cause of the universe, it is called *prakṛti* by those who are knowledgeable.[104]

In the verses that follow, the subsumption of Sāṃkhya categories is apparent. Viṣṇu engages himself in the creation of the three worlds, and three forms evolve from him: time (*kāla*), *puruṣa,* and *prakṛti.* When *prakṛti* is agitated, *mahat* evolves; from *mahat* evolves *buddhi,* from which *ahaṃkāra* originates in turn. The rest of the *tattvas* then arise in succession.[105] Although Viṣṇu's *śakti* is identical with him on the highest level as *vidyā,* it is also distinct from him and is evolved from him as primordial *prakṛti.*

The different levels of identification of the different feminine principles associated with Viṣṇu and the corresponding stages in creation in this section of the Nārada Purāṇa can be schematized as follows:

Stages of Manifestation

The Feminine Principle	*Creation*
Śakti/māyā as the inherent energy of Viṣṇu, identified as various goddesses (Umā, Lakṣmī, Durgā, etc.)	The initial impulse toward creation that is represented by the activation of Viṣṇu's *śakti/māyā* as *avidyā*
Prakṛti as the manifestation of *śakti/māyā,* distinct from Viṣṇu	The beginning of primary creation through the agitation of *prakṛti* and the evolution of the *tattvas*

The third *pāda* of the first part (Pūrva-Khaṇḍa) and the second part (Uttara-Khaṇḍa) of the Nārada Purāṇa contain materials that elevate Kṛṣṇa, one of the most important incarnations of Viṣṇu, to supreme status and identify his consort Rādhā with Kṛṣṇa's *māyā* and with *prakṛti.*[106] We are told that in Goloka, Kṛṣṇa's heaven, Kṛṣṇa dwells eternally as supreme Brahman (Parabrahman), who is beyond attributes. On this highest level, Rādhā is one with Kṛṣṇa. Rādhā abides with Kṛṣṇa in the same body, and it is said that there is no difference at all between them—a common Purāṇic formula, as previously mentioned. Kṛṣṇa is like the substance of which Rādhā is the attribute, and they are as inseparable as milk and its color or earth and its smell.[107] One passage describes this highest level of Rādhā's identity as beyond *prakṛti,* existing in the form of consciousness (*cidrūpa*).[108] Just as Viṣṇu's *śakti,* which is equated with several different goddesses, is described in the earlier portions of the text as both identical with Viṣṇu on the highest level and distinct from him when evolved out of him at the time of creation, Rādhā, too, is described as both identical with Kṛṣṇa on the highest level and distinct from him when she is separated from him. She is said to be produced from half of his body, and she becomes manifest as Mūlaprakṛti Īśvarī, the goddess primordial Prakṛti. As such, Rādhā is described as being of the nature of the visible and invisible worlds (*dṛśyādṛśyasvarūpinī*) and is called the maker of the universe (*jagatkartrī*) and the mother (*sūtikā*) of all.[109]

The highest, eternal form of Rādhā gives rise to five goddesses who are described as her five manifestations: Lakṣmī, Durgā, Sāvitrī, Sarasvatī, and a second form of Rādhā herself. These five goddesses are called collectively the cause of creation (*sṛṣṭikāraṇa*).[110] So Rādhā is also conceived to be the Great Goddess of whom other goddesses are lesser forms. In fact, the text asserts that she springs forth from Kṛṣṇa's body and becomes the source of not only other goddesses, but also the cowherdesses who sport with Kṛṣṇa. These are her partial incarnations (*aṃśa*) and are identified as her own individual *śakti*s:

> Sanatkumāra said: Oh Nārada, listen! I will narrate the greatly wondrous origin of the partial incarnations (*aṃśa*) of Rādhā, her *śakti*s, along with the (appropriate) mantra recitation. That (goddess) whom I call Rādhā originates from half of Kṛṣṇa's body. She is eternal, residing in Goloka together with Kṛṣṇa. . . . Mahālakṣmī arose from the left side of Rādhā . . . (and) the cowherd-maidens arose from the pores of Rādhā's skin.[111]

Although Rādhā is the chief female deity in this section of the Purāṇa, Durgā is also sometimes elevated to supreme status. The ascendency of Durgā is in fact asserted in this same passage. Various male divinities are described as evolving from Kṛṣṇa's person and are subsequently paired with their corresponding female consorts, who emerge from the body of either Kṛṣṇa or Rādhā. Viṣṇu/Nārāyaṇa, for example, is manifested from Kṛṣṇa's left side; analogously, Lakṣmī, Viṣṇu's consort, springs from Rādhā's left side (see above), and Kṛṣṇa gives her to Nārāyaṇa. Śiva is created when Kṛṣṇa divides himself in two, and Śiva takes as his wife Durgā, who is also manifested from Kṛṣṇa's person.[112] When she emerges from Kṛṣṇa, Durgā is lauded as the source of all other female divinities and as *māyā/prakṛti*:

> Meanwhile, oh Brahmin, Durgā, the eternal *māyā* of Viṣṇu, suddenly became manifest from the body of Kṛṣṇa. She—Mūlaprakṛti Īśvarī—was in the form of the seed of all goddesses, perfect, having splendor as her own form, and consisting of the three *guṇas*.[113]

Different passages use similar or identical epithets to describe Rādhā, calling her Mūlaprakṛti, the eternal *māyā* of Viṣṇu and the inherent *māyā* of Kṛṣṇa. Thus the ultimate identity between the two goddesses is made implicitly.[114] The integration of Durgā into this material is probably attributable at least in part to the influence of the Devī-Māhātyma. This passage makes a self-conscious attempt to model itself on the Great Goddess tradition and thus adopts not only some of the Devī-Māhātmya's themes but also its Great Goddess, who is associated primarily with Śiva and is named Durgā.

Although the Nārada Purāṇa does not explicitly link the materials pertaining to Rādhā and Kṛṣṇa with stages of cosmogony, the similarity between the two different accounts in this text that we have explored—that of Viṣṇu's *śakti*/Viṣṇu and that of Rādhā/Kṛṣṇa—suggests an underlying structural parallel between the members of each pair. In the first case, the material is integrated into an account of primary creation, but in the second case, it is not. Furthermore, the Purāṇa also contains a creation narrative immediately preceding the description of the ultimate unity of Rādhā and Kṛṣṇa that incorporates Kṛṣṇa into a Sāṃkhya-type description of cosmogony. Kṛṣṇa is described as the supreme lord who is present at the time of creation. He deposits his *śakti* into *prakṛti*, causing the evolution of the *guṇas*, which are described as Kṛṣṇa's rays (*aṃśu*) or bodies. This causes the evolution of *mahat* from the *guṇas*, and the rest of creation follows.[115] This *śakti* seems to be different from *prakṛti*, since Kṛṣṇa deposits the former in the latter, yet the two principles are also identified with one another, just as Rādhā is described as both the form of consciousness beyond *prakṛti* as well as *prakṛti*.

The elevation of Kṛṣṇa and Rādhā to supreme status and their identities and roles in cosmogony are most elaborately depicted in the Brahmavaivarta Purāṇa (ca. 1400–1600 C.E.), which also includes much Rādhā-Kṛṣṇa material similar to that which is in the Nārada Puraṇa. In this Purāṇa, the celebration of the feminine principle in cosmogony is even stronger than in most of the others that we have seen thus far. There are several different accounts of creation in this text, all of which explicitly ascribe an active role to certain goddesses at the level of primary creation. It is notable that the cosmogonies that are found in the Brahmavaivarta Purāṇa leave out the description of the evolution of the *tattvas* that we have seen in some of the other Purāṇas in favor of more purely mythological explanations of cosmogony.

There are several different accounts of creation in this text. According to one account, Ātman splits himself into two parts in the beginning of creation by the power of yoga. The right side is called *puruṣa,* and the left, *prakṛti.* The significance of *prakṛti* in the process of creation is recounted in a passage where Nārāyaṇa explains to Nārada the significance of the term *prakṛti* according to some rather creative etymology.

> Oh child, who is fit to describe the essence of *prakṛti*? Nevertheless, I will describe it to you as I heard it from the mouth of Dharma. *Pra-* means distinguished (*prakṛṣṭa*), and *-kṛti* means creation (*sṛṣṭi*). Which goddess is distinguished in creation, she is called Prakṛti. According to scripture (*śruti*), *pra-* means the preeminent *guṇa sattva, -kṛ-* means the middle *guṇa rajas,* and *-ti* means *tamas.* She, therefore, who has the three *guṇas* as her own form is possessed of all powers (*śakti*) and is preeminent in causing creation; therefore, she is called Prakṛti. *Pra-* means first, and *-kṛti* means creation. And that goddess who is first in creation is therefore called Prakṛti.[116]

Just as Kṛṣṇa is eternal, so is Prakṛti, for the two are indissolubly connected. Kṛṣṇa cannot create without her, for she is also his creative power, *śakti.* In order to explain the nature of this *śakti,* the text again resorts to folk etymology. We are told that *śak-* means majesty (*aiśvarya*), and *-ti* means strength (*parākrama*); hence Śakti is the bestower of all majesty and strength.[117] Although the equation of *prakṛti/śakti* with *māyā* is found in the text, the Goddess's manifestation as *māyā* is subordinated.

The relationship between Kṛṣṇa and the goddess Prakṛti/Śakti is quite complex. In his excellent and careful study of the Brahmavaivarta Purāṇa, C. Mackenzie Brown differentiates among four types of relational models or analogies that are found in the text and are used to describe the relationship between Kṛṣṇa and his female counterpart: (1) substance and attribute, (2) efficient and material cause, (3) support and supported or container and contained (*ādhāra* and *ādheya*), and (4) "soul" (*ātman*) and body.[118] Brown argues that, as substance and attribute, Kṛṣṇa and the goddess Prakṛti/Śakti are described as existing together like milk and its whiteness, water and its coolness, smell in the earth, burning in fire, and so on. Such descriptions are also found in the Nārada Purāṇa, as we have seen. Brown points out that in some passages of the Brahmavaivarta Purāṇa, Prakṛti is described not just as an attribute but also as the activating energy, *śakti,* of the substance that represents Kṛṣṇa and without which the substance could not properly function or function at all.[119] As this *śakti,* Prakṛti also represents the power that is needed to bring forth and make manifest the essence or the very life of the substance with which she is linked:

> She (is the one) who has the form of the burning quality in fire and radiance in the sun, the lustre in the moon and in the lotuses, exceedingly beautiful; whose own form consists of all the powers (*śakti*) in Śrī Kṛṣṇa, the supreme Self (Paramātman), by means of whom,

> too, the Self is possessed with power (*śakti*), and the world also; and without whom the whole world, though living, remains as if dead.[120]

As efficient and material cause of creation, Kṛṣṇa and Prakṛti are like goldsmith and gold, or potter and clay. This model tends to emphasize the materiality of Prakṛti over her nature as power, which is emphasized more in the substance-attribute metaphor. Nevertheless, Prakṛti's power in relation to her mate is not forgotten, for when Kṛṣṇa possesses the material with which to create, this gives him the ability to act on his creative impulses. Kṛṣṇa declares:

> Just as a potter with clay is always possessed of the power (*śaktimat*) to make a pot, thus am I together with you, who are Prakṛti, (possessed of the power) to create creation. Without you, I am inert and am always powerless. You have all powers (*śakti*) as your own form; come into my presence.[121]

Prakṛti represents the material that Kṛṣṇa then manipulates in order to bring about creation or the energy, *śakti*, which he employs in the creative process.

In passages that describe their relationship according to the third type of model, as support and supported or container and contained (*ādhāra* and *ādheya*), Kṛṣṇa and Prakṛti are less rigidly cast in their roles. Whereas some passages assert that Kṛṣṇa is the support of the world, which is the manifestation of Prakṛti, other passages interpret Prakṛti to be the support. As the womb of creation, she is that which supports and contains Kṛṣṇa, who is in the form of seed and thus resides within her.[122] As "soul" (*ātman*) and body, they are inseparably united not only within the body of Kṛṣṇa himself but on all levels of creation as well:

> Without the body, where is the soul (*ātman*)? And where is the body without the soul? There is pre-

eminence of both, Oh Goddess; without you now, whence the world? Nowhere is there separation of us two. . . . Where there is soul, there also is body.[123]

On the highest level, *prakṛti* is both an impersonal principle and the Great Goddess, the Mahādevī who transcends all other female divinities and is their source. When the goddess Prakṛti is *nirguṇa,* without qualities, she is the counterpart of Kṛṣṇa's *nirguṇa* form. It is in fact remarkable that the Brahmavaivarta Purāṇa identifies a level of Prakṛti that is *nirguṇa,* since Sāṃkhya describes *prakṛti* as inherently possessed of *guṇas* and is thus usually described as *triguṇā,* "having three *guṇas,*" by nature. Yet we are told:

> As the power (*śakti*) of burning in fire and the radiance in the sun, oh sage, as the whiteness in milk and coldness in water, as sound in the sky and smell in the earth, thus always are Nirguṇa Brahman and Nirguṇā Prakṛti.[124]

The postulation of a level of Prakṛti that is beyond qualities, hence beyond the three *guṇas*, is probably a reflection of the fact that Prakṛti is equated with the *śakti* of Kṛṣṇa/Brahman. The notion of a *śakti* inherent in Brahman does not involve any postulation of qualities whatsoever. If Brahman is in his *nirguṇa* state, it thus follows that his inherent *śakti* must also be *nirguṇa.* Since Prakṛti is here identified with Kṛṣṇa/Brahman's *śakti,* the significance of the principle is reinterpreted to conform to the new context.

As *saguṇā,* Prakṛti is Mūlaprakṛti Īśvarī, the goddess primordial Prakṛti.[125] She assumes five forms in the process of creation and becomes manifest as the goddesses Durgā, Rādhā, Lakṣmī, Sarasvatī, and Sāvitrī.[126] Besides taking on different manifestations in the form of different goddesses, Prakṛti is also the source of all human women, who are descended from her parts or digits.[127] Essentially, all female forms are her portions. The five different goddesses who spring out of Prakṛti appear to be simply her partial incarnations, but in fact Rādhā and Durgā are often identified with her. Brown has pointed out that the identification of both Rādhā and Durgā with Prakṛti indicates the essential identity of the two goddesses with one another, an identification that we have also seen made implicitly in the Nārada Purāṇa. In this case, the text proposes the equation between the two explicitly.[128] The final ascendency of either Rādhā or Durgā as the chosen form depends on the perspective of the believer:

> She who is merged into Kṛṣṇa's breast is the goddess Mūlaprakṛti. The wise call her Durgā, the eternal Viṣṇumāyā. . . . Vaiṣṇavas call her Mahālakṣmī, the supreme Rādhā.[129]

Because of the Vaiṣṇava orientation of the Brahmavaivarta Purāṇa, it ultimately favors Rādhā as the supreme feminine principle and goddess. As such, Rādhā is both *nirguṇa* and *saguṇa*:

> [Y]ou are the goddess Mūlaprakṛti; you are *saguṇa* by a digit (*kalā*), but you yourself are *nirguṇa* alone.[130]

As in the Nārada Purāṇa, however, it is sometimes Durgā, not Rādhā, who is elevated to this status. In the Brahma-Khaṇḍa, for example, Hari (Kṛṣṇa) is said to be present at the time of creation. When he decides to create, the *guṇas* emerge from his right side. The *tattvas* are then evolved from the *guṇas*. Nārāyaṇa also comes out of his right side; Maheśa (Śiva) emerges from the left; and Brahmā comes out of his abdomen. Various other beings also spring from Kṛṣṇa's body, including the goddess Mūlaprakṛti, who springs from his intellect (*buddhi*). This goddess is described as the root cause of the universe and is identified as Durgā. It is through her that the world becomes possessed of power (*śaktimat*). Rādhā emerges quite a bit later from Kṛṣṇa's left side.[131] Durgā is said to be Prakṛti, but she is also supreme Śakti, and it is said that at a future time she will emerge from the accumulated energy (*tejas*) of the gods.[132] The influence of the Devī-Māhātmya is again apparent here.

The role of Prakṛti in creation is also described in an account that Brown calls creation by copulation and that he differentiates from the division of Prakṛti into the five goddesses described above, denoted by Brown as the divisional manifestation of Prakṛti.[133] When Kṛṣṇa desires to create, he divides himself into two parts. The right side becomes the male Puruṣa, who is the second self of Kṛṣṇa, and the left becomes the female Prakṛti.[134] When he sees his female counterpart, Kṛṣṇa (Puruṣa) is overtaken with lust.

> The eternal one, greatly lustful and possessed by unrestrained desire, beheld her. She was exceedingly desirable (and) as beautiful as a Champaka tree. Her buttocks were like the disk of the full moon; that beautiful woman had hips that were like the stem of a very lovely plantain tree and two breasts that were shaped like beautiful coconuts. She was endowed with a voluptuous shape but was slender-waisted. She was a gorgeous woman.[135]

Kṛṣṇa succumbs to his passion. The two make love, and Kṛṣṇa discharges semen into her womb. Prakṛti sweats and breathes hard during the lovemaking; her perspiration becomes the cosmic waters, and her breath becomes the wind and the life-breath (*prāṇa*) of all living creatures. The semen deposited in the womb of the Goddess is fruitful and forms an egg. Distressed by the egg, she casts it into the cosmic waters. Kṛṣṇa becomes angry and curses her so that neither she nor the other celestial nymphs who are her portions will ever again produce offspring.[136]

In this account, the familiar theme of the interaction of Puruṣa and Prakṛti providing the initial impulse that spurs the genesis of the cosmos is reinterpreted and clad in more colorful mythological clothing than the other accounts that we have seen. Prakṛti is not only clearly female, but she is also the sexual partner of the supreme male being, who makes love to her and impregnates her. The primordial oceans are explicitly connected to her by being identified as her bodily fluid. There is a related account in Nārada Purāṇa, Uttara-Bhāga 58.24-38, according to which seven oceans are born from Rādhā's womb during the course of creation. They have divine physical bodies. When they become hungry and need to be nourished at Rādhā's breast, she is not to be found anywhere. In fact, she is off making love with Kṛṣṇa. Crying out for their mother, the seven oceans force their way into the general area where Rādhā and Kṛṣṇa are indulging in their amorous dalliance. One of the sons interrupts them, and Rādhā becomes angry. She banishes them to the earth, where they become the terrestrial oceans and seas.

The account of *pratisarga* that follows the story of creation by copulation is somewhat different from the more common accounts that are given in many of the other Purāṇas and does not mention Śatarūpā at all. The cosmic egg lies in the primordial waters for a lifetime of Brahmā; after this, it hatches and splits in two. The child born from the egg is called Mahāvirāṭ. Abandoned by his parents, he lies helpless in the midst of the waters and begins to cry from hunger.

> Now that egg remained in the water for a period of time equal to the lifetime of Brahmā. When the time was right, all at once he split into two parts, (and) from the middle of the egg a single child as splendid as a thousand-million suns (emerged). And that child, having no shelter, abandoned by his father and mother and afflicted by hunger, immediately (began) screaming loudly.[137]

Brahmā is born from the abdomen of Virāṭ, and Śiva is then produced from Brahmā's forehead. They both enter the waters and penetrate Virāṭ, who immediately shrinks in size. Brahmā, who appears to be the second self of Virāṭ, then enters the lotus that springs out of the navel of Kṛṣṇa, who is sleeping in the cosmic ocean. Brahmā wanders in the stalk of the lotus for many *yugas* but cannot find its limit. Understanding Kṛṣṇa's greatness, Brahmā then proceeds to worship him and obtains a boon, by means of which he is able to create the worlds.[138] Given the strong preoccupation with the feminine principle and different goddesses on the level of primary creation, it is notable that the Brahmavaivarta Purāṇa does not elaborate more fully on the role of the feminine in the *pratisarga*.

As Brown notes, there is a strong tendency in this Purāṇa to elevate Prakṛti to an equal status with Kṛṣṇa or even to postulate her superiority to him, but—as is always the case in Vaiṣṇava and Śaiva texts—ultimately the goddess is subordinate to her male counterpart on the ontological level, and it is Prakṛti's equality with Kṛṣṇa that is called into question throughout the text, not his equality with her. Prakṛti's significance lies less in her ultimate ontological status than in her dynamic role in the process of creation.[139]

The different levels of the Goddess and the corresponding stages of creation in the Brahmavaivarta Purāṇa can be schematized as follows:

Stages of Manifestation

The Goddess	*Creation*
Rādhā as Kṛṣṇa's inherent *śakti*, also called Nirguṇā Prakṛti	Kṛṣṇa's inital impulse to create
Rādhā as Saguṇā Prakṛti, the material principle that emerges from Kṛṣṇa but is distinct from him	The emergence of the *guṇas* from Kṛṣṇa's body or creation through copulation of Kṛṣṇa (Puruṣa) and Prakṛti
Rādhā/Durgā as the Great Goddess Prakṛti who is the source of other goddesses	The manifestation of different goddesses from the goddess Prakṛti

ŚAIVA PURĀṆAS AND ŚAIVA SECTIONS OF CROSS-SECTARIAN PURĀṆAS

Just as various Vaiṣṇava Purāṇas equate certain creative principles with the female counterpart of Viṣṇu or his incarnations, Śaiva Purāṇas do the same with respect to the consorts and wives of Śiva. As the Brahmavaivarta Purāṇa personalizes *prakṛti* so that she becomes the goddess Prakṛti, the Śaiva Purāṇas tend to personalize *śakti,* although *prakṛti* is also personalized. We will focus our analysis on the Śaiva sections of the Kūrma Purāṇa and the Liṅga and Śiva Purāṇas.

The Kūrma Purāṇa contains an account of creation on the secondary level that absorbs principles from primary creation. In this account, Brahmā produces Rudra out of his mouth. At Brahmā's command, Rudra splits himself into male and female forms. The male portion divides into eleven parts that become the eleven Rudras, and the female half becomes many different goddesses of variable character.[140] These themes are familiar from other accounts of the *pratisarga* contained in some of the Purāṇas examined above. Yet in this text, as in the Vāyu Purāṇa's account narrated above, it is the female half of Rudra, not Brahmā, who is the focus of attention.

The female who springs from Rudra is called Īśānī, "female sovereign," and is described as Māheśvarī, Śāṃkarī, or Śivā—the female counterpart of Maheśvara or Śaṃkara, which are epithets of Śiva, or Śiva himself—and as the supreme goddess who creates the world. Though singular, she has different forms as different goddesses; they represent portions of her and are the *śakti*s inherent in creation.[141] In her different forms as various *śakti*s, she pervades the world.

> Śivā is all pervading, endless, beyond the *guṇa*s, absolutely without parts, one but abiding in many portions, having the form of knowledge, exceedingly desirous, without any peer. . . . That one Māheśvarī Śakti

> (appears as) many in combination with (her various) attributes; she plays in his [Śiva's] presence with an all-inclusive form. She does it all. This world is her creation. . . . [S]he is the Devī, the sovereign over all, and the stimulator of all beings.[142]

As the supreme Śakti, she is also identified with Viṣṇu's *māyā*, with which he deludes. As Śakti in the form of *māyā*, she is also called upon to manifest the universal form (*vaiśvarūpya*) of Śiva. Thus she is linked with both Viṣṇu and Śiva.[143]

As Śiva's counterpart, this goddess Śakti is equal to him in the process of creation, and everything is said to spring from Śiva and Śakti. Śiva is *śaktimat*, "possessed of *śakti*," and all other *śakti*s and possessors of *śakti* are born of the goddess Śakti. Although Śiva and Śakti are said to be equal, there appears to be some distinction between them. Whereas Śiva is described as the enjoyer (*bhoktṛ*), Śakti is that which is enjoyed (*bhogya*). Śiva is the thinker, whereas Śakti is the thought.[144] The goddess associated with Śiva is said to have a status that is more or less equal to his, yet this is not quite the case. Here again, the supreme Goddess is ultimately subordinate to the god with whom she is associated.

On the level of primary creation, Śakti is higher than *prakṛti* and is described as the source of both *prakṛti/pradhāna* and *puruṣa*. The text asserts that in proximity to Śiva, Śakti, who is called Māyā in this passage, splits herself and becomes *pradhāna* and *puruṣa*.[145] As Śiva's *śakti*, she is beyond *pradhāna/prakṛti*, yet she becomes *prakṛti* at the beginning of creation, and it is said that Śiva produces the entire world, beginning with *pradhāna* (= *prakṛti*), depending on her.[146] In other words, as *śakti* she is the presupposition of creation, that upon which creation depends. Although the text does not incorporate the evolution of the *tattva*s into this discussion of creation, we are told that Śakti is the source of not only *pradhāna* and *puruṣa* but also *mahat*, as well as various other creations.[147]

The Goddess's role in cosmogony is the same as in the other Purāṇas that we have explored. As Prakṛti represents the agency through which Kṛṣṇa creates in the Brahmavaivarta Purāṇa, for example, Śakti in this context is the means through which Śiva creates. The different levels of the Goddess and the corresponding stages of creation in this part of the Kūrma Purāṇa can be schematized as follows:

Stages of Manifestation

The Goddess	*Creation*
Śivā/Śakti as Śiva's inherent energy (*śakti*), also called *māyā*	The presupposition of creation
Śakti as *prakṛti/pradhāna*	The dawn of manifest creation

The cosmogony of the Liṅga Purāṇa, which is also Śaiva in orientation, has many similar themes but emphasizes the identity of the feminine principle as *prakṛti* rather than *śakti*, thus stressing materiality over creative power. Śiva, who is devoid of any mark or characteristic (*aliṅga*), is described as the root of manifest *pradhāna* or *prakṛti*, which is characterized (*liṅga*).

> The noncharacterized (*aliṅga*) is the root of the characterized (*liṅga*). That which is characterized is called the unmanifest (*avyakta*, = *prakṛti*). The noncharacterized is called Śiva, and the characterized is said to be related to Śiva (Śaiva). They call that which is characterized *prakṛti* and *pradhāna*; but the highest entity, the noncharacterized—which is without attributes, unchanging, undecaying, free from smell, color, and taste, (and) devoid of sound, touch, and so forth—is named Śiva.[148]

Prakṛti originates from the body of the *aliṅga* Śiva of its own accord (*svayam*). The agency by means of which Śiva produces *prakṛti* is designated as *māyā*. *Māyā* is the power by which the noncharacterized (Śiva) becomes characterized (*prakṛti*), but *māyā* is not explicitly identified with *prakṛti*. It is said that *prakṛti* is originally unmanifest, but when gazed at by Śiva, it becomes possessed of the *guṇas*. This latter form of *prakṛti* is called Śaivī, "the female form pertaining to Śiva."[149]

Śaivī Prakṛti is the source of the cosmos. She is called the unborn (*ajā*), unique mother of the universe consisting of red, white, and black colors, the three colors of the *guṇas* of *prakṛti*—a description that clearly refers to that of the unborn (*ajā*) red, white, and black female found in Śvetāśvatara Upaniṣad 4.5. At the time of creation, it is said that *mahat* is evolved out of the *guṇas* of *prakṛti* at Puruṣa's command. *Mahat* enters the unmanifest form of *prakṛti*; the triple *ahaṃkāra* evolves out of *mahat*, and the evolution of the rest of the *tattvas* ensues. The *tattvas* then give rise to a cosmic egg.[150]

As Śaivī, Prakṛti is the female counterpart of Śiva. She is his feminine side, and it is she who gives rise to creation. She is also the Great Goddess, Mahādevī, who is the source of all goddesses and who has many forms. As the Mahādevī, she is also known as Umā, Śivā, and so on. Śiva explains the nature of the goddess Prakṛti, repeating again the theme of the unborn (*ajā*) tricolored female:

> O Lord Brahmā, the Great Goddess (Maheśvarī) Prakṛti, your source/mother (*prasūti*), and that of Viṣṇu and the other gods, has been apportioned out. . . . Those knowing the truth call her by various names: the one possessing four-faces, the origin/womb (*yoni*) of the universe, primordial cow, the foundation, Gaurī, Māyā, Vidyā, Kṛṣṇā, Haimavatī, Pradhāna, or Prakṛti. (They call her) unborn (*ajā*), singular, red, white, and black, creating all beings as having the same form as her.[151]

Although she appears to be subordinate to Śiva, since he creates her, the text asserts that ultimately there is no difference between them.[152] Once again, however, the alleged equality between the two appears to be somewhat equivocal, for it is the Goddess's status in relation to Śiva that is called into question and not his status in relation to her.

As in the section of the Kūrma Purāṇa discussed above, the account of secondary creation in this text identifies the female half of Rudra as this Great Goddess. At the beginning of creation, Brahmā creates Rudra with a body that is half male and half female. He commands Rudra to divide himself, which Rudra does. The female portion becomes the mother of the universe and the source of all women in the three worlds.[153] A different account of secondary creation repeats the same general theme. Upset with his self-generated creation, which is not bearing progeny, Brahmā becomes angry. Rudra springs forth from Brahmā's mouth in a form that is half male, half female. The female half becomes Umā; she in turn makes other goddesses and human women. Śiva calls her unborn (*ajā*) Māyā.[154] The term "unborn" (*ajā*) used in relation to a goddess thus appears once again. Prakṛti is also called *ajā*, indicating that Umā, who is Māyā, is also identified with Prakṛti, since all three are given this same epithet. Yet another account asserts that the Great Goddess sharing half of Śiva's body divides into two portions, white and black. From both parts, thousands of goddesses are born and pervade all of creation.[155]

The different levels of the Goddess and the corresponding stages of creation in the Liṅga Purāṇa can be schematized as follows:

Stages of Manifestation

The Goddess	*Creation*
Śaivī Prakṛti as unmanifest *prakṛti,* inherent within the body of Śiva	The presupposition of creation

The manifestation of Prakṛti by means of *māyā* or by means of Śiva's glance	Evolution of *mahat* out of the *guṇas* of *prakṛti* and the entrance of *mahat* into unmanifest *prakṛti*
Prakṛti/Śivā/Umā as the Great Goddess who is the source of all other goddesses	Manifestation of different goddesses from the goddess Prakṛti

Many of the cosmogonic themes found in the Liṅga Purāṇa are also found in the Śiva Purāṇa (ca. 800–1000 C.E.), though in a slightly different form. In this Purāṇa's account, Nirguṇa Brahman alone exists at the beginning of creation and is described as incomprehensible to the mind and beyond description. The text emphasizes the unfathomable nature of Brahman by using negative language reminiscent of that used in the Upaniṣads to describe Brahman as "not this . . . not that" (*neti . . . neti*). Having no form, it is said that Brahman wishes to create one and therefore produces a form with qualities (*saguṇa*) called Īśvara or Sadāśiva, which is Brahman's second self. These categories are obviously borrowed from Vedānta. When Īśvara is created, Parabrahman becomes veiled (*antar* √*dhā*).[156]

Without affecting his body in any way, Īśvara/Sadāśiva emits the goddess Śakti from himself. Śakti is called by many names, including Pradhāna, Prakṛti, and Māyā. She is the goddess of all (Sakaleśvarī), the prime cause (*mūlakāraṇa*), the generator of everything. Together, the two create the realm of Śiva, Śivaloka. Śiva then creates Viṣṇu, who undertakes austerities. Water currents begin to flow from the body of Viṣṇu. It is said that this flowing forth of water is the result of Śiva's *māyā,* although the precise nature of the effect of *māyā* on Viṣṇu is not explained. Brahman (Śiva) in the form of the waters then pervades the entire void. Meanwhile, the *tattva*s are evolved from *śakti/prakṛti,* and Viṣṇu goes to sleep in the waters of Brahman.[157] There is another account of the manifestation of Śakti that adopts the Madhu-Kaiṭabha story of the manifestation of the Goddess from the Devī-Māhātmya. When the world is under water during the dissolution, two *asuras*, Madhu and Kaiṭabha, are born of the dirt in the ear of Viṣṇu. Seeing Brahmā seated on his lotus, they attempt to kill him. Brahmā, afraid, invokes the Goddess. He calls her by several names and lauds her as the mother of the three deities (Brahmā, Viṣṇu, and Śiva), the protectress of the gods, the *māyā* of Viṣṇu, and so forth. The goddess then manifests herself as Mahākālī.[158]

Śakti is Śivā, the female side of Śiva. One passage asserts that although Śakti appears to be born from Śiva in his form as Sadāśiva, she is not really born but is simply manifested from him. In truth, it is said, she is part of Śiva and is as eternal and all-pervasive as he is:

> Hara, the most excellent lord, sent forth a goddess from a portion of his body. Those who are knowledgeable about Brahman say that this goddess, who is endowed with divine attributes, is the highest *śakti* of that supreme Śiva, the highest Self. Bhavānī (= Śivā) is that goddess who manifested from the body of Śiva and in whom there is found no birth, death, old age, and so forth. . . . She is the Goddess who, pervading this whole world with her might, stands (in it). That goddess wondrously appeared as if she were embodied. And she deludes this whole world with *māyā*. Although (it appears that) she was born from the lord (Īśvara, = Śiva), in reality she is not born.[159]

This Śakti is the source of the manifest cosmos and has several forms. In this text, usually the primary consort of Śiva—Umā or Durgā—is identified as Prakṛti or Śakti, and other goddesses are seen as being her manifestations. In one passage, for example, the goddess Umā, who is called the Great Goddess (Parameśvarī), is identified as Prakṛti.

She is the source of Vāc, Lakṣmī, and Kālī, the wives of Brahmā, Viṣṇu, and another wife of Śiva himself. These three are her *śaktis*.[160] Śakti is reborn as Satī and Pārvatī,[161] and these two goddesses are also lauded as primordial Prakṛti or Śakti. In one passage, for example, Satī, like Umā, is called Parameśvarī and is identified as primordial Śakti; elsewhere, Pārvatī is lauded as the Mahādevī, the primordial Śakti who is Śivā.[162]

One account of secondary creation identifies Śatarūpā as an embodiment of Śakti.[163] Brahmā, frustrated by the inability of his mind-born progeny to further his creation, appeals to the Goddess. Complaining that the sons he has created thus far are not fruitful, he wishes to increase the population through sexual reproduction. He has a problem, however, for women have not yet been created. Śakti must create them, for Brahmā seems unable to do so. Women are *śaktis*, and as such are portions of Śakti. Brahmā remarks:

> The imperishable race of women has not yet gone forth from you. Thus, I have no power (*śakti*) to create the race of women. Indeed, the origin of all *śaktis* is from you. Therefore, I pray to you (who are) bestowing all the *śaktis* of everyone everywhere, granting wishes, Māyā, the goddess of the gods (Sureśvarī).[164]

To solve the problem, Śakti creates a form of herself that she gives to Brahmā. Having secured her, Brahmā divides himself in half; one part becomes male, and the other part becomes the female Śatarūpā.[165] Although Śatarūpā is not explicitly identified with the female form given to Brahmā by Śakti, this is implied.

The different levels of the Goddess and the corresponding stages of creation in the Śiva Purāṇa can be schematized as follows:

Stages of Manifestation

The Goddess	*Creation*
Śakti as the inherent energy (*śakti*) of Śiva	The presupposition of creation
Śakti as Prakṛti/Pradhāna/Māyā, manifested from the body of Śiva	The separation of Śakti from the body of Īśvara/Sadāśiva at the dawn of creation
Śakti/Umā, etc. as the Great Goddess who is the source of other goddesses	Manifestation of different goddesses from the Goddess
Śakti as Śatarūpā	Secondary creation (*pratisarga*)

ŚĀKTA PURĀṆAS

The Vaiṣṇava and the Śaiva Purāṇas that we have explored thus far incorporate the feminine principle into the mechanisms of creation by identifying a creative principle, either *prakṛti, māyā,* or *śakti,* with a goddess who is conceived to be the Great Goddess. Although the Goddess is supreme as a goddess, however, she is nevertheless subordinate to the god, either Viṣṇu/Kṛṣṇa or Śiva, who is extolled as the highest divinity and who is identified as Brahman. In the Śākta Purāṇas and Śākta sections of other Purāṇas, the Goddess herself is the highest divinity and is the source of all other gods, including Viṣṇu and Śiva. The Goddess therefore takes the place held by Viṣṇu in the Vaiṣṇava Purāṇas and Śiva in the Śaiva Purāṇas. Nevertheless, as in the other texts that we have explored above, she is still called Prakṛti, Māyā, or Śakti, and she is described as the source of all manifest forms, whether male or female. Thus her essential nature as the cause of creation does not change, although she is conceived to be greater than any other divinity. We will focus our analysis on the Devī-Bhāgavata Purāṇa, one of the most celebrated of the Śākta Purāṇas.[166]

The Devī-Bhāgavata Purāṇa follows in the tradition of the Devī-Māhātmya in identifying the Goddess as the ultimate overlord of creation. She is described as the highest, primordial (*ādya*) Śakti, the mother of all the worlds, eternal and omnipresent, the ultimate support of all that exists.[167] The Goddess is both *nirguṇa* and *saguṇa*, and the text makes a distinction between these two aspects of the Goddess.[168] In her *nirguṇa* state, she has a form that is beyond the three *guṇas*; she is supreme reality itself and transcends all qualities. When her *nirguṇa* aspect is emphasized in the text, she is frequently called Nirguṇā Śakti or Mahāmāyā, but, as in the Brahmavaivarta Purāṇa, the epithet Nirguṇā Prakṛti is also used to describe this level of her being.[169] Whereas descriptions of her *nirguṇa* form tend to delineate Śakti and Mahāmāya as something that the Great Goddess is, descriptions of her *saguṇa* form tend to use the terms *śakti* and *māyā* to denote something that she possesses.

The Goddess also has a *saguṇa* form, and in this state she is often depicted as a great cosmic queen. She is described as sitting on a throne composed of Brahmā, Viṣṇu, and Śiva in their various forms, thus emphasizing her superiority over the male gods.[170] She dwells in Maṇidvīpa, "the island of gems," which is her supreme abode. Her form is overwhelming, even to the gods. One passage describes Brahmā's impression of the Goddess when he, Viṣṇu, and Śiva are transported up to Maṇidvīpa in the Goddess's celestial chariot. They see first a couch with a jeweled carpet spread over it. Then they catch sight of the figure seated on the couch:

> A beautiful woman was seated on that most excellent of couches, wearing a red garland and red clothes, anointed with red sandalwood paste, red-eyed, having a beautiful face, red-lipped, glorious, equal in splendor to ten millions of lightning flashes and ten millions of beautiful women. . . . Such a one had never been seen before.[171]

The Goddess assumes her *saguṇa* form when she engages in creation. As in the Devī-Māhātmya, the Goddess plays three cosmogonic roles. On one level, she is the efficient cause of creation, the willful agent who catalyzes the whole cosmogonic process. The epithets Śakti and Mahāmāyā are often used to denote her in her role as the active creator of the universe. Yet she is also the material basis of creation, *prakṛti* or *mūlaprakṛti*. And, finally, she is embodied as creation itself.

When the Goddess wishes to create the cosmos, she does so without effort or desire. Although she is the cause of creation, she herself remains unchanged (*nirīha*).[172] It is said that with one portion she remains Nirguṇā Śakti, but she also becomes three *śakti*s that are involved in creation: sattvic *śakti*, rajasic *śakti*, and tamasic *śakti*. The names of these three creative powers reveal the influence of Sāṃkhya categories, for they are named after the three *guṇa*s of *prakṛti*. The Goddess transforms herself into these three forms when she desires to create. Her sattvic aspect becomes Mahālakṣmī, that is, Lakṣmī in a universal form. Her rajasic aspect becomes Sarasvatī, and her tamasic aspect becomes Mahākālī:

> Śivā is beyond attributes (*nirguṇa*), eternal, constant, all-pervading, unchanging. She is the support of all that must be realized by means of yoga, and she abides as the fourth state of consciousness (*turīya*). Her sattvic, rajasic, and tamasic *śakti*s are the three female forms Mahālakṣmī, Sarasvatī, and Mahākālī.[173]

Because these goddesses are manifestations of the Goddess herself, the relationship between them and their spouses—Brahmā, Viṣṇu, and Śiva—is the opposite of that which we have seen in the Vaiṣṇava and Śaiva Purāṇas, for the goddesses function at a higher level than their husbands. The superior status of the Goddess over the three male divinities is again affirmed when it is said that the assuming of female form by these three *śakti*s for purposes of creation is deemed *sarga*, primary creation, whereas the further resolution of them into the male deities Brahmā, Viṣṇu, and Śiva is called *pratisarga*, secondary creation. Thus the three gods are subordinated to their female counterparts.[174] In another passage, the creative supremacy of the Goddess over other gods is asserted in a somewhat different manner. The text states that although those who are knowledgeable in the tradition say that Brahmā is the creator of the universe, they also say that he is born from the navel-lotus of Viṣṇu. Thus, it appears that Brahmā cannot create independently and so cannot be the true creator. Again, Viṣṇu, from whose navel Brahmā is born, lies asleep on his serpent, Śeṣa, during the period of dissolution. Therefore, he cannot be the creator of the universe. Śeṣa, too, lies on the waters. As liquid cannot rest without a vessel, there must be some support that is sustaining the waters. This support is identified as the Goddess herself.[175]

A different account of the mechanisms of creation draws more upon the basic conceptual framework of Advaita Vedānta but subsumes Sāṃkhya categories as well. It is said that before the universe is created, only the Goddess exists as supreme Brahman (Parabrahman). As such, she is beyond all qualities (*nirguṇa*). She is incomprehensible, undefinable, and unparalleled, and she possesses a single inherent power (*śakti*) called *māyā*. The *māyā* of the Goddess is also beyond qualification: it is neither existent, nor nonexistent, nor both:

> The Goddess said: . . . Formerly, I alone existed. There was nothing else whatsoever. . . . At that time, my own form was named intellect (*cit*), consciousness (*saṃvid*), and supreme Brahman. I am incomprehensible, undefinable, unparalleled. . . . My perfect (*siddha*) *śakti* is known as *māyā*. It is neither existent, nor nonexistent, nor both, nor self-contradictory. This indefinable entity always exists.[176]

United with her power (*śakti*) of *māyā*, Devī acts as the source of creation.[177] There are two types of *māyā* that are described as different kinds of causes and play different roles in cosmogony. It is said that when the Goddess's *māyā* is united with intelligence (*caitanya*), it acts as the instrumental or efficient cause (*nimitta*) in creation, but when it transforms into the manifest world, it is the material cause (*samavāya*).[178] It appears to be the Goddess's inherent *māyā*, not the Goddess herself, who is both the efficient and the material cause of creation, but the Goddess is said to be ultimately identical with her *māyā*, for on the highest level of reality there is no difference between them.[179] Another passage also enumerates two levels of *māyā*, one of which is described as purely sattvic and the other of which is described as mixed with the *guṇas* and is equated with *avidyā*. *Māyā* is identified here with *prakṛti*.[180] Elsewhere, the two aspects of the Goddess's *māyā* are described as "inward facing" (*antarmukhā*) and "outward facing" (*bahirmukhā*).[181] In all cases, the latter form of *māyā* takes on the role of *prakṛti* as the material source of the world.

As Prakṛti, the Goddess is the material ground of the manifest cosmos, and she is described as the root of the tree of creation and the cause of all that exists.[182] As primordial cause, she contains the effect, creation itself, latent within her. After she creates the cosmos, it is said that she then enters into it or assumes its form.[183] Thus the universe is simply a transformation of the Goddess herself. This equation of the Goddess with the manifest universe is dramatically illustrated in a passage in which diverse parts of the cosmos are equated with different parts of her body. The sun and moon are equated with her eyes and the quarters with her ears. The universe is said to be her heart, the earth her loins, and the midregions her navel. Different gods and portions of the worlds are also equated with her different body parts.[184]

While conceding to the ultimate identity of all forms of the Goddess, the Devī-Bhāgavata Purāṇa nevertheless asserts a hierarchical relationship among her different aspects. As Nirguṇa Brahman, she is essentially primordial or Nirguṇā Śakti, Mahāmāyā, or Nirguṇā Prakṛti, beyond attributes, beyond the *guṇas*, and without any qualification whatsoever. As Saguṇa Brahman, she is said to be endowed with the *śakti* of *māyā*, a creative power that participates in both her transcendent and immanent forms. As the principle of *prakṛti*, finally, she both activates and is identified with the creative *māyā* with which she is endowed.

The different levels of the Goddess and the corresponding stages of creation in the Devī-Bhāgavata Purāṇa can be schematized as follows:

Stages of Manifestation

The Goddess	*Creation*
The Goddess as Parabrahman, Primordial or Nirguṇā Śakti, Mahāmāyā, or Nirguṇā Prakṛti	Beyond creation
The Goddess as Saguṇa Brahman, the possessor of creative powers (*śakti*s) that she activates or the possessor of a single inherent creative power called *māyā*	The initial impulse toward creation that is represented by the activation of the Goddess's creative *śakti*s
The Goddess as Prakṛti or *avidyā/bahirmukhā māyā*	The beginning of the differentiation of creation

In the Purāṇas, many of the disparate elements that we have explored in the previous two chapters pertaining to the identity of the Great Goddess and her nature as *śakti*, *māyā*, and *prakṛti* are woven together in elaborate but fairly consistent ways in the context of cosmogonic narratives.

Vedic themes and structures are joined with others that are derived from speculative and philosophical discourse, and a new narrative emerges. The marriage of mythological and philosophical motifs provides a context for pairing divinities with principles, and a Great Goddess is born.

CHAPTER FOUR

Concluding Remarks

Resume

Before moving on to assess the implications of the observations made in the preceding pages, first it might be helpful to review and summarize the essential points that have been made. This is perhaps most effectively done in terms of four different types of questions that have been asked and the answers to them that we have found. These questions address four different types of issues with respect to the rise of the Great Goddess in Brahmanical Hinduism: contextual, thematic, historical, and interpretive.

- *Contextual*: In what context is the theology of the Great Goddess formulated? What are the mechanisms by means of which she is formulated?
- *Thematic*: What makes the Great Goddess "Great"? Why is she *the* Goddess and not just *a* goddess?
- *Historical*: Where do the conceptual formulations associated with the Goddess come from, and how does this whole symbolic complex come about?
- *Interpretive*: Why is the Goddess formulated in the specific ways in which she is formulated?

CONTEXTUAL ISSUES

Within Brahmanical Hinduism, the essential identity of the Great Goddess is expounded in the Purāṇas, mythological works dating from about the third century C.E.–ca. the sixteenth century C.E. More specifically, the Goddess is integrated into the accounts of creation found in several of the Purāṇas and is often described as an essential cog in the cosmogonic wheel. Although the Purāṇas are a heterogeneous mix of many elements, they all contain accounts of primary and secondary creation (*sarga* and *pratisarga*) that participate in the same essential cosmogonic patterns.

THEMATIC ISSUES

The Goddess is *the* Goddess, not just *a* goddess, because of certain kinds of equations that are made in the Purāṇic myths of creation. The Goddess is identified with cosmogonic principles that are unique and transcend the particular identity of individual divinities. Since she is equated with such principles, the Goddess is also seen as transcending any particular identity.

Three patterns appear throughout the Purāṇas. (1) The Goddess is described as the active dimension of Nirguṇa Brahman or the power inherent within Brahman that is responsible for creation itself. She is the creative impulse that sets in motion the mechanisms of the cosmogonic process and then sustains the universe once it has been created. In this capacity, she is called *śakti.* (2) The Goddess is also the principle of materiality that is the basis of the phenomenal-empirical world, the ground of all things. As such, she is called *prakṛti.* (3) Finally, the Goddess is identified as *māyā,* which lies between *śakti* and *prakṛti.* When *māyā* denotes the creative or delusive power by means of which creation is effected, it is identified or allied with *śakti.* When the term *māyā* is used to indicate the material principle of creation, it is identified or allied with *prakṛti*. In all cases, when the Goddess is identified with these principles, she plays both a cosmogonic and a cosmological role.

As a cosmogonic agent, the Goddess as *śakti*, *prakṛti*, and/or *māyā* is the immediate source of the created universe. In this capacity she is identified as an impersonal principle active in primary creation, that is, in the creation of the various categories that form the foundation of the manifest world. In Vaiṣṇava and Śaiva contexts where either Viṣṇu or Śiva is identified as Brahman, she plays a creative role on two different levels.

On the highest level, the Goddess is the inherent creative power or *śakti* of the Absolute. She exists within Nirguṇa Brahman as his inseparable dimension or aspect. As *śakti*, she is the impelling cause of creation, the impulse that sets the cosmogonic process in motion. Thus, for example, in the Kūrma Purāṇa Viṣṇu describes Lakṣmī, his supreme (*paramā*) *śakti*, as consisting of or absorbed in himself, and the Śiva Purāṇa asserts that Sadāśiva creates Śakti by manifesting her from himself. When this level of the Goddess is also identified with the principle *māyā*, it is generally construed as encompassing both the creative and delusive capacities possessed by Brahman. This level of the Goddess's identity corresponds to the initial stage of cosmogony in which the first impulse toward creation arises within the Absolute.

On a lower level, once the Goddess is separated out from Nirguṇa Brahman and becomes an independent entity, she is identified as the material principle of creation, *prakṛti*. As such, she is the immediate source of the manifest cosmos. When this level of the Goddess is identified with *māyā*, it is generally construed as a material principle distinct from Brahman in which the drama of continual birth and rebirth (*saṃsāra*) unfolds. This level of the Goddess's identity corresponds to the activation of the creative impulse inherent within the Absolute and the commencement of the mechanisms of cosmogony.

The roles of the Goddess in the Purāṇas as both *śakti/māyā* and *māyā/prakṛti* are structured according to patterns that can be traced back to Vedic literature. The double function of the Goddess in Purāṇic accounts of primary creation parallels the roles of various Vedic goddesses as both the impelling and the material causes of creation. In the Vedic texts these two levels of the feminine principle are most clearly combined in accounts of the creative role of the goddess Vāc found in the Brāhmaṇas. On one level, Vāc exists as an inherent aspect of Prajāpati, the creator. When she is separated from him and sent forth, she becomes the material foundation of creation, usually identified as the cosmic waters. These two aspects of Vāc's identity correspond to those of the Goddess.

In the Vaiṣṇava and Śaiva Purāṇas, the two levels of the Goddess and the stages of primary creation (*sarga*) to which they correspond can be generally schematized as follows:

Stages of Manifestation

The Goddess	*Creation*
The Goddess (Lakṣmī, Rādhā, Śakti, etc.) as the inherent energy (*śakti* or *māyā*) of Brahman	The initial impulse toward creation that is represented by the activation of the *śakti* inherent within Brahman
The Goddess as the material foundation of the cosmos (*prakṛti* or *māyā*) that is distinct from Brahman	The beginning of the creative process

Śākta texts such as the Devī-Bhāgavata Purāṇa postulate a third level of the Goddess that lies beyond either of these two levels. Since the Goddess herself is identified as Nirguṇa Brahman, she is equated with the Absolute, in which capacity she is called Śakti, Nirguṇā Śakti, primordial (*ādya*) Śakti, Mahāmāyā, Nirguṇā Prakṛti, and so forth. As Nirguṇa Brahman, the Goddess is the eternal, unchanging Absolute.

This level of the Goddess's identity transcends the other two levels that we find in Vaiṣṇava and Śaiva contexts. Second, the Goddess is also described as the possessor of creative powers or *śaktis* by means of which she creates the universe. Finally, she is also identified as *prakṛti*. These latter two stages correspond to the stages of creation described above. The levels of the Goddess in the Devī-Bhāgavata Purāṇa and the stages of primary creation with which they are correlated can therefore be schematized as follows:

Stages of Manifestation

The Goddess	*Creation*
The Goddess as Primordial or Nirguṇā Śakti, Māyā, or Prakṛti	Beyond creation and the process of cosmogony
The Goddess as the possessor of creative powers (*śakti* or *māyā*) that she activates	The initial impulse toward creation that is represented by the activation of the *śakti* inherent within the Goddess
The Goddess as the material foundation of the cosmos (*prakṛti* or *māyā*)	The beginning of the creative process

This depiction of the Goddess is in fact far less common in the Purāṇas as a whole than the portrayal of her as subordinate to Viṣṇu or Śiva.

In secondary creation, that is, in the formation and differentiation of the manifest cosmos, the function of the Goddess as *prakṛti* is embodied first in the function of the cosmic waters during the creation or re-creation of the worlds, and second in the function of Śatarūpā during the creation of progeny. The Vedic theme of the cosmic waters as material matrix of creation is adopted by the Purāṇic cosmogonies, although in a post-Vedic context the waters are rarely identified explicitly with the Goddess. One notable exception to this rule is the Garuḍa Purāṇa, which counts the waters as a manifestation of Lakṣmī. Śatarūpā represents the same principle on a more differentiated level. As *prakṛti* functions as the material principle on the level of primary creation and the waters function as the material matrix of creation during the differentiation of the worlds, Śatarūpā functions as the source of individual progeny.

HISTORICAL ISSUES

Śakti, māyā, and *prakṛti* are important creative principles in pre-Purāṇic speculative and philosophical Brahmanical literature, as explored in the second chapter of this study. Yet in these earlier contexts, they are often not associated with any goddess, nor are they feminine principles, although they are grammatically feminine terms. So how does this equation of *śakti, māyā,* and *prakṛti* with the Goddess come about?

The formation of this symbolic complex reflects a larger pattern concerning Purāṇic cosmogony. As we have seen, the Purāṇas tend to adopt theories of creation or cosmogonic themes that are already current in the Brahmanical tradition and incorporate other elements into these already existing structures such that the older creation motifs are recast and woven together to suit the particular perspective of the Purāṇas. Thus, for example, the cosmogonic mechanism postulated in Sāṃkhya whereby creation is viewed as arising from the evolution of *prakṛti* is adopted by many of the Purāṇas but given a theistic cast. Similarly, the notion of creation as activated by the inherent power or *śakti* of the Absolute is also absorbed but reinterpreted and reworked. In this way, older Brahmanical structures are retained but then modified to suit the concerns of newer scriptural environments. As part of this process, the Brahmanical tradition subsumes what appears to be a primarily non-Brahmanical tendency to elevate female divinities to supreme status by equating certain unique principles—*śakti, māyā,* and *prakṛti*—which are already present in the earlier layers of the Brahmanical tradition with the goddesses appropriate to the perspective of the given text. Thus, although the impulse to elevate the feminine principle may be largely non-Brahmanical, the means by which it is elevated are borrowed directly from Brahmanical orthodoxy.

INTERPRETIVE ISSUES

Why is the Goddess consistently identified in many of the Purāṇas as *śakti/māyā/prakṛti*? Why this particular configuration? Such a question is particularly interesting in light of the fact that many of the other great Asian traditions—including the Buddhist tradition, which originated in India—see the feminine as the material principle but generally ascribe it a passive, not an active, role in creation.

As we have seen in the first and second chapters, the support for this particular complex comes from cosmogonic themes found not only in philosophical and epic materials but even in the Vedas. Many myths or mythic motifs found in the Vedas identify the impelling cause of creation as feminine. Thus, for example, Virāj, Vāc, and Śacī/Indrāṇī are described in the Vedic literature as the energizing principle that sets the processes of creation into motion. Other passages associate different goddesses—primarily the goddess earth (Pṛthivī), the waters (*ap*), and Aditi—with materiality. Although no Great Goddess is postulated in these texts, different goddesses are depicted as playing an active creative role. Thus, the support for identifying the impelling and material causes of creation with a goddess can be found in the mythology of the Vedas.

The Upaniṣads and philosophical schools systematically articulate theories that identify various principles as impelling or material causes of creation. These principles are depicted as impersonal, although their roles parallel those of the various goddesses postulated in Vedic cosmogonies. In the Purāṇas, these different themes and theories of creation are then blended together. The confluence of these streams of thought with other non-Brahmanical streams results in the postulation of personalized goddess-principles that are portrayed as (a) the power that provides the initial cosmogonic impulse and sustains the universe once it has been created; and (b) the material foundation of creation.

Perhaps one explanation for why this particular combination is not found as clearly or prevalently in some of the other Asian traditions—such as Buddhism, which rejects the Vedas—is that there is little or no inherent mythological, conceptual, scriptural, and/or ideological support for such a complex of associations. In Brahmanical Hinduism, on the other hand, the seeds of the active/material depiction of the feminine principle are firmly planted in the earliest layers of the tradition and are nurtured by later developments.

Further Implications of the Study: Historical and Socio-Political Implications

In light of the results that we have found, it would be useful to examine a bit more closely some of the implications of this study. We will explore what the continuities and discontinuities with respect to the formulation of the portrayal of the Goddess might tell us about the tangible historical and socio-political factors that may have participated in the creation of her theology.

During the postclassical and medieval periods in India, the Brahmanical tradition was increasingly challenged by non-Brahmanical trends that called into question the validity of the core "orthodox" tradition. The greatest challenge came from the increasing attention placed on devotion to various divinities that were not part of the Vedic-Brahmanical tradition. The rise of *bhakti* as an expression of spirituality and the related rise and spread of non-Brahmanical devotional movements offered an alternative to the hierarchical, caste-conscious religiosity of the Brahmin priests and provided a vehicle for the expression of more popular religious values. In the face of such challenges, the Brahmanical tradition absorbed and accommodated elements of non-Brahmanical religiosity in order to escape becoming completely irrelevant.

As has been noted by numerous scholars, those elements that were absorbed by the Brahmanical tradition in post-Vedic times include the celebration of various non-Vedic goddesses. But it is noteworthy that despite the appearance of new non-Vedic female divinities in post-Vedic literature, nevertheless, as we have noted in this study, they are subsumed to some extent under Vedic-Brahmanical structures, some of which can be traced back to even the earliest layer of Vedic literature, the Saṃhitās. Hence, there is a certain amount of structural continuity within the Brahmanical tradition, although there is discontinuity on the level of specific narrative elements and emphases. The theology of the Goddess is constructed in such a way that it accommodates non-Brahmanical devotional impulses while maintaining and upholding the religious authority of the Brahmanical tradition. It does this by retaining "orthodox" ideas and structures yet reconceptualizing them vis-à-vis more popular tendencies. The Brahmanical tradition thus is able to maintain its authority and, at the same time, to strengthen its appeal.

It is most likely the case, therefore, that there was no recognition of the Great Goddess until she was constructed through the Brahmanical system's accommodation of non-Brahmanical impulses. The notion of a single Great Goddess hinges at least in part on the identification of a female divinity with unique, cosmic principles—*śakti*, *māyā*, and *prakṛti*—which, as we have seen, are borrowed from philosophy. The systematic articulation of these principles arises first within the context of the orthodox philosophical schools, which are the domain of Brahmin priests educated in the Brahmanical Sanskritic tradition, and which then provide the conceptual frameworks that make a Great Goddess possible. What we see in the construction of the theology of the Goddess is a kind of continual reworking of different narrative elements and structures in a network of themes and variations. The themes are generally orthodox; the variations are, at least to some extent, shaped by influences coming in from outside the orthodox tradition. The impulse to revere goddesses highly, then, which appears to be more part of the non-Brahmanical traditions of India than of Brahmanical orthodoxy, is absorbed into Brahmanical structures so that tensions between the orthodox system and nonorthodox systems are mitigated.

Further Implications of the Study: Cultural Implications

THE RELATIONSHIP BETWEEN GODDESSES AND WOMEN

Before concluding, it would be fruitful to turn from textual analysis to cultural analysis and to explore some of the possible implications of the theology of the Goddess on the social level. In other words, how might the conception of the Great Goddess as *śakti/māyā/prakṛti* translate on the human level into certain Hindu attitudes toward women?

In asking such a question, one must first evaluate the extent to which a formulation such as the one explored in this study may reflect or be reflected in social practice. Much contemporary scholarship has called into question the importance of texts and textual formulations in the values, beliefs, and experiences of most human beings. With respect to the Hindu tradition, it must be said that the vast majority of Indians—past and present, Hindu or not—have no knowledge of Sanskrit and have never read a single word of the Brahmanical canon. While acknowledging the tenuous relationship between literature and life, however, it is important to note that the types of texts in which we find formulations of the Great Goddess are not just mere texts but scriptures of the Brahmanical tradition. They thus carry a great deal of authority. Furthermore, the concepts surrounding the Great Goddess that we have explored in this study are not just scriptural but also cultural. Brahmanical values and formulations including those pertaining to the feminine represent a strong current in the cultural stream of contemporary Hindu India. The recognition of a Great Goddess and her identity as *śakti/prakṛti/māyā* are found throughout India even today and are integrated into the spiritual lives of Hindus on many levels of Indian society. Related perceptions of female gender are also integrated, often unconsciously, into people's awareness.

Another objection could also be raised, namely, that it is not at all clear that a strong Goddess tradition such as the one that we find in India has anything at all to do with real gender relationships. It is certainly the case that in India, strong goddesses do not generally cash out in a less sexist society than our own or an acceptance of more dominant or "liberated" social roles for women. In speaking of the Devī-Māhātmya, for example, Coburn notes:

> [O]ne of the clear early lessons emerging from feminist study is that one cannot assume that the existence of goddesses, or Goddess texts, in a given culture correlates with favorable social status for women. . . . [T]he Devī-Māhatmya is part of a broader Indian context whose thinking about gender is shaped by many factors other than the fact that the Devī-Māhātmya happens to be a text praising the Goddess.[1]

Furthermore, worship of Hindu goddesses or the Great Goddess does not seem to be the special domain of women in Indian society, nor is the Goddess tradition itself necessarily seen as particularly empowering for females. Kathleen Erndl has noted, for example, that worship of the Goddess in India is not really a strong part of Indian feminist discourse, although in certain contexts the Goddess can serve as a source of spiritual empowerment for women.[2] Similarly, in her own research on interpretations of the

Devī-Māhātmya, Cynthia Ann Humes has found that most of her contemporary Hindu informants view the Great Goddess and human females as being quite different, although some highly educated and Westernized women see the Goddess as an empowering role model.[3]

It is of course important to take such objections seriously. Nevertheless, we must also take seriously the assertions and perceptions of aspects of the tradition that postulate a connection between the divine female and the human female. Even in the Vedic period, for example, the sacrificer's wife was identified with the wife of the gods and the goddess earth during the soma sacrifice.[4] In many of the Purāṇas, women are said to be portions (*aṃśa*) of the Goddess or of her various manifestations. And in his recent fieldwork, William S. Sax has noted parallels between the mythology and pilgrimage rituals pertaining to the cult of the mountain goddess Nandādevī and the lives of the women who worship her.[5] While not claiming to speak for the experiences of all, or even most, Hindu women, it is nevertheless possible to explore the gender values *supported by* and *reflected in* formulations of the Goddess and goddesses and suggest some of the ways in which the influence of such values might be manifest in certain social tendencies.

If we accept that there may well be some kind of connection, we might then begin by asking the following question: Why is it in fact the case that women in India are not necessarily more socially "liberated" or "empowered" than they are in other societies that lack a strong goddess tradition, such as ours? As is evidenced by the various goddess cults that have sprung up in the United States in recent years, many contemporary Western feminists posit a clear relationship between strong reverence for female divinity or divinities and the empowerment of human females. The basic assumption of this type of model is that powerful goddesses mean powerful women, and if women have divine females as role models, women will be more liberated and/or empowered. Yet this does not seem to be the case in India.

There are at least two ways of approaching such a question. One way is to call into question the way in which Western scholars, and especially Western feminists, understand such notions as "liberation" and "empowerment." It is certainly a form of cultural imperialism to insist that other societies conform to our own cultural norms and expectations; hence, although we might perceive Indian women to be oppressed according to our own social and economic standards, it is perhaps incorrect to assume that Indian women themselves feel oppressed or think of themselves as oppressed. Scholars sympathetic to such a perspective have emphasized the ways in which Indian women interpret their own roles, rituals, and practices as empowering, if not socially then at least spiritually.[6]

Another approach, and the one that we will take, is to postulate that despite the reverence for the Goddess in Brahmanical Hinduism, there may be underlying views of female gender as a category that support both a strong goddess tradition and traditional cultural norms for women and that may in fact help limit the social choices that women have. In order to make such a connection, however, we must clearly distinguish between those aspects and qualities of the Great Goddess that are related to her femaleness and those that transcend it.[7] As Nirguṇa Brahman, the Goddess is beyond all qualities and therefore transcends any gender category. But as a cosmogonic agent, the Goddess is clearly female.

As we have seen, the Great Goddess functions in primary creation on essentially two different levels: as creative/delusive power (*śakti*) and as materiality (*prakṛti*). The principle of *māyā* is subsumed under either level or both levels. And in the Brahmanical tradition, these principles are regarded with a deep ambivalence. Let us consider each in turn.

THE AMBIGUOUS GODDESS

Śakti/Māyā

As *śakti/māyā*, the Goddess plays a creative role, as we have seen. But this role can be seen as both positive and negative. When *śakti* is identified with *māyā*, it is not only a power of creation, but also a power of delusion that is often seen to be negative. The Nārada Purāṇa's account of creation, for example, as we have seen, adopts the categories of Advaita Vedānta such that *śakti* is equated with *māyā* and is said to be of two natures: knowledge (*vidyā*) and ignorance (*avidyā*). As knowledge, it leads to Brahman, but in its capacity as ignorance (*avidyā*), which is that aspect of *māyā* that leads to the continual round of birth and rebirth, it causes suffering and prevents the realization of Brahman. In her capacity as the power (*śakti*) of *māyā*, therefore, the Goddess sometimes has negative connotations.

As pure *śakti*, raw power, the Goddess is not only a cosmogonic force but a cosmological one as well. She pervades creation and sustains it. And as a power active in the world, she is not only creative, but can also be destructive. This aspect of the Goddess is expressed in her many terrible forms and can have either positive or negative connotations. As David Kinsley notes, these forms are usually associated with war, blood, death, and so forth, and they often arise in the context of the Goddess's role as the protector of the cosmos who destroys negative forces and is therefore beneficial to creation.[8] So, for example, the Goddess in her form as Durgā is celebrated in the Devī-Māhātmya as the destroyer of demons, which is one of her main functions. In her destructive capacity, she protects and maintains the cosmos by restoring order. The Goddess is also said to be the destroyer of ignorance. This function is performed above all by the goddess Kālī, who is one of the Goddess's most terrifying and uncontrollable manifestations. Kālī not only destroys demons but also devours them. Yet Kālī's wild behavior can be beneficent, especially to those who seek to destroy their attachment to the world, for she also brings about favorable spiritual transformation:

> Her raised and bloodied sword suggests the death of ignorance, her disheveled hair suggests the freedom of release, and her girdle of severed arms may suggest the end of grasping. As death or the mistress of death she grants to him who sees truly the ultimate boon of unconditioned freedom, release from the cycle of *saṃsāra,* release from pain, sorrow, and not-knowing.[9]

Although the destructive forms of the Goddess can be directed toward positive goals, they can also be directed toward negative goals and can therefore cause suffering. Śītalā, for example, is a goddess associated with illness, especially smallpox. Furthermore, even when performing a positive function in battle against demons, the Goddess's destructive manifestations can become threatening and dangerous; Kinsley notes that in such contexts the Goddess delights in blood and death, and when she goes berserk on the battlefield she threatens not only her enemies but also her allies and even the stability of the world itself.[10] According to one account in the Liṅga Purāṇa, for example, after Kālī defeats a demon she goes out of control and threatens to destroy the entire universe.[11] As a destructive power, the Goddess is often associated with the forces that can easily lead to disorder.

Prakṛti/Māyā

Not only is it the Goddess who as *śakti* makes creation possible, but it is the Goddess who in her capacity as *prakṛti/māyā* essentially *is* creation. Since the manifest world of differentiated forms evolves from unmanifest, undifferentiated *prakṛti,* who is the Goddess, the world is essentially her embodiment. And we find that in the Brahmanical tradition there is a deep ambivalence toward this aspect of the Goddess as well.

Depending on the perspective, creation itself can be seen as good or bad, liberating or binding. More popular strands of Hinduism celebrate creation and adopt a positive attitude toward the world. Creation is that in and through which one encounters the divine. This more positive attitude is reflected in the reverence expressed for sacred natural sites in India. India herself is felt to be a goddess, Bhārat Mātā ("mother India"), as well as a sacred land filled with sites that possess sacred power. These sites are places where one can "cross over" (√*tṛ*) to the divine and are thus called *tīrtha*s. Many *tīrtha*s are specifically associated with the Goddess and are therefore called "seats" of her power (*śākta pīṭha*).[12]

In stark contrast to this celebratory attitude toward the manifest world, the ascetic and philosophical strands of Hinduism tend to adopt a much more negative attitude. Physical creation is viewed not as something to be celebrated but rather as something that causes suffering. In these environments, the ultimate goal of human existence is to achieve liberation (*mokṣa*) from the world through various techniques, including ascetic practices that emphasize renunciation of the world. In the quest for liberation, *prakṛti* represents bondage and is therefore that which one must escape. In this capacity, the equation of *prakṛti* with *māyā* is often emphasized, for creation itself is felt to be ultimately illusory and represents above all that which prevents one from seeing the true nature of Brahman.

In summary, then, the Brahmanical tradition regards the principles that the Goddess embodies with a great deal of ambivalence. First, as *śakti/māyā*, the Goddess is the creative power that is needed for creation to take place, but she is also the power of delusion that prevents one from realizing Brahman. Furthermore, in her cosmological role, she is the force that maintains creation. But she can also be destructive power. Second, as creation itself, which is a manifestation of *prakṛti*, she is that through which one encounters the divine, but she is also that from which one seeks liberation, especially as the embodiment of *māyā*. Depending on the role she adopts and the way in which she is manifest, the Goddess can be creative or destructive, beneficent or terrible, liberating or binding.

THE AMBIGUOUS FEMALE: FROM DIVINE TO HUMAN

This ambivalence toward the different expressions of the feminine principle is reflected in attitudes toward human women. Women are often said to be portions (*aṃśa*) of the Goddess or of her various manifestations as different goddesses, and women, like the Goddess, are also embodiments of both power and materiality, *śakti* and *prakṛti*. So the ambivalence expressed with respect to the principles that the Goddess embodies also applies to attitudes toward human women. As an embodiment of *śakti*, a woman can be either creative or destructive; as *prakṛti*, she can be either liberating or binding. Thus, for example, the Brahmanical tradition is filled with tales of goddesses and women who act both as instruments of salvation and as temptresses who lure sages and ascetics away from their spiritual practices and impede their progress toward liberation. When left to her own devices, the female can go either way. And because she is ambiguous, a woman is always capable of regressing into her least savory aspects. In her regressive capacity, which is an inherent part of the female, she is dangerous. As Wadley notes, danger is the essence of femaleness as it underlies Brahmanical Hindu religious beliefs about women.[13]

The ambiguity and danger inherent within femaleness appear to be at least in part a function of the intermediate position that the female occupies. Sherry Ortner has remarked that in many societies, women are seen as dangerous by virtue of being closer to nature than men, who are more fully allied with the processes of culture. Women occupy an intermediate position between nature and culture and therefore mediate between the two.[14] The progressive aspects of the female are expressed in those tendencies inherent in female gender that lead from nature, which is associated with chaos and represents disorder, toward culture, which represents order. Women's regressive tendencies are those that lead in the other direction. In the Brahmanical tradition, the intermediacy of the feminine is also reflected on the level of the divine in the transitional place of the Goddess in the process of cosmogony. Between the Absolute and the relative world lies the Goddess, who effects the transition. Since she lies between them, she is the gateway to both. Therefore, she can conduce either to the realization of Brahman and thus liberation (*mokṣa*) or to bondage in the snares of the phenomenal-empirical world, the continual round of birth and rebirth (*saṃsāra*), as the Nārada Purāṇa indicates.[15] Because the female principle is transitional she is ambiguous, and because she is ambiguous she is also dangerous.[16]

The intermediate position of the female also means that she straddles the fence between auspiciousness and inauspiciousness. Veena Das has noted that in Indian culture, the category "auspicious" (*śubha/maṅgala*) tends to be associated with all that is on the side of life, the future, and the right side of the body, whereas the category "inauspicious" (*aśubha/amaṅgala*) tends to be associated with death, termination, and the left side of the body.[17] Auspicious/inauspicious are not static qualities, however, but fluid categories that appear to be associated more with processes or events taken in context rather than objects; thus auspiciousness can easily give way to inauspiciousness unless it is reiterated and reinforced.[18] In this regard, Frédérique Marglin notes that female power, *śakti*, is a transformative force that unites auspiciousness and inauspiciousness, allowing events to be resolved in either direction. She remarks, "Female power, *śakti*, signifies the potency of the joining of both auspiciousness and inauspiciousness."[19] The female as *śakti* has the potential to become inauspicious or to make things become inauspicious; this potential contributes to her dangerousness.

So, we might ask, how does the human female, who also embodies *śakti and prakṛti,* manage to subvert the negative tendencies inherent within her very being and promote her positive aspects? The way in which both goddesses and women are viewed is determined above all by the manner in which they channel their essential character. On both divine and human levels, the paradigms are substantially the same, for both microcosm and macrocosm, society and cosmos, are said to participate in the same essential patterns.

The ambiguity inherent in the Goddess and her manifestations is strongly linked to sexuality and sexual roles. Lawrence Babb was one of the first to note that in both Hindu social and religious symbolism, marriage seems to domesticate the potentially destructive power that females embody, and many other scholars have confirmed Babb's initial observations.[20] Wadley, for example, remarks that Hindu goddesses who are married and have thus transferred control of their sexuality to their husbands are generally benevolent, whereas independent goddesses who control their own sexuality tend to be dangerous and potentially malevolent; David Shulman also notes that the dangerous and sinister aspects of the Goddess are transmuted into positive, beneficent qualities in the context of marriage and domestication.[21] Sax summarizes the issue quite well:

> The benign, gentle forms of the goddess are, like Hindu brides, quite literally bound: their toes, ankles, waists, fingers, wrists, and especially their hair are bound with rings and bangles and cloth, as if their *śakti* could somehow be dammed up like water. They are like good Hindu wives: meek, submissive, and docile. They have transferred their female energy to their husbands. By contrast, the blood-drinking goddesses are all unmarried. Their hair is loose and flowing, they are unbound, their sexuality is uncontrolled by any male, and it is therefore considered dangerous and threatening.[22]

In a similar vein, Wendy Doniger O'Flaherty notes that Indian goddesses can be divided into two categories, one beneficent and the other malevolent, which she calls the categories "goddesses of the breast" and "goddesses of the tooth." Beneficent goddesses are generally married and remain subservient to their husbands, whereas those who are potentially malevolent dominate their consorts. Thus, beneficent goddesses are sexually controlled by their husbands, whereas potentially malevolent goddesses are sexually more free. This distinction is also expressed in terms of rank, for goddesses in the first group tend to be high-ranking, whereas those in the second group tend to be low-ranking.[23]

Recently, the simple model of married/benevolent female versus single/malevolent female has been questioned. C. Mackenzie Brown, for example, challenges the universality of this "marriage control model," as he terms it, and questions whether it fits the portrayal of the Goddess in the Devī-Māhātmya and the Devī-Bhāgavata Purāṇa.[24] Based on his own observations about the portrayal of the goddess Santoṣī Mā on film, Stanley Kurtz also argues that this model has its limitations. Kurtz has noted that it is primarily the nurturing, motherly qualities of a goddess, either married or unmarried, over any other that cause that goddess to be seen as benevolent and the lack of such qualities that causes her to be seen as malevolent. The favorable portrayal of an individual goddess, then, may have less to do with whether or not she is a wife than with whether or not she is a nurturing, motherly female. Hence Kurtz wants to graft a motherly/unmotherly model onto the marriage control model.[25]

One must be mindful of these scholars' objections, for the marriage control model may in fact need to be modified, as Kurtz has suggested. In this regard, an order/disorder dynamic may underlie both the married/unmarried and the motherly/unmotherly paradigms. When a goddess is portrayed as threatening patterns of order, regardless of whether she is married or unmarried, she is viewed as dangerous, unmotherly, and malevolent. Likewise, when a goddess is portrayed as upholding order, regardless of whether she is married or unmarried, she tends to be viewed as nurturing, motherly, and benevolent. Even destructive goddesses are viewed as "good" if they uphold patterns of order. The goddess Durgā, for example, who is unmarried and destructive, helps maintain order by destroying the forces that threaten the world; hence she is viewed as benevolent and is frequently invoked as "mother."

The Goddess and her manifestations, then, are viewed in a positive light when their natures are channeled in a way that creates order, as in the function of the Goddess in the creation of the cosmos, or maintains/restores order, as in Durgā's role as the destroyer of demons. In such cases, goddesses are considered to be good, even when they are destructive. When a goddess is unchanneled or is channeled in a way that leads to disorder or the destruction of order, she is bad. Some goddesses, most notably Kālī, seem to embody both of these tendencies. Generally, then, the positive outlets for the nature of the ambiguous female on the divine level consist in those that harness the feminine principle in ways that lead to creation of the cosmos on the one hand, or maintenance of the cosmos on the other.

What about the human level? The interpretation of female gender as a category implicates many dimensions of experience, yet the representation of the essence of the feminine as *śakti* and *prakṛti* on the human level, as on the divine level, is strongly linked to female sexuality.[26] Not surprisingly, the Brahmanical tradition tends to view women's sexuality with great suspicion. Sexuality is, on one level, pure *śakti,* raw power, expressed as unmediated libidinal desire, and the uninhibited expression of sexual desire is seen as not only inappropriate for women, but also potentially harmful. Social treatises describe female sexuality as being so uncontrollable and irresponsible that women are apt to place sexual gratification above family well-being. The Manu-Smṛti, for example, claims that because of their passion for men and their natural heartlessness, women are prone to be disloyal to their husbands.[27] The *Strīdharmapaddhati* of Tryambaka, the only major extant trea-tise fully devoted to discussion of the nature (*svabhāva*) and duties (*dharma*) particular to women, confirms this view.[28] I. Julia Leslie notes in her discussion of this text that "in the human realm, as in the divine, the untamed female nature—with all the negative associations of female sexuality—is antisocial, elemental, and dangerous."[29] Sax notes also that women's sexual desires are commonly believed to threaten men's well-being, both with respect to their physical vitality, which is correlated with their supply of semen, and their spiritual discipline, which emphasizes renunciation of sexual desire.[30] The drive of female desire creates a condition of inherent danger to social order, for a woman's desire for sex may lead her to engage in "inappropriate" sexual conduct, that is, to engage in sex outside of socially sanctioned circumstances. Such conduct, in turn, may lead to disastrous consequences.

The danger inherent in female sexuality can also be attributed in part to the exchange of bodily fluids that takes place during intercourse. O'Flaherty emphasizes the ambiguous nature of the fluids that issue forth from a woman's body. Milk, which flows from the breasts and symbolizes the maternal role of the female, is generally good, although it becomes ambiguous when attributed with erotic qualities. Sexual fluid, on the other hand, which flows from the genitals and symbolizes the sexual role of the female, is generally bad and potentially dangerous. This danger can be realized when there is an imbalance in the sexual fluids of a man and woman engaging in coitus. In such a situation, the man may be adversely affected.[31]

In Brahmanical Hinduism, one of the greatest dangers with respect to female sexuality lies in the female's vulnerability to ritual pollution through sex, which in turn leads to disorder or matter out of place. This aspect of female gender can be attributed especially to her nature as *prakṛti*, which is commonly described as the "field" (*kṣetra*) that is opposed to pure consciousness, *puruṣa*, which is the "knower of the field" (*kṣetrajña*) and is often allied with male gender. In a similar vein, women, who embody *prakṛti*, are described metaphorically as the field in which men plant the seed during insemination.[32] As the field, a woman can become polluted, whereas the seed is not vulnerable to pollution in the same way. Therefore, for the female, sexual promiscuity is a sure road to pollution, for sex with different partners leads to exchange of bodily substance, which in turn leads to pollution of the "field."

Such concerns about pollution tie into concerns about caste and caste purity. Ronald Inden and McKim Marriott have proposed that caste hierarchy, which has traditionally structured social order in Hindu India, is governed by the differentiation of all living beings into unique genera (*jātis*), each of which is thought to have a defining encoded substance or "substance-code." These defining particles of substance are transmitted genetically from one generation to the next. When bodily substances are improperly mixed, the coded substance defining the caste is altered.[33] Since the woman, as the field, is the fertile matrix in which the child gestates, she must maintain purity of substance-code in order to maintain purity of her offspring and, thus, purity of caste. Mixture of caste is mixture of substance-code; it is matter out of place and thus represents disorder. Regulation of female sexuality is vital to the stability of society, for breakdown of caste is said to lead to breakdown of the social order.

The crux of the matter, then, is the way in which female sexuality is employed and expressed. When it conduces to order, it is good; when it conduces to disorder, it is bad. The association of free use of female sexuality with chaos and matter out of place, which represents disorder and threatens cultural institutions, provides a support for ethical and moral evaluations of female sexuality that are simply not applicable to men. Women who enjoy sex and use their sexuality primarily to satisfy themselves are potentially bad since they threaten social order, whereas men who do the same are not subject to such judgments. If it is to be beneficent, female sexuality must be given an outlet in society that establishes or reinforces the human social order in the same way that the essence of the Goddess is channeled in a way that establishes or reinforces cosmic order. In other words, the channeling of female sexuality must parallel the channeling of the Goddess's essence in the creation or maintenance of the cosmos. A woman's proper role in Hindu society, then, is to direct her essence, her sexuality, into the creation and maintenance of the social order. The threatening aspects of her nature, those that lead to disorder, are therefore neutralized.

Women and Creation of the Social Order

Acceptable expressions of the female's essence are located above all in prescribed roles that provide a socially constructive outlet for female sexuality, that is, one that literally helps to construct society as the Goddess constructs the world. In order for this sexuality to be constructive, it must be brought under control, and its dangerous aspects—those that lead to disorder—must be neutralized through the imposition of order. The best way to do this is, of course, through marriage. Whenever a woman properly transfers control of her essential nature to a male through marriage, she may be viewed as benevolent.[34] The importance of marriage for females is reflected in the fact that the dominant norms for the Hindu woman concern her role as a good wife (*pativratā*) who remains at all times devoted to her husband. Even her spiritual life should be directed into this role. In her research on votive observances among North Indian women, Mary McGee has found that a married woman's auspiciousness or marital felicity (*saubhāgya*) is particularly related to her performance of votive rites on behalf of her husband and family:

> The *dharma* of women is summarized in the role of the devoted wife (*pativratā*) whose duties and devotions are directed solely towards the well-being of her husband. In many ways, the life of the *pativratā* is the *vrata* [vow] *par excellence* of women. It is through fulfilling this *vrata* of service and devotion to the husband that a woman is rewarded in this world and the next. The life of the *pativratā* allows a woman the opportunity to pursue three of the four aims of Hindu life (*puruṣārtha*)—religious duty (*dharma*), wealth (*artha*), and pleasure (*kāma*)—while striving for a moral perfection leading to the fourth, liberation (*mokṣa*).[35]

As a proper wife, a woman is not only devoted to her husband, but in fact also becomes part of him, just as the Goddess is originally part of her male consort in many of the Purāṇas. The loss of a woman's identity to her husband is noted by Vanaja Dhruvarajan in her study of women's lives in an Indian village in south-central India. Dhruvarajan notes that a wife refers to her husband as "my lord," or, using the formal third person, as "they," whereas a husband refers to his wife as "she who is mine" or "she who shares half of my being."[36]

The ideology concerning the duties and conduct of a proper wife or *pativratā* emphasizes both the subordination of the woman to her husband and, most important, her sexual continence. A good wife is above all a chaste wife. A woman who uses her sexuality for any purpose other than providing for her husband's pleasure and bearing his children threatens not only the welfare of her husband but also the stability of society. Correct use of sexuality in marriage maintains order, whereas any other use of sexuality leads to disorder. In this regard, Wadley notes:

> The powers of the chaste woman have no equal. Most critically, these are powers that are bound: they are powers that are built upon a culturally perceived morality, they are powers of order. The benevolent woman and the benevolent goddesses are those who maintain order and who are themselves regulated.[37]

Thus, for example, Sītā, the wife of Rām, who guards her chastity against the advances of a demon and remains faithful to her husband even when threatened with death, represents the highest standard for a good Hindu bride.[38]

The fulfillment of a married woman's role occurs when she becomes a mother, especially a mother of male children, who are much more valued than female children. Children represent an expression of female sexual functioning that is not only socially acceptable, but also desirable and necessary. As a wife who is also a mother, a woman lies at the threshold between nature and culture: the processes of reproduction are natural, but the result of these processes—namely, the child and the family constituted by children and parents—is also a social-cultural unit.[39] The function performed by a mother guarantees the survival of the family line and of the community and therefore reinforces the social order. Hence also Kurtz's observation that it is primarily the motherly qualities of a goddess that determine her beneficence.

In an interesting way, the standard life pattern of an Indian woman as a wife who then becomes a mother parallels the role of the feminine principle in cosmogony. In the patterns that we have seen in the Purāṇic accounts of creation, the Goddess brings about the creation of the manifest world through her transition from pure power to material matrix, from which ordered forms then arise. In this regard, the role of the Goddess in cosmogony represents the quintessential paradigm for the constructive, beneficent expression of the feminine principle, for in cosmogony the Goddess is always cast in a good role, since she is channeling her essential character into a creative act that leads to order. This is also the pattern reflected in the culturally sanctioned trajectory of human women, who channel their *śakti* in the form of sexuality to their husbands, and then, as mothers, become the material matrix from which progeny spring. The production of progeny parallels the production of the cosmos. It is therefore not surprising that in India, a new wife is often not fully accepted into her husband's family until she becomes a mother, for until she has children, she has not yet completed her trajectory.

Women and Maintenance of the Social Order

What about females who do not follow this standard pattern? Goddesses who sublimate their essential nature and channel it into roles in politics, art, academic activity, and so forth are generally viewed as beneficent. Such activities direct female essence into constructive outlets that strengthen and reinforce culture. Thus we find in the Brahmanical tradition a rich mythology of goddesses who are associated with various forms of cultural activity, such as Sarasvatī, the goddess of knowledge and patroness of the arts and sciences, and Durgā, the leader of armies. These different goddesses contribute to the maintenance of society and, therefore, are also expressions of properly channeled feminine nature. To what extent are these divine expressions of the feminine principle seen as examples that women should emulate? One might argue that such goddesses provide empowering role models for human women. In this regard, scholars have pointed out that India is one of the few democratic countries to have been ruled by a woman, Indira Gandhi, who was especially revered because of her power and was even depicted by one artist as Durgā riding on her tiger.[40] Women who become educators could invoke the model of Sarasvatī, who is usually depicted in iconography alone even though she is married to the god Brahmā.

It must be said, however, that there are comparatively few women who have been able to appropriate effectively these more independent roles. Benevolent and submissive goddesses like Sītā are the ones that are generally upheld as the best exemplars of proper female behavior; independent goddesses, however, even when they are "good," are not usually interpreted in this way, and dangerous goddesses like Kālī are usually understood primarily as metaphors for spiritual, mental, or physical processes but certainly not as role models for behavior. Even Indira Gandhi was likened to Durgā by others only after she became prime minister of India as a way of making sense of her role, but she herself did not uphold Durgā as a role model either for her own conduct or for that of other women. One reason behind such distinctions may be that a strong, independent female is still thought to possess a free-floating chaotic potential, whereas a married female who is controlled by her husband is far less likely to be able to give expression to such a potential. Thus the role of a woman as wife and mother has been the dominant cultural norm for the proper expression of female gender in traditional Indian society, as in most societies.

The idea that women are concrete expressions of both *śakti* and *prakṛti* continues to influence—and, one might argue, restrict—the roles that women play in contemporary Indian society, the activities in which they participate, and, most important, the amount of choice that they have in their lives. The question is, to what extent could this system function as a positive paradigm for Indian women that recognizes their power and gives it a place, and to what extent is it a paradigm created by males that inherently represents women as unstable and dangerous? In other words, is the paradigm itself inherently repressive, or does the problem lie more in the ways in which the images have been used and interpreted? Is it possible for Indian women to claim their power from within the tradition in a way that increases the amount of choice they have in their lives? Or must they reject all traditional conceptions of femaleness in search of freedom from gender definition if they are to undertake new roles?

One important issue in evaluating these different possibilities is how the more independent but "good" images of the female embodied by goddesses like Durgā and Sarasvatī may be more self-consciously and consistently appropriated by Indian women as effective role models. Until recently, the social institutions that dominated India have not really provided paths for women to follow in pursuit of nontraditional options. Although the divine models may have been there as potential resources, the situation "on the ground" has not provided any possibility for women to appropriate them. As India changes, more options are becoming available. It is now possible for Hindu women not only to consciously draw upon goddess mythology in redefining their place in society, but also to pursue the options that this mythology, coupled with institutional support, provides. As Wadley notes, as women take more powerful positions in India, they can find validation for their new roles in long-standing Hindu textual traditions.[41]

Further potential lies in how the relationship between the more dangerous goddesses and women might be reconsidered. The range of ways in which goddesses have been interpreted from role model to metaphor is not inherent in the goddess materials themselves but rather appears to reflect social agendas that aim to keep women bound to traditional roles. Why not recast this paradigm in favor of a new one that is more radical and empowering for women? Why not, for example, invoke Kālī not as a metaphor but as a kind of role model? As a goddess associated with transformative processes, Kālī could well serve as a symbol of women's desire to transform and empower both their own lives and Hindu culture in general.

No matter what the answers ultimately may be, we cannot ignore the fact that in India, despite the rich tradition of goddess reverence, the human female has been and continues to be tremendously undervalued. As traditional institutions such as caste change, it would seem logical that the regulation of women and the danger that women's control over their own nature represents to social order should begin to change. Such transformations, however, appear to be slow in coming. The lack of support for fast or pervasive change in the status of women in contemporary India is not surprising given the larger social, mythological, and ideological concerns to which conceptions about female gender have been tied for centuries, and it appears that the freedoms accorded generously to Indian men probably will not easily be extended to women. Despite such obstacles, however, we must nevertheless recognize that the Brahmanical Hindu tradition supports a rich mythology pertaining to goddesses and postulates an important place for the feminine principle in its understanding of cosmogony and cosmology. The problem appears to lie more in the ways that the images of the different goddesses and the Great Goddess have been interpreted and applied and the emphases that have been given to the various dimensions of the feminine than in the very symbols that the tradition itself has generated. If this is the case, then it may very well be possible for Indian women to appropriate these images in ways that are more empowering than the ways in which they have been appropriated in the past.

Notes

Introduction

1. Sir Monier Monier-Williams, *A Sanskrit-English Dictionary*, rev. ed. (Delhi: Motilal Banarsidass, 1988), p. 654.

2. Thomas Coburn, *Devī-Māhātmya: The Crystallization of the Goddess Tradition* (Delhi: Motilal Banarsidass, 1984), p. 186.

3. Monier-Williams, *Sanskrit-English Dictionary*, p. 1044.

4. Susan S. Wadley, "Women and the Hindu Tradition," in *Women in India: Two Perspectives*, edited by Doranne Jacobson and Susan S. Wadley (Columbia, Mo.: South Asia Books, 1977), p. 115.

5. See David Kinsley, *The Sword and the Flute: Kālī and Kṛṣṇa; Dark Visions of the Terrible and the Sublime in Hindu Mythology* (Berkeley and Los Angeles: University of California Press, 1975), pp. 109–114, 133–139, and *Hindu Goddesses: Visions of the Divine Feminine in the Hindu Religious Tradition* (Berkeley and Los Angeles: University of California Press, 1986), pp. 133–137; P. G. Layle, *Studies in Devī-Bhāgavata* (Bombay: Popular Prakashan, 1973), pp. 147–169; and Coburn, *Devī-Māhātmya*, pp. 123–127, 146–153, 180–186.

6. In dating Tantric literature from the ninth century, I am following Teun Goudriaan. Other scholars have argued for earlier dates. For a discussion of the dating of the Tantric literature and a summary of different scholars' views, see Sanjukta Gupta and Teun Goudriaan, *Hindu Tantric and Śākta Literature*, vol. 2, fasc. 2 of *A History of Indian Literature* (Wiesbaden: Otto Harrossowitz, 1981), pp. 19–21.

7. The term "cosmology" refers to reflection regarding the

general nature and structure of the created universe. "Cosmogony," on the other hand, refers to accounts of the act of creation or birth (*gonos*) of the cosmos itself.

8. The history of this literature is extremely complex and cannot be undertaken in any detail here. There are many standard works available that provide elaborate discussions of this history. See, for example, Arthur Berriedale Keith, *The Religion and Philosophy of the Veda and Upaniṣads,* Harvard Oriental Series, vols. 31–32 (Cambridge: Harvard University Press, 1925); Maurice Winternitz, *A History of Indian Literature,* translated by V. Srinivasa Sarma and Subhadra Jha, 3 vols. (Delhi: Motilal Banarsidass, 1985-1988); Erich Frauwallner, *History of Indian Philosophy,* translated by V. M. Bedekar, 2 vols. (Delhi: Motilal Banarsidass, 1973); and Ludo Rocher, *The Purāṇas,* vol. 2, fasc. 3 of *A History of Indian Literature,* (Wiesbaden: Otto Harrassowitz, 1986).

9. For more discussion of these texts, see James Santucci, *An Outline of Vedic Literature,* (Missoula, Mont.: Scholars Press, 1976).

10. For more on the oral nature of the Purāṇas, see C. Mackenzie Brown, "Purāṇa as Scripture: From Sound to Image of the Holy Word in the Hindu Tradition," *History of Religions* 26, no. 1 (August 1986): 68–86.

11. This view is particularly strong in the school of Pūrva-Mīmāṃsā philosophy.

12. See Thomas B. Coburn, "The Study of the Purāṇas and the Study of Religion," *Religious Studies* 16, no. 3 (September 1980): 341–352.

13. C. Mackenzie Brown, *The Triumph of the Goddess: The Canonical Models and Theological Visions of the Devī-Bhāgavata Purāṇa* (Albany: State University of New York Press, 1990), p. 5.

14. Ibid., p. 3.

15. Ibid., p. 4.

16. Vincent B. Leitch, *Deconstructive Criticism: An Advanced Introduction* (New York: Columbia University Press, 1983), p. 59. See also Umberto Eco, *Role of the Reader: Explorations in the Semiotics of Texts* (Bloomington: Indiana University Press, 1979), p. 21: "Intertextual knowledge . . . can be considered a special case of overcoding and establishes its own intertextual frames (frequently identified with genre rules). . . . Intertextual frames . . . are already literary 'topoi,' narrative schemes."

17. A. K. Ramanujan has also discussed intertextuality in relation to Indian texts. See A. K. Ramanujan, "On Folk Mythologies and Folk Purāṇas," in *Purāṇa Perennis: Reciprocity and Transformation in Hindu and Jaina Texts,* edited by Wendy Doniger (Albany: State University of New York Press, 1993), p. 105.

18. J. C. Heesterman, "Veda and Dharma," in *The Concept of Duty in South Asia,* edited by Wendy Doniger O'Flaherty and J. Duncan M. Derrett (New Delhi: Vikas Publishing House, 1978), p. 80.

19. Brian K. Smith, *Reflections on Resemblance, Ritual, and Religion* (New York and Oxford: Oxford University Press, 1989), p. 20. Smith quotes Louis Renou, *The Destiny of the Veda in India,* edited and translated by Dev Raj Chanana (Delhi: Motilal Banarsidass, 1965), p. 2.

20. Although the categorization of Vedic scripture as *śruti* and post-Vedic Brahmanical scripture as *smṛti* is a traditionally accepted schema, these categories are actually somewhat fluid, and scriptures that are traditionally categorized as *smṛti,* such as the Purāṇas, sometimes claim divine or *śruti* status. Coburn, for example, notes that there is a tradition that views the Purāṇas as having a divine origin. See Coburn, "Study of the Purāṇas and the Study of Religion," pp. 343–344.

21. Barbara A. Holdrege, *Veda and Torah: Transcending the Textuality of Scripture* (Albany: State University of New York Press, forthcoming).

22. Ibid., ms. pp. 8–9.

Chapter One. The Feminine Principle in the Vedas

1. F. B. J. Kuiper, "Cosmogony and Conception: A Query," *History of Religions* 10, no. 2 (November 1970): 98–104.

2. W. Norman Brown, "Theories of Creation in the Rig Veda," *Journal of the American Oriental Society* 85, no. 1 (January–March 1965): 27.

3. David Kinsley makes the point that there is no one Great Goddess in the Vedic literature and that the expression of a single Mahādevī is a much later product of a carefully articulated theology. See Kinsley, *Hindu Goddesses,* p. 18. Although I agree overall with Kinsley, it is important to note that one can find underlying thematic patterns that are clearly associated with many different

female divinities and characterize more than one goddess.

4. See, for example, Ṛg-Veda 7.49.1–4, 10.9.1–7; Atharva-Veda 1.5.1, 1.6.3–4.

5. See, for example, Ṛg-Veda 4.3.12.

6. All translations throughout the book are my own unless otherwise indicated.

7. See, for example, Ṛg-Veda 4.3.12; Vājasaneyi Saṃhitā 6.27, 10.7; Taittirīya Saṃhitā 1.2.1, 1.3.8; Atharva-Veda 1.4.3, 1.6.1.

8. See, for example, Ṛg-Veda 1.95.4–5, 1.143.1, 2.35.2–13, 7.9.3, 10.8.5.

9. Ṛg-Veda 1.22.6, 6.50.13.

10. Ṛg-Veda 10.63.2.

11. Ṛg-Veda 6.50.7, 10.30.10, 10.9.5.

12. Kuiper, "Cosmogony and Conception," pp. 100–104. See also H. W. Bodewitz, "The Waters in Vedic Cosmic Classifications," *Indologica Taurinensia* 10 (1982): 49–50.

13. Ṛg-Veda 10.72 also describes the gods assembling in the waters (*salila*), presumably before the dawn of creation as they are described as drawing forth from the ocean the sun, which was hidden in the ocean. Without the sun, there can be no light, and the primordial phase of creation is elsewhere (e.g., 10.129) described as being characterized by lack of light.

14. Or, perhaps, beheld together.

15. Franklin Edgerton has provided fine translations for some of the hymns discussed in this chapter, including this one. In such cases, I follow fairly closely, although not exactly, his translations. See Franklin Edgerton, *The Beginnings of Indian Philosophy: Selections from the Rig Veda, Atharva Veda, Upaniṣads, and Mahābhārata* (Cambridge, Mass.: Harvard University Press, 1965).

16. Atharva-Veda 4.2.8.

17. Taittirīya Saṃhitā 5.6.4.2–3.

18. See, for example, Ṛg-Veda 10.9.1, 3.

19. Ṛg-Veda 1.144.2.

20. See, for example, Ṛg-Veda 6.51.5, 10.18.10; Vājasaneyi Saṃhitā 2.10, 9.22; Atharva-Veda 12.1.63.

21. In this hymn, the earth is associated with the plants (*oṣadhi*) with which the waters are associated in the Taittirīya Saṃhitā.

22. Atharva-Veda 12.1.2–17.

23. Atharva-Veda 12.1.17.

24. Atharva-Veda 12.1.7–10, 12.1.6.

25. Atharva-Veda 5.25.2, 6.17.1, 12.1.43.

26. Atharva-Veda 12.1.1.

27. Ṛg-Veda 1.159.2, 1.185.4. See also Kinsley, *Hindu Goddesses*, p. 8.

28. Ṛg-Veda 1.185.7.

29. See, for example, Maitrāyaṇī Saṃhitā 1.6.3 and Kāṭhaka Saṃhitā 8.2. This theme is then picked up in later accounts of creation.

30. Ṛg-Veda 1.159.2.

31. Atharva-Veda 12.1.12.

32. See, for example, Ṛg-Veda 1.153.3, 8.90.15.

33. Atharva-Veda 6.120.2; Atharva-Veda 7.6.2, 7.6.4 and Vājasaneyi Saṃhitā 9.5; Ṛg-Veda 2.27.7 (literally, having kings as sons or having princely sons [*rājaputra*]). See also Kinsley, *Hindu Goddesses*, pp. 9–10.

34. See, for example, Atharva-Veda 12.1.61, 13.1.38; Vājasaneyi Saṃhitā 13.18.

35. Ṛg-Veda 1.185.3. See also Atharva-Veda 12.3.11.

36. Atharva-Veda 7.6.2.

37. Ṛg-Veda 1.89.10.

38. The term used here is *vāja*, which can also mean wealth or treasure.

39. F. Max Müller, trans. *Vedic Hymns*, Sacred Books of the East, vol. 32 (1891; reprint, Delhi: Motilal Banarsidass, 1964), p. 248. For a brief review of various scholarly opinions about the nature of Aditi, see A. A. Macdonell, *Vedic Mythology* (1898; reprint, Delhi: Motilal Banarsidass, 1974), p. 123.

40. Müller, *Vedic Hymns*, p. 241.

41. Ṛg-Veda 10.130.5.

42. Ṛg-Veda 10.90.5.

43. In some passages *virāj* is an epithet applied to Indra, Prajāpati, and Parameṣṭhin. See also W. D. Whitney, *Atharva-Veda-Samhita*, Harvard Oriental Series, vols. 7–8 (1905; 2d Indian reprint ed., Delhi: Motilal Banarsidass, 1971), vol. 2, p. 508. Atharva-Veda 8.9.10 asks, "who understands (*pra* √*vid*) the pairness (*mithunatva*) of Virāj?" Whitney understands *mithunatva* to refer especially to the condition of being a pair of opposite sexes.

44. For more on Virāj and her role in this hymn, see also

André Padoux, *Vāc: The Concept of the Word in Selected Hindu Tantras*, translated by Jacques Gontier (Albany: State University of New York Press, 1990), pp. 9–10. In discussing Atharva-Veda 8.9 and 8.10, Padoux says, "There *virāj* appears as the cosmic cow, identical with Vāc, whose calf is Indra and who is once described—becoming masculine for the occasion—as "the father of *brahman*. . . . " *Virāj*, therefore, is identified with *vāc*. Moreover (in accordance with its etymology, vi plus the root RĀJ), she appears as an active principle, ruling, luminous, nourishing, and feminine, as a creative energy which might already, because of this aspect and role, prefigure the *śakti* of the later periods (and furthermore, this is an energy which is the Word)."

45. Edgerton suggests for this last verse, "She is the one who knows that upon which we both may subsist, let us invoke her."

46. See also Jan Gonda, 'The 'Original' Sense and the Etymology of Skt. *māyā*," in *Four Studies in the Language of the Veda*, Disputationes Rheno-Trajectinae, vol. 3 (The Hague: Mouton, 1959), p. 155. Gonda comments upon the cited passage as follows:

> The text recites the curious migrations and metamorphoses of Virāj . . . which here is considered the first principle, the universe in the beginning. She came, successively, to the asuras, the Fathers, men etc., and each of these categories of beings calls her by a special name which of course is nothing but an aspect of her nature and essence. Moreover, each class of creature milks her and her milk—upon which these beings are stated to subsist—is mostly identical with the 'idea' or 'substance' indicated by that name. . . . The conclusion must be that there is, in the view of the author, a special relation between asuras and *māyā*, for they call to her "O *māyā*," and she yields them *māyā*, upon which the asuras are said to subsist.

47. Gonda (ibid.) characterizes her as "a creative principle representing also the idea of ruling far and wide, being the sum of all existence, the hypostatization of the conception of the universe as a whole."

48. See Atharva-Veda 8.10.22ff., where Virāj is described in conjunction with milking-pails and calves of different varieties. See also Atharva-Veda 9.2.5, where she is explicitly identified as a cow and is also called Vāc.

49. Atharva-Veda 9.10.24.

50. Atharva-Veda 8.9.8–10.

51. Atharva-Veda 8.9.11.

52. See also Holdrege, *Veda and Torah*, ms. p. 42.

53. Ṛg-Veda 10.71.1.

54. Ṛg-Veda 10.71.3–4. See also Holdrege, *Veda and Torah*, ms. p. 43.

55. W. Norman Brown has published an excellent study and careful translation of this hymn, and I have followed his translation fairly closely. See W. Norman Brown, "Agni, Sun, Sacrifice, and Vāc: A Sacerdotal Ode by Dīrghatamas (Rig Veda 1.164)," *Journal of the American Oriental Society* 88, no. 2 (April–June 1968): 217.

56. Ṛg-Veda 10.125.3–8.

57. See also Brown's translation in "Agni, Sun, Sacrifice, and Vāc," pp. 216–217. For a discussion regarding the translation of the term *akṣara* ("syllable, imperishable"), see J. A. B. van Buitenen, "Akṣara," *Journal of the American Oriental Society* 79, no. 3 (July–September 1959): 176–187. Note that the term *salila* (pl. *salilāni*) is also the term used for the primordial waters in 10.129.3.

Vāc is not explicitly identified in the hymn with the buffalo, but Sāyana equates the two.

58. See, for example, Taittirīya Saṃhitā 2.1.6; Vājasaneyi Saṃhitā 10.30.

59. See, for example, Ṛg-Veda 6.61.4, 6; Vājasaneyi Saṃhitā 21.32–33.

60. See, for example, Ṛg-Veda 10.30.12–13; Vājasaneyi Saṃhitā 20.75.

61. Ṛg-Veda 2.41.17.

62. Ṛg-Veda 6.61.11–12.

63. Ṛg-Veda 2.41.16, 6.61.2, 6.61.8, 7.95.1.

64. See, for example, Ṛg-Veda 1.13.9, 1.142.9, 9.6.8, 10.110.8, 10.17.7. The identities of the other two goddesses fluctuate, but they are usually called Iḷā and Mahī or, in Vājasaneyi Saṃhitā, Iḍā and Bhāratī.

65. Ṛg-Veda 1.3.12, 6.49.7.

66. For more detailed speculation on this problem, see S. K. Das, *Śakti or Divine Power* (Calcutta: University of Calcutta, 1934), pp. 34ff.

67. Ṛg-Veda 8.89.11.

68. Macdonell, *Vedic Mythology*, p. 58.

69. See Das, *Śakti or Divine Power*, p. 11. He has found that *śacībhis*, the instrumental plural of *śacī*, is used over thirty times in the Ṛg-Veda.

70. See also Das, *Śakti or Divine Power*, p. 12; and Macdonnell, *Vedic Mythology*, p. 57.

71. Das, *Śakti or Divine Power*, pp. 15–16.

72. Although I include in this section references to two of the Āraṇyakas, the Śāṅkhāyana Āraṇyaka and the Aitareya Āraṇyaka, the predominant emphasis is on the Brāhmaṇas.

73. Jaiminīya Brāhmaṇa 1.237.

74. Śatapatha Brāhmaṇa 6.8.2.2.

75. Śatapatha Brāhmaṇa 7.4.1.6.

76. Śatapatha Brāhmaṇa 6.1.3.11, 6.8.2.3.

77. Śatapatha Brāhmaṇa 1.1.1.14.

78. See, for example, Aitareya Brāhmaṇa 2.16, Śatapatha Brāhmaṇa 14.3.2.13.

79. See above, p. 39.

80. Kauṣītaki Brāhmaṇa 25.1.

81. Śatapatha Brāhmaṇa 1.1.1.18.

82. Jaiminīya Brāhmaṇa 1.140; Śatapatha Brāhmaṇa 6.8.2.3.

83. Śatapatha Brāhmaṇa 9.4.1.10.

84. Pañcaviṃśa Brāhmaṇa 7.8.1.

85. See, for example, Śatapatha Brāhmaṇa 7.4.2.6 and 7.4.1.8.

86. Śatapatha Brāhmaṇa 7.3.1.20.

87. Śatapatha Brāhmaṇa 14.1.3.25.

88. See, for example, Śatapatha Brāhmaṇa 5.3.1.4, 6.5.3.1, 4.6.9.16.

89. See, for example, Śatapatha Brāhmaṇa 2.2.1.19, 5.3.1.4, 6.5.4.2, 7.4.2.7; Kauṣītaki Brāhmaṇa 6.14.

90. Śāṅkhāyana Āraṇyaka 7.16 (7.15).

91. Śatapatha Brāhmaṇa 6.5.2.20.

92. See, for example, Śatapatha Brāhmaṇa 8.3.2.13, 8.5.2.2, 13.6.2.3, 13.7.1.2.

93. See, for example, Śatapatha Brāhmaṇa 5.2.2.13–14, 5.3.4.25, 5.4.5.7, 13.1.8.5, 14.2.1.12; Jaiminīya Brāhmaṇa 1.82; Pañcaviṃśa Brāhmaṇa 6.7.7.

94. Śatapatha Brāhmaṇa 11.1.6.3.

95. See also Jaiminīya Brāhmaṇa 1.104, where Prajāpati again creates through speech.

96. For a more detailed exploration of this association, see S. K. Lal, *Female Divinities in Hindu Mythology and Ritual* (Poona: University of Poona, 1980), pp. 159–160.

97. Śāṅkhāyana Āraṇyaka 7.1.

98. Śatapatha Brāhmaṇa 12.8.2.6, 8.6.3.22. Aitareya Āraṇyaka 1.3.2 and Aitareya Brāhmaṇa 5.23 and 5.33 also pair off mind and speech.

99. Śatapatha Brāhmaṇa 1.4.4.1, 1.4.4.7.

100. Śatapatha Brāhmaṇa 3.2.4.11, 1.4.5.11. Śatapatha Brāhmaṇa 4.6.7.5, however, gives speech its due by arguing that mind cannot be made known without speech. See also Śatapatha Brāhmaṇa 1.4.4.5–7, 10.5.3.3–4; and Lal, *Female Divinities,* p. 160.

101. See, for example, Pañcaviṃśa Brāhmaṇa 7.6.17, 16.10.8, 18.6.11; Jaiminīya Brāhmaṇa 1.128; Aitareya Brāhmaṇa 4.28. For the equation between Vāc and the earth, see note 88 above. The *rathantara* is also identified in Pañcaviṃśa Brāhmaṇa 7.7.16 as procreative energy or semen (*prajanana*).

102. For more detail, see Lal, *Female Divinities,* p. 160.

103. See also Holdrege, *Veda and Torah,* ms. p. 47.

104. Jaiminīya Brāhmaṇa 1.128. In Jaiminīya Brāhmaṇa 1.270, speech is again correlated with earth, but mind is correlated not with heaven but with the waters:

> And he combines the divine *dhūr*s with the human *dhūr*s. The mind is a human *dhūr,* the waters (*ap*) are a divine *dhūr.* . . . Speech is a human *dhūr,* the earth a divine *dhūr* (the term *dhūr* refers to a particular set of Gāyatrī verses).

105. Śatapatha Brāhmaṇa 7.5.1.31, 8.5.2.3, 11.2.4.9, 11.2.6.3. In at least one place, Śatapatha Brāhmaṇa 12.9.1.13, Indra is equated with mind.

106. Jaiminīya Brāhmaṇa 1.128.

107. Jaiminīya Brāhmaṇa 1.19; Śatapatha Brāhmaṇa 1.5.1.21. Or, the offering spoon (*sruk*) is Vāc, the dipping spoon (*sruva*) is breath/Prajāpati (Śatapatha Brāhmaṇa 6.3.1.8–9).

108. See also Śatapatha Brāhmaṇa 1.4.4.4–5, 6.3.1.9.

109. See Śatapatha Brāhmaṇa 11.1.6.3; Pañcaviṃśa Brāhmaṇa 7.6.1–3; and Pañcaviṃśa Brāhmaṇa 20.14.2, cited above.

110. Śatapatha Brāhmaṇa 2.4.4.2.

111. Śatapatha Brāhmaṇa 10.5.2.14.
112. Bṛhadāraṇyaka Upaniṣad 4.2.2-3.
113. Bṛhadāraṇyaka Upaniṣad 3.6, 5.5.1.
114. Aitareya Upaniṣad 1.1.3–4. The formation of creation from the body of a primal man, Puruṣa, is first recounted in Ṛg-Veda 10.90.
115. Aitareya Upaniṣad 1.1.4.
116. Śatapatha Brāhmaṇa 10.6.5.1–2.
117. Śatapatha Brāhmaṇa 10.6.5.4–5.
118. See also Holdrege, *Veda and Torah*, ms. p. 51: "In the first phase of creation the Creator, desiring to have a 'second self' (*dvitīya ātman*), enters into union with Vāc by means of his mind (*manas*). The seed becomes the year, which is consistently identified with Prajāpati in the Brāhmaṇas. In the second phase, which is distinguished from the first phase by the period of a year, a child, representing the 'second self' of the Creator, is born and cries out, producing speech (*vāc*). This speech represents the second phase of Vāc, and it is from this expressed level of speech that the *ṛks*, *yajuses*, *sāmans*, meters, sacrifices, human beings, and animals are brought forth."
119. Bṛhadāraṇyaka Upaniṣad 1.5.11.
120. Chāndogya Upaniṣad 1.13.2.

Chapter Two. Prakṛti, Māyā, *and* Śakti: *The Feminine Principle in Philosophical Discourse*

1. See Coburn, *Devī-Māhātmya*, p. 181.
2. Ibid. See also *Nirukta* 2.2, 28. Coburn also notes that the term occasionally just means "the norm, the usual way." He cites as evidence the Śaṅkhāyana Śrauta-Sūtra 6.1.2, 14.1.1.
3. See, for example, Śaṅkhāyana Śrauta-Sūtra 1.16.1–2. See also the commentary on Āpastamba's Yajña Paribhāṣā-Sūtra 114 in *The Gṛhya-Sūtras*, Sacred Books of the East, edited by F. Max Müller, translated by Hermann Oldenberg, vol. 30 (1892: reprint, Delhi: Motilal Banarsidass, 1964), p. 346; and Samiran Chandra Chakrabarti, *The Paribhāṣās in the Śrautasūtras* (Calcutta: Sanskrit Pustak Bhandar, 1980), pp. 131–134.
4. Louis Renou, "Les connexions entre le rituel et la grammaire en sanskrit," *Journal Asiatique* 233 (1941–1942): 143–

144, reprinted in *A Reader on the Sanskrit Grammarians*, edited by J. F. Staal (Cambridge, Mass.: MIT Press, 1972), p. 457 (translation mine).

5. See Mīmāṃsā-Sūtra 1.1.10. A similar use of the term occurs in Nyāya-Sūtra 2.2.41 and 2.2.54, where the term *prakṛti* is used to refer to the nonmodified form of Sanskrit letters.

6. We find an association of *prakṛti* with some notion of materiality in the Vaiśeṣika-Sūtras, the foundational text of Vaiśeṣika philosophy, where in sūtra 8.2.5 earth (*pṛthivī*) is cited as the material basis or material cause (*prakṛti*) of smell, but the association here is limited in its sense and application and does not seem to have any larger philosophical or cosmological force.

7. Renou, "Les connexions," pp. 456–457.

8. Gerald J. Larson, *Classical Sāṃkhya*, 2d ed. (Delhi: Motilal Banarsidass, 1979), p. 75.

9. Ibid., p. 76.

10. Ibid., p. 95.

11. This section is selective and will focus only on passages and motifs that are immediately relevant to the project at hand. Readers interested in a fuller historical treatment are referred to Larson's *Classical Sāṃkhya* and E. H. Johnston's *Early Sāṃkhya: An Essay on Its Historical Development According to the Texts* (London: Royal Asiatic Society, 1937).

12. See chapter one, pp. 27-28, 45.

13. Taittirīya Upaniṣad 2.1.

14. Chāndogya Upaniṣad 6.6.4–5.

15. See also Larson, *Classical Sāṃkhya*, pp. 30, 83–84.

16. Note also that Virāj is identified with food in the Brāhmaṇas.

17. See also Larson, *Classical Sāṃkhya*, pp. 83–86. Larson notes that there are also passages in the Atharva-Veda that may be sources for the later *guṇa* theory, but the passages that he cites are quite obscure.

18. The Chāndogya Upaniṣad probably dates from around 800–600 B.C.E., whereas the Śvetāśvatara dates around 400 years later (400–200 B.C.E.). See Gerald J. Larson and Ram Shankar Bhattacharya, eds., *Sāṃkhya: A Dualist Tradition in Indian Philosophies*, vol. 4 of *Encyclopedia of Indian Philosophies* (Delhi: Motilal Banarsidass, 1987), p. 14.

19. Śvetāśvatara Upaniṣad 4.5. See also Larson, *Classical Sāṃkhya*, pp. 84–85.

20. Śvetāśvatara Upaniṣad 4.5–6. The reference to the image of the two birds is clearly inspired by Ṛg-Veda 1.164.20, which presents the same image of two birds.

21. Maitri Upaniṣad 6.10.

22. In his translation of this Upaniṣad, Robert E. Hume interprets "from this" (*asmāt*) as meaning "from Brahman," and "the other" (*anya*) as referring to the individual soul. See Robert E. Hume, trans., *The Thirteen Principal Upaniṣads*, 2d ed., 4th impression (Delhi: Oxford University Press, 1988), p. 404.

23. Śvetāśvatara Upaniṣad 1.10.

24. Śvetāśvatara Upaniṣad 1.8–9.

25. See also Larson, *Classical Sāṃkhya*, pp. 113–114.

26. The evolution of the term *prakṛti* within the context of the development of proto-Sāṃkhya materials in not only the Mokṣadharma and Bhagavad-Gītā sections of the Mahābhārata but also the *Caraka* and *Suśruta Saṃhitās* and the *Buddhacarita* of Aśvaghoṣa, has been covered extensively elsewhere. See, for example, Larson, *Classical Sāṃkhya*, especially pp. 103ff., and "Part One: Introduction to the Philosophy of Sāṃkhya," in Larson and Bhattacharya, *Sāṃkhya*, pp. 7–15; Surendranath Dasgupta, *A History of Indian Philosophy*, 5 vols. (1922; reprint, Delhi: Motilal Banarsidass, 1988), vol. 1, pp. 213ff., vol. 2, pp. 428–29. We will not attempt to reproduce here in any great detail the work of these other scholars but will rather focus on materials that are immediately relevant to the present discussion.

27. All numbers refer to the passages in the Sanskrit critical edition. Unfortunately, the best complete available translation of the Mahābhārata, that of Pratap Chandra Roy, is based not on the critical edition but on the Bombay edition of the text. See Roy's *The Mahabharata of Krishna-Dwaipayana Vyasa*, 2d ed., 12 vols. (Calcutta: Oriental Publishing Co., 1883–1896). The passage cited is found in section 4 of Roy's translation.

28. Section 5 in Roy's translation.

29. Erich Frauwallner notes that the Mahābhārata adheres to a theory of evolution of the five elements that he calls the Accumulation Theory, according to which "every element possesses, besides its own special quality, still the total qualities of the forego-

ing element out of which it has sprung." See Frauwallner, *History of Indian Philosophy,* vol. 1, pp. 96–97. References to the five gross elements are found already in two of the early Upaniṣads, the Tattirīya (2.1) and the Aitareya (3.5.3). See Larson, *Classical Sāṃkhya,* p. 90.

30. Section 183 in Roy's translation.

31. Section 202 in Roy's translation.

32. Section 233 in Roy's translation.

33. Literally, attain the state of earthness (*bhūmitvamupayānti*).

34. Section 340 in Roy's translation.

35. Section 343 in Roy's translation.

36. Whenever the name of a principle is used as an epithet of a divinity, I capitalize it. Thus I capitalize the term *puruṣa* here because it is an epithet of Hari (Viṣṇu).

37. See chapter one, p. 26.

38. Section 187 in Roy's translation.

39. Section 304 in Roy's translation.

40. Section 306 in Roy's translation.

41. 12.206.7–8 (section 213 in Roy's translation).

42. Surendranath Dasgupta equates the *mahat brahman* with *prakṛti.* See Dasgupta, *History of Indian Philosophy,* vol. 2, p. 462.

43. Ibid., p. 463.

44. Bhagavad-Gītā 7.5.

45. See also Coburn, *Devī-Māhātmya,* p. 184.

46. Larson, *Classical Sāṃkhya,* pp. 10–13.

47. See Larson and Bhattacharya, *Sāṃkhya,* p. 49.

48. Larson, *Classical Sāṃkhya,* p. 11.

49. Sāṃkhya-Kārikā 8. See also ibid., p. 164.

50. Italics are mine. I have followed Larson's translation of this passage fairly closely (ibid., pp. 260–261).

51. Sāṃkhya-Kārikā 19.

52. Sāṃkhya-Kārikā 20. See also Larson, *Classical Sāṃkhya,* pp. 173–175.

53. Sāṃkhya-Kārikā 59. See also Debiprasad Chattopadhyaya, *Lokāyata: A Study in Ancient Indian Materialism* (New Delhi: People's Publishing House, 1959), pp. 61–62.

54. J. Gonda, *Change and Continuity in Indian Religion,* Disputationes Rheno-Trajectinae, vol. 9 (The Hague: Mouton, 1965), p. 166.

55. Gonda, "'Original' Sense and the Etymology of Skt. *māyā*," pp. 119–194.

56. Teun Goudriaan, *Māyā Divine and Human* (Delhi: Motilal Banarsidass, 1978), p. 2. For a discussion of various scholars' interpretations of the meaning of *māyā* in the early tradition, see L. Thomas O'Neil, *Māyā in Śaṅkara: Measuring the Immeasurable* (Delhi: Motilal Banarsidass, 1980), pp. 29–39.

57. Goudriaan, *Māyā*, pp. 2–3.

58. Ibid., p. 4.

59. For discussion and references, see Paul David Devanandan, *The Concept of Māyā* (London: Lutterworth Press, 1950), pp. 20–21.

60. Praśna Upaniṣad 1.15–16.

61. *Brahma-Sūtra Bhāṣya* 1.1.12. See also 3.2.11.

62. See, for example, *Brahma-Sūtra Bhāṣya* 1.1.12–15, 3.2.11–21. See also Karl H. Potter, ed., *Advaita Vedānta up to Śaṃkara and His Pupils*, vol. 3 of *The Encyclopedia of Indian Philosophies* (Princeton, N.J.: Princeton University Press, 1981), p. 74.

63. *Brahma-Sūtra Bhāṣya* 1.1.12.

64. See, for example, *Brahma-Sūtra Bhāṣya* 1.1.12, 3.2.11-15. See also Eliot Deutsch, *Advaita Vedānta: A Philosophical Reconstruction* (Honolulu: University of Hawaii Press, 1969), p. 12.

65. *Brahma-Sūtra Bhāṣya* 2.1.33.

66. See, for example, *Brahma-Sūtra Bhāṣya* 3.2.21, as well as the introduction (*upodghāta*).

67. *Brahma-Sūtra Bhāṣya* 2.1.14.

68. *Brahma-Sūtra Bhāṣya* 1.1.20. See also 3.2.17.

69. See Devanandan, *Concept of Māyā*, p. 107.

70. Devanandan (ibid., p. 103) summarizes his own and other scholars' views regarding this point:

> Śaṅkara uses the term [*sic*] *Avidyā* and *Māyā* indiscriminately, and it is difficult to see just how he distinguished the two. Not only does he use them interchangeably, he attributes to Avidyā the same functions which he ascribes to Māyā. Thibaut concludes that Śaṅkara identifies them both. Deussen holds that to Śaṅkara Avidyā is the causal principle of the world of appearance while Māyā is the effect, the appearance itself. It is true that later Vedāntin [*sic*] of the school of Śaṅkara make some distinction; in Śaṅkara's own thinking, however, Māyā is both a principle of creation as well as the creation itself. But it

is Māyā as a principle of creation that is obviously identified with Avidyā. Radhakrishnan offers another interpretation. "Avidyā and Māyā," says he, "represent the subjective and the objective sides of the one fundamental fact of experience. It is called avidyā, since it is dissolvable by knowledge; but the objective series is called māyā, since it is coeternal with the supreme personality."

71. *Brahma-Sūtra Bhāṣya* 1.4.3. See also 2.2.2.

72. *Brahma-Sūtra Bhāṣya* 1.4.1–7.

73. See page 68.

74. *Brahma-Sūtra Bhāṣya* 1.4.9.

75. *Brahma-Sūtra Bhāṣya* 1.4.10.

76. Dasgupta, *History of Indian Philosophy,* vol. 1, p. 418.

77. Brahma-Sūtra 3.2.3.

78. See Chandradhar Sharma, *A Critical Survey of Indian Philosophy* (Delhi: Motilal Banarsidass, 1987), chapters six, fourteen, and fifteen.

79. Coburn, *Devī-Māhātmya,* pp. 148–149.

80. See chapter one, pp. 47-53. The cosmogonic implications of the union of Indra/Indrāṇī are described in Śatapatha Brāhmaṇa 10.5.2.9–12.

81. See Śvetāśvatara Upaniṣad 6.8, where God's *śakti* is also described as various (*vividhā*).

82. See also Das, *Śakti or Divine Power,* p. 49.

83. Śvetāśvatara Upaniṣad 1.4–6. The term *preritṛ* probably refers to God himself.

84. See Hume, *Thirteen Principal Upaniṣads,* pp. 394–395; and S. Radhakrishnan, *The Principal Upaniṣads* (London: George Allen and Unwin, 1953), pp. 711–713.

85. See also the argument presented by Coburn in *Devī-Māhātmya,* pp. 150–151. I disagree with Coburn, who argues that the identification of *śakti* and *prakṛti* is implicit in this passage.

86. As Das remarks, in the Śvetāśvatara Upaniṣad we find for the first time the notion of an absolute God, designated sometimes by the generic term *deva* but also construed in personal terms as Īśvara, who is associated with a *śakti* belonging to him alone as his own power. See Das, *Śakti or Divine Power,* p. 57.

87. For a discussion of the doctrine of *śakti* in Mīmāṃsā and Nyāya, see Prabhat Chandra Chakravarti, *Doctrine of Sakti in Indian*

Literature (Patna: Eastern Book House, 1940), pp. 34–44.

88. See Dasgupta, *History of Indian Philosophy,* vol. 1, pp. 279–280, 305; and Sharma, *Critical Survey of Indian Philosophy,* p. 175. Dasgupta locates the Vaiśeṣika-Sūtras before Caraka, whom he dates in the first century, since Caraka "not only quotes one of the *Vaiśeṣika sūtras,* but the whole foundation of his medical physics is based on the Vaiśeṣika physics." He believes that the sūtras are probably pre-Buddhistic. Sharma asserts that the Vaiśeṣika system is "certainly not later than Buddhism and Jainism."

89. Vaiśeṣika-Sūtra 1.1.2–4.

90. Vaiśeṣika-Sūtra 5.1.15, 5.2.2, 5.2.7, 5.2.17.

91. Vaiśeṣika-Sūtra 5.2.18. See also Dasgupta, *History of Indian Philosophy,* vol. 1, pp. 283, 292. Dasgupta observes that the categories that are unexplained by known experience are attributed to *adṛṣṭa* and constitute "the acts on which depend all life-processes of animals and plants, the continuation of atoms or the construction of the worlds, natural motion of fire and air, death and rebirth." Commenting on this particular passage, he observes that "with the absence of *adṛṣṭa* there is no contact of body with soul, and thus there is no rebirth, and therefore mokṣa (salvation)."

92. Vaiśeṣika-Sūtra 6.2.2.

93. Vaiśeṣika-Sūtra 10.2.8. See also Dasgupta, *History of Indian Philosophy,* vol. 1, pp. 282–283.

94. For a discussion of the place of cosmogonic elements in early Vaiśeṣika, see Frauwallner, *History of Indian Philosophy,* vol. 2, pp. 61–64; and Nandalal Sinha, trans., *The Vaiśeṣika Sūtras of Kaṇāda [with the commentary of Śaṅkara Miśra and extracts from the gloss of Jayanārāyaṇa, together with notes from the commentary of Candrakānta and an introduction by the translator]* (Delhi: S. N. Publications, 1986), pp. xxx–xxxiii. In later Nyāya-Vaiśeṣika, the cosmogonic import of the *adṛṣṭa* is clearly designated in the work of Praśastapāda (ca. sixth century). For discussion of such later formulations, see Dasgupta, *History of Indian Philosophy,* vol. 1, pp. 323–325; and Frauwallner, *History of Indian Philosophy,* vol. 2, pp. 146–147.

95. *Ślokavarttika, Codanāsūtra* 199.

96. *Ślokavarttika, Śūnyavāda* 249–254.

97. See, for example, *Ślokavarttika, Vanavāda* 86 and *Sambandhākṣepaparihāra* 11. See also Das, *Śakti or Divine Power,* pp. 227–228.

98. See Gaṅgānātha Jhā, *Pūrva-Mīmāṃsā in Its Sources,* 2d ed.

(Varanasi: Banaras Hindu University, 1964), p. 55; and A. B. Keith, *The Karma-Mīmāṃsā* (Calcutta: Association Press, 1921), pp. 52, 55.

99. Yoga-Sūtra 4.34.

100. There has been much scholarly analysis of the notion of *māyā* as *śakti* in Śaṅkara's thought, and I will not attempt to reproduce such discussion here. For a good summary, see chapter five, "The Māyā Vāda in Śaṇkara," in Devanandan, *Concept of Māyā*; and "Śakti in Different Schools of Vedānta," in Chakravarti, *Doctrine of Śakti in Indian Literature.* See also O'Neil, *Māyā in Śaṅkara.*

101. See Gerald J. Larson, "The Sources for *Śakti* in Abhinavagupta's Kāsmīr Śaivism: A Linguistic and Aesthetic Category," *Philosophy East and West* 24, no. 1 (January 1974): 48. As Larson notes, the meaning of any phrase in Sanskrit is expressed by the inflection of the words, since syntax has very little importance in the construction of sentences or phrases.

102. *Vākyapadīya* 1.1. See also Gaurinath Sastri, *The Philosophy of Word and Meaning* (1959: reprint, Calcutta: Sanskrit College, 1983), p. 20.

103. *Vākyapadīya* 1.2. See also Sastri, *Philosophy of Word and Meaning,* pp. 15–16.

104. *Vākyapadīya* 1.3. See also Sastri, *Philosophy of Word and Meaning,* pp. 28–29.

105. *Vākyapadīya* 1.44ff. and 2.31; and Sastri, *Philosophy of Word and Meaning,* pp. 66–67.

106. *Vākyapadīya* 1.142. There is some variation on the numbering of this verse in the various editions of the *Vākyapadīya,* and it is sometimes listed as 1.143.

107. *Vṛtti* on 1.142 (143). The *vṛtti* is usually attributed to Bhartṛhahri himself, although there is some disagreement about this. For a discussion of the various positions and arguments regarding the authorship of the *vṛtti,* see K. A. Subramania Iyer, trans., *The Vākyapadīyā of Bhartṛhari with the Vṛtti, Chapter I* (Poona: Deccan College Postgraduate and Research Institute, 1965), pp. xvi–xxxvii.

108. See also Harold G. Coward, *Bhartṛhari* (Boston: Twayne Publishers, 1976), pp. 47–48.

109. Besides those studies mentioned in notes above or below, see also, for example, Douglas Renfrew Brooks, *The Secret of the Three*

Cities: An Introduction to Hindu Śākta Tantrism (Chicago: University of Chicago Press, 1990); Mark S. G. Dyczkowski, *The Aphorisms of Śiva: The Śiva Sūtra with Bhāskara's Commentary, the Vārttika* (Albany: State University of New York Press, 1992) and *The Doctrine of Vibration: An Analysis of the Doctrines and Practices of Kashmir Shaivism* (Delhi: Motilal Banarsidass, 1989); and Paul Muller-Ortega, *The Triadic Heart of Śiva* (Albany: State University of New York Press, 1989).

110. Sanjukta Gupta, Dirk Jan Hoens, and Teun Goudriaan, *Hindu Tantrism* (Leiden: E. J. Brill, 1979), p. 17.

111. See Padoux, *Vāc*, pp. 23–24.

112. Gupta and Goudriaan, *Hindu Tantric and Śākta Literature*, p. 9.

113. Ernest A. Payne, *The Saktas: An Introductory and Comparative Study* (1933; reprint, New York and London: Garland Publishing, Inc., 1979), p. 72.

114. See Padoux, *Vāc*, pp. 45–46.

115. Lakṣmī Tantra 11.1–2.

116. Lakṣmī Tantra 31.77.

117. See, for example, Lakṣmī Tantra 4.5, 14.3, 18.20.

118. Lakṣmī Tantra 21.4–6. In her translation of this text, Sanjukta Gupta indicates that the *kalās* are the six divine attributes of Viṣṇu-Nārāyaṇa: knowledge (*jñāna*), sovereignty (*aiśvarya*), power (*śakti*), strength (*bala*), virility (*vīrya*), and energy (*tejas*). See Sanjukta Gupta, trans., *Lakṣmī Tantra: A Pāñcarātra Text* (Leiden: E. J. Brill, 1972), pp. 114–115, n. 2. For further discussion of creation according to Pāñcarātra, see also Gupta's "The Pāñcarātra Attitude to Mantra," in *Understanding Mantras*, edited by Harvey P. Alper (Albany: State University of New York Press, 1989), pp. 224–248, especially pp. 224–225, 228–229; and F. Otto Schrader, *Introduction to the Pāñcarātra and the Ahirbudhnya Saṃhitā*, 2d ed. (Madras: The Adyar Library and Research Centre, 1973).

119. Lakṣmī Tantra 18.19ff.

120. *Parātrīśikā-Vivaraṇa* of Abhinavagupta, p. 29 of the Sanskrit text given in *Parātrīśikā-vivaraṇa: The Secret of Tantric Mysticism*, edited by Bettina Bäumer, translated by Jaideva Singh, Abhinavagupta's Sanskrit text edited by Swami Lakshmanjee (Delhi: Motilal Banarsidass, 1988). This book has also been published in identical form in the United States as *A Trident of Wisdom* (Albany: State University of New York Press, 1989). I have followed fairly closely

Singh's translation (p. 77 of the English translation).

121. *Parātrīśikā-Vivaraṇa*, pp. 29–30 of the Sanskrit text (pp. 77–80 of Singh's translation). See also pp. 3–4 (pp. 8–12 of Singh's translation).

122. See also Padoux, *Vāc*, especially pp. 78–80.

Chapter Three. The Feminine Principle in Purāṇic Cosmogony and Cosmology

1. Mahābhārata, Śalya-Parvan 41.31 and Harivaṃśa 2.3.13, 18.

2. Evidence of this kind of tradition appears in the Harivaṃśa and especially in the Devī-Māhātmya, which is usually dated around the sixth century.

3. Kinsley, *Hindu Goddesses*, p. 132.

4. I am borrowing the metaphor of crystallization from Thomas Coburn, who has subtitled his first study of the Devī-Māhātmya "the crystallization of the Goddess tradition."

For the dates of the various Purāṇas, see Rocher, *The Purāṇas*. Rocher summarizes various scholars' arguments concerning the dating of the Purāṇic literature, and the dates that I give are generally derived from Rocher's discussions, unless otherwise noted. It must be said that many of the Purāṇas cannot be dated with any precision; many appear to have been compiled slowly over the course of many centuries, and the age of several of the Purāṇas is greatly contested.

5. In Coburn's study of the Devī-Māhātmya, he examines all the epithets used to describe the Goddess. He notes that the term *mahāmāyā* occurs seven times, *prakṛti* three times, and *śakti,* four times. For his remarks on these three epithets of the Goddess, see his *Devī-Māhātmya,* pp. 123–127, 180–186, 146–153.

The best available translation of the Devī-Māhātmya is Thomas Coburn's translation found in his book *Encountering the Goddess: A Translation of the Devī-Māhātmya and a Study of Its Interpretation* (Albany: State University of New York Press, 1991), pp. 32–84.

6. Devī-Māhātmya 1.48 (1.66).

7. Devī-Māhātmya 1.49–78 (1.67–104). This story first appears in the Mahābhārata, where it is told from a Vaiṣṇava perspective. For a history of this story, see Coburn, *Devī-Māhātmya,* pp. 211–221. See also Veena Dās, "The Goddess and the Demon—An

Analysis of the Devi Mahatmya," *Manushi,* no. 30 (1985): 30. The story is also repeated with some variations in other Purāṇas, including the Śiva Purāṇa, Umā-Saṃhitā 45.47–69, recounted below, and the Devī-Bhāgavata Purāṇa, I.6–7. For a comparison of the versions in the Devī-Māhātmya and the Devī-Bhāgavata as well as a detailed discussion of the myth, see Brown, *Triumph of the Goddess,* pp. 83–94.

Both Brown and Coburn discuss at greater length this story as well as the two other main stories of her exploits—her victory over the demon Mahiṣa and her defeat of Śumbha and Niśumbha. See Brown, *Triumph of the Goddess,* pp. 81–131; and Coburn, *Devī-Māhātmya,* pp. 209–241, and *Encountering the Goddess,* pp. 22–24.

8. Devī-Māhātmya 2.1–12 (2.1–13). This story reappears in variable form in several other Purāṇas as well.

9. Devī-Māhātmya 11.3–4 (11.4–5).

10. Throughout this chapter, I capitalize the names of cosmic principles, such as *prakṛti, māyā, mahāmāyā, śakti,* and so forth, when they are used as epithets of the Great Goddess and designate her status as an independent, supreme goddess. Similarly, I capitalize *puruṣa* when it is used as an epithet of the god identified as Brahman.

11. See, for example, Devī-Māhātmya 1.47 (1.64), 4.6 (4.7).

12. Devī-Māhātmya 11.10 (11.11).

13. Devī-Māhātmya 5.18 (5.32–34), 1.63 (1.82).

14. Thomas Coburn, "Consort of None, *Śakti* of All: The Vision of the *Devī-Māhātmya,*" in *The Divine Consort: Rādhā and the Goddesses of India,* edited by John S. Hawley and Donna Marie Wulff (Berkeley: Berkeley Religious Studies Series, 1982; reprint, Boston: Beacon Press, 1986), p. 160.

15. Devī-Māhātmya 1.42–43 (1.55–56).

16. See Coburn, "Consort of None," pp. 155–156.

17. Devī-Māhātmya 1.59 (1.78). See also Coburn, "Consort of None," p. 156.

18. Coburn, *Encountering the Goddess,* p. 16.

19. Manu-Smṛti 1.5–13. See Holdrege, *Veda and Torah,* ms. pp. 85–86.

20. Matsya Purāṇa 2.25–32. The dates that I give for this Purāṇa are those proposed by P. V. Kane, but other scholars propose dates ranging from the fourth century B.C.E. to 1250 C.E.

See Rocher, *The Purāṇas,* p. 199.

21. See Holdrege, *Veda and Torah,* ms. pp. 111–115.

22. There is some dispute in the Purāṇas themselves with respect to exactly which texts should be included in which list. The main disagreement concerns whether the Śiva Purāṇa should be included as a Mahā-Purāṇa replacing the Vāyu Purāṇa or whether it should be classified as an Upa-Purāṇa. If we include both, the result is a list of nineteen Purāṇas: Agni, Bhāgavata, Bhaviṣya, Brahma, Brahmāṇḍa, Brahmavaivarta, Garuḍa, Kūrma, Liṅga, Mārkaṇḍeya, Matsya, Nārada, Padma, Skanda, Śiva, Vāmana, Varāha, Vāyu, and Viṣṇu.

23. The dates that I give for this Purāṇa are those proposed by P. V. Kane, but other scholars propose dates ranging from 700 B.C.E. to ca. 1045 C.E. See Rocher, *The Purāṇas,* p. 249.

24. See, for example, Viṣṇu Purāṇa, 1.3. Such time calculations are found in most of the Purāṇas, with some variation in the length of the individual *yugas*.

25. Brown, *Triumph of the Goddess,* pp. 7–8. Brown is not alone in his frustrations. Many of the Purāṇas cannot be dated with any real precision. Scholars disagree about when they were recorded, and much of the material found in these texts remained oral for a long time before it was written down. It is thus difficult to determine the relative age of the various texts.

26. The dates that I give for this Purāṇa are those proposed by P. V. Kane, but other scholars propose dates ranging from the fourth century B.C.E. to 1000 C.E. See Rocher, *The Purāṇas,* p. 157.

27. These are the dates proposed by R. C. Hazra, *Studies in the Purāṇic Record on Hindu Rites and Customs,* 2d ed. (Delhi: Motilal Banarsidass, 1975), p. 144. Hazra also notes that the Uttara Khaṇḍa is a later addition. See also Rocher, *The Purāṇas,* p. 177. The Garuḍa Purāṇa appears to have been compiled over a long period of time in several stages. Many scholars have proposed that the date of the text as a whole cannot be fixed. Rather, they have dated different sections of the text separately, ranging from the first century C.E. up to the eleventh century.

28. Although the Devī-Bhāgavata is generally held to be an Upa-Purāṇa and is not included in most lists of the Mahā-Purāṇas, I nevertheless include it in my analysis because of its importance in the Śākta tradition. Furthermore, Brown has argued in his

introduction to *Triumph of the Goddess* that the status of the Devī-Bhāgavata is actually somewhat open to discussion (see especially pp. 5–6, 17–24). In this book, Brown also shows that the Devī-Bhāgavata is heavily influenced by the Devī-Māhātmya, the Brahmavaivarta Purāṇa, and the Bhāgavata Purāṇa, all of which are included in the standard list of Mahā-Purāṇas. The form and content of the Devī-Bhāgavata are thus shaped substantially by the Mahā-Purāṇic tradition.

29. For an extensive discussion of the relationship between the Devī-Māhātmya and the Devī-Bhāgavata Purāṇa, see Brown, *Triumph of the Goddess,* especially pp. 81–176.

30. Madeleine Biardeau, *Cosmogonies Purāṇiques,* Études de Mythologie Hindoue, tome 1 (Paris: École Française D'Éxtrême Orient, 1981), pp. 14–24. See also Greg Bailey, *The Mythology of Brahmā* (Delhi: Oxford University Press, 1983), pp. 85–103.

31. "[L]es deux entités sont très exactement complémentaires . . . et ne peuvent être pensées l'une sans l'autre." See *Cosmogonies Purāṇiques,* p. 14.

32. Ibid. Biardeau gives the following list:

Pradhāna	**Puruṣa**
Brahman	Brahmā
Prakṛti	Svayambhū
	Īśvara
	Nārāyaṇa
Avyakta	Vyaktāvyakta
Jagadyoni	Jaganmaya
Sadasadātmaka	Sthūlasukṣmātman
Sadasatpara	Ekānekasvarūpa
	Sṛjya, Sargakartṛ
	Hiranyagarbha

33. See, for example, Viṣṇu Purāṇa 1.2.29–49; Brahma Purāṇa 1.34–36; and Vāyu Purāṇa 4.15–61. Biardeau discusses the evolution of the *tattvas* in fair detail. See Biardeau, *Cosmogonies Purāṇiques,* pp. 16–24.

34. See, for example, Brahmāṇḍa Purāṇa 1.1.3.13.

35. Brahma Purāṇa 1.34, 1.38–39.

36. Mārkaṇḍeya Purāṇa 46.9.

37. Viṣṇu Purāṇa 1.2.21; Mārkaṇḍeya Purāṇa 46.12.

38. See Daniel P. Sheridan, *The Advaitic Theism of the Bhāgavata Purāṇa* (Delhi: Motilal Banarsidass, 1986), especially chapter two.

39. Bhāgavata Purāṇa 2.5.4–5.

40. Bhāgavata Purāṇa 1.3.30–31.

41. The description of *māyā* as having three *guṇas* is found elsewhere in the text as well. See, for example, 2.5.18, 3.5.26, and 11.6.8. As discussed in chapter two, the description of *māyā* as possessed of three *guṇas* is also found in Bhagavad-Gītā 7.14.

42. Bhāgavata Purāṇa 3.5.23–27.

43. See Sheridan, *Advaitic Theism*, pp. 31–35. Sheridan emphasizes that the term *māyā* is used in the Bhāgavata Purāṇa to indicate the creative power of Bhagavān. The term *śakti* is also used to designate this creative power. The association of Viṣṇu/Bhagavān with a fundamental energy that is the source of creation is found throughout the text. See, for example, 2.5.5, "You create all beings . . . having taken hold of your own power (*ātmaśakti*)"; and 8.1.13, "By means of his own power (*ātmaśakti*), which is uncreated, he brings about the creation, and so forth (*janmādi*) of the world."

44. Bhāgavata Purāṇa 3.5.28–29.

45. See, for example, Bhāgavata Purāṇa 2.9.33.

46. In terms of the major schools of Vedānta philosophy, this position of both identity and difference represents the position of the school of Viśiṣṭādvaita Vedānta, the prime exponent of which is Rāmānuja. It should also be said that Rāmānuja takes the theistic tendency found in the narrative Brahmanical tradition more seriously than do other philosophers and attempts to reconcile philosophical absolutism with personal theism.

47. Kūrma Purāṇa 2.3.1–15.

48. Kūrma Purāṇa 2.3.21–22.

49. Kūrma Purāṇa 2.4.18–19.

50. Kūrma Purāṇa 2.4.20–23.

51. Kūrma Purāṇa 2.6.5–9, 51.

52. See also Bailey, *Mythology of Brahmā*, pp. 103–121; and Biardeau, *Cosmogonies Purāṇiques*, pp. 44-90.

53. See, for example, Agni Purāṇa 17.9–10; Brahma Purāṇa 1.40–42; Matsya Purāṇa 2.28–32; Viṣṇu Purāṇa 1.2.50ff.

54. See, for example, Brahmāṇḍa Purāṇa 1.1.5.1–28; Vāyu Purāṇa 6.6–32; Padma Purāṇa 1.3.25–56; Viṣṇu Purāṇa 1.4.1–8

and 45–52; Mārkaṇḍeya Purāṇa 47.6–14.

55. Viṣṇu Purāṇa 1.4.7–8.

56. Viṣṇu Purāṇa 1.4.11–52.

57. Bhāgavata Purāṇa 3.8.10–3.10.9.

58. See, for example, Brahmāṇḍa Purāṇa 1.1.5.29–58; Vāyu Purāṇa 6.38–60; Padma Purāṇa 1.3.61–82; Viṣṇu Purāṇa 1.5.1–26.

59. Although it is not explicitly stated that the *kaumāra* creation consists of the mind-born progeny of Brahmā, this does in fact seem to be the case. Biardeau also believes that this is probably so. See Biardeau, *Cosmogonies Purāṇiques,* p. 48. See also Mahābhārata 12.176.2–16, quoted on pp. 76-77, where the creator Mānasa is said to create by means of his mind.

60. See, for example, Vāyu Purāṇa 9.2–22; Brahmāṇḍa Purāṇa 1.2.8.2–30; Padma Purāṇa 1.3.84–97; Viṣṇu Purāṇa 1.5.28–67.

61. Brahma Purāṇa 1.52–53.

62. See, for example, Brahmāṇḍa Purāṇa 1.2.9.31–36.

63. Viṣṇu Purāṇa 1.7.9–13. See also Mārkaṇḍeya Purāṇa 50.4–10; Padma Purāṇa 1.3.172–173.

64. See, for example, Viṣṇu Purāṇa 1.7.14–17; Mārkaṇḍeya Purāṇa 50.11–15; Padma Purāṇa 1.3.174–179.

65. Matsya Purāṇa 3.30–32.

66. Matsya Purāṇa 3.33–35.

67. Matsya Purāṇa 3.43–47.

68. Padma Purāṇa 1.6.2.

69. Brahma Purāṇa 1.56–59.

70. Brahma Purāṇa 1.99–107. See also Brahmāṇḍa Purāṇa 1.2.9.37–38; Vāyu Purāṇa 10.12–13.

71. Brahmāṇḍa Purāṇa 1.2.9.14–15, 32–33.

72. Vāyu Purāṇa 9.75–85.

73. Brahma Purāṇa 34.24–25.

74. Bhāgavata Purāṇa 6.19.11–13.

75. Kūrma Purāṇa 1.1.34–38.

76. Kūrma Purāṇa 1.1.57–58.

77. Kūrma Purāṇa 1.2.7–10.

78. Kūrma Purāṇa 1.4.5ff.

79. These are the dates proposed by Hazra, who dates different chapters and sections of the Purāṇa separately. He argues that this section, the "Triśakti-Māhātmya," is quite late but not later than 1400 C.E. See Hazra, *Studies in the Purāṇic Records,* pp. 103–106. Not

all scholars agree with Hazra. In his own discussion of this passage, for example, Brown gives various scholars' views on its age and acknowledges the dates given by Hazra, but he himself dates this section no later than the ninth century C.E. See Brown, *Triumph of the Goddess,* pp. 135–136, 268, n. 21.

80. Varāha Purāṇa 89.3–28 in the Sanskrit edition, 90.3–28 in *Varaha Purāṇa,* translated by S. V. Iyer, Ancient Indian Tradition and Mythology Series, vols. 31–32 (Delhi: Motilal Banarsidass, 1985). For this Purāṇa, the numbering of passages in the English translation deviates slightly from the numbering given in the critical Sanskrit edition. I provide first the reference for the passage in the Sanskrit text and then, in parentheses, the corresponding passage in the translation.

81. Varāha Purāṇa 89.27–29 (90.29–32).

82. Varāha Purāṇa 90.1–12 (91.1–12).

83. Varāha Purāṇa 95.59–61 (96.63–65).

84. Varāha Purāṇa 94.57 (95.62), (144.47). The identification of the Vaiṣṇavī *śakti* as Mahāmāyā, the mother of the universe (*jaganmātṛ*), Prakṛti, and Pradhāṇa is quoted in the translation in 144.47 but does not appear in the text of the critical edition. It is, however, cited on page 803 of the critical edition as a variant found in the printed Veṅkateśvara edition of the Varāha Purāṇa (Bombay: Veṅkateśvara Press, 1929).

85. Varāha Purāṇa 89.34–36 (90.37–39).

86. Varāha Purāṇa 89.37–41 (90.40–45).

87. Varāha Purāṇa 21.5–6 in both the Sanskrit edition and the translation.

88. Varāha Purāṇa 21.2–13 in both the Sanskrit edition and the translation.

89. The six *guṇa*s are: *jñāna* (knowledge), *aiśvarya* (lordship), *śakti* (power), *bala* (strength), *vīrya* (virility or energy), and *tejas* (splendor). For more on the six *guṇa*s, see Schrader, *Introduction to the Pāñcarātra,* pp. 37–39.

90. Garuḍa Purāṇa 3.3.12–14.

91. Garuḍa Purāṇa 3.3.15–16.

92. Garuḍa Purāṇa 3.3.19.

93. Garuḍa Purāṇa 3.3.24–25.

94. Garuḍa Purāṇa 3.3.25–26.

95. Garuḍa Purāṇa 3.3.57–58. Cf. Bhāgavata Purāṇa 3.5.23–27

discussed above, pp. 133-134.

96. Garuḍa Purāṇa 3.4.1–3. Śrī is another name for Lakṣmī, and Bhū is the same as Pṛthivī, the goddess earth. See also 3.11.4–5 cited below, which states that *prakṛti* assumes the forms of Lakṣmī and the earth (= Śrī and Bhū).

97. Garuḍa Purāṇa 3.4.4–6, 10–11. Note that the correlation of *guṇas* and gods found here is different from that found in the Varāha Purāṇa, where Brahmā is associated with the sattvic goddess and Viṣṇu is associated with the rajasic goddess.

98. Garuḍa Purāṇa 3.5.1ff.

99. Garuḍa Purāṇa 3.11.1–5.

100. Nārada Purāṇa, Pūrva-Khaṇḍa 3.3–6.

101. Nārada Purāṇa, Pūrva-Khaṇḍa 3.7–9.

102. Nārada Purāṇa, Pūrva-Khaṇḍa 3.10–12.

103. Nārada Purāṇa, Pūrva-Khaṇḍa 3.13–15. In his translation of this text, G. V. Tagare notes that "Although the *purāṇa*-writer appears to give synonyms of *Vaiṣṇavī śakti,* he is actually describing or summarizing the various aspects of this potency. Thus *Māyā* emphasizes the illusive power, *Vidyā,* the Spiritual Knowledge, *Avidyā,* Nescience, *Parā Prakṛti,* the Supreme Primordial nature, and the *Śaktis* of various gods like Brāhmī, Aindrī, etc. are given to emphasize that whatever feats these gods achieve are due to the motive force of Viṣṇu." See *The Nārada Purāṇa,* translated by G. V. Tagare, Ancient Indian Tradition and Mythology Series, vols. 15–19 (Delhi: Motilal Banarsidass, 1980–1982), vol. 15, p. 97, n. 4.

104. Nārada Purāṇa, Pūrva-Khaṇḍa 3.27.

105. Nārada Purāṇa, Pūrva–Khaṇḍa 3.28–32.

106. These sections appear to be late additions and might be dated after 1000 C.E. See Hazra, *Studies in the Purāṇic Records,* pp. 129–133.

107. Nārada Purāṇa, Uttara-Khaṇḍa 59.2–9.

108. Nārada Purāṇa, Uttara-Khaṇḍa 59.8.

109. Nārada Purāṇa, Pūrva-Khaṇḍa 83.10–11, 83.44, 82.214.

110. Nārada Purāṇa, Pūrva-Khaṇḍa 83.32.

111. Nārada Purāṇa, Pūrva-Khaṇḍa 83.9–13, 16.

112. Nārada Purāṇa, Pūrva-Khaṇḍa 83.13–28.

113. Nārada Purāṇa, Pūrva-Khaṇḍa 83.17–18.

114. See, for example, Nārada Purāṇa, Pūrva-Khaṇḍa 83.44–47.

115. Nārada Purāṇa, Uttara-Khaṇḍa 58.45ff.

116. Brahmavaivarta Purāṇa, Prakṛti-Khaṇḍa 1.4–8.

117. Brahmavaivarta Purāṇa, Prakṛti-Khaṇḍa 2.10.

118. C. Mackenzie Brown, *God as Mother: A Feminine Theology in India; An Historical and Theological Study of the Brahmavaivarta Purāṇa* (Hartford, Vt.: Claude Stark and Co., 1974), pp. 123–139. I have reversed the order to emphasize that in the first pair, the active pole of *prakṛti/śakti* is emphasized, whereas in the other three, it is the material dimension that is emphasized.

119. Brown, *God as Mother,* pp. 128–129.

120. Brahmavaivarta Purāṇa, Prakṛti-Khaṇḍa 2.74–76.

121. Brahmavaivarta Purāṇa, Prakṛti-Khaṇḍa 55.86–87.

122. See Brown, *God as Mother,* pp. 130–132.

123. Brahmavaivarta Purāṇa, Kṛṣṇa-Janma-Khaṇḍa 6.215–216. See also ibid., pp. 132–133.

124. Brahmavaivarta Purāṇa, Brahma-Khaṇḍa 28.23–24. For a discussion of *nirguṇa* as an epithet of *prakṛti,* see Brown, *God as Mother,* pp. 134–136.

125. See, for example, Brahmavaivarta Purāṇa, Prakṛti-Khaṇḍa 1.12.

126. For a detailed discussion of the five forms of *prakṛti* and the historical roots of this concept, see Brown, *God as Mother,* pp. 142–167.

127. Brown notes that sometimes not just women but all beings, both male and female, are said to be derived from Prakṛti. He cites as an example Prakṛti-Khaṇḍa 12.14. See ibid., p. 195.

128. Ibid., p. 121. See also Prakṛti-Khaṇḍa 55.52, 65.25–26.

129. Brahmavaivarta Purāṇa, Prakṛti-Khaṇḍa 54.88–91.

130. Brahmavaivarta Purāṇa, Prakṛti-Khaṇḍa 55.77.

131. Brahmavaivarta Purāṇa, Brahma-Khaṇḍa 3.1ff., 5.25–26.

132. Brahmavaivarta Purāṇa, Brahma-Khaṇḍa 6.56.

133. See Brown, *God as Mother,* chapter nine.

134. Brahmavaivarta Purāṇa, Prakṛti-Khaṇḍa 2.27–29.

135. Brahmavaivarta Purāṇa, Prakṛti-Khaṇḍa 2.30–32.

136. Brahmavaivarta Purāṇa, Prakṛti-Khaṇḍa 2.33–53. See also Prakṛti-Khaṇḍa 54.112–117 and Gaṇeśa-Khaṇḍa 45.21ff. In this last passage, it is Durgā who is equated with *prakṛti,* and the account of Prakṛti's division into five goddesses and the model of creation by copulation are conflated. After Kṛṣṇa makes love to the goddess and various creations come into being, she then

divides herself further into five goddesses.

137. Brahmavaivarta Purāṇa, Prakṛti-Khaṇḍa 3.1–3.

138. Brahmavaivarta Purāṇa, Prakṛti-Khaṇḍa 3.48ff. This passage resembles the above-discussed account of the *pratisarga* found in the Bhāgavata Purāṇa, where Brahmā, who is identified as the second self of Viṣṇu, dives into the waters hoping to find the ground from which the lotus has sprung. Failing to find the bottom of the cosmic ocean, he propitiates Viṣṇu-Nārāyaṇa.

139. Brown, *God as Mother,* pp. 140–141. See also Brown, *Triumph of the Goddess,* pp. ix–x.

140. Kūrma Purāṇa 1.11.2–6.

141. Kūrma Purāṇa 1.11.7–13.

142. Kūrma Purāṇa 1.11.22–30.

143. Kūrma Purāṇa 1.11.34–35.

144. Kūrma Purāṇa 1.11.42–47.

145. Kūrma Purāṇa 1.11.40–41.

146. Kūrma Purāṇa 1.11.224.

147. Kūrma Purāṇa 1.11.222.

148. Liṅga Purāṇa 1.3.1–3.

149. Liṅga Purāṇa 1.3.4–12.

150. Liṅga Purāṇa 1.3.12–28. Cf. the discussion of Śvetāśvatara Upaniṣad 4.5 in chapter two, p. 68. There is another account of creation in chapter seventy of the Purāṇa that proposes a Sāṃkhya-type cosmology without interpreting *prakṛti* as feminine.

151. Liṅga Purāṇa 1.16.32–35.

152. Liṅga Purāṇa 1.87.13.

153. Liṅga Purāṇa 1.5.27–31.

154. Liṅga Purāṇa 1.41.39–56.

155. Liṅga Purāṇa 1.70.325–344.

156. Śiva Purāṇa, Rudra-Saṃhitā 1.6.8–18.

157. Śiva Purāṇa, Rudra-Saṃhitā 1.6.19–59.

158. Śiva Purāṇa, Umā-Saṃhitā 45.47–67. Although this account occurs in a Śaiva Purāṇa, it is Śākta in orientation, for the Goddess is extolled as the highest reality. Primordial Śakti is described as the great Brahman who alone creates, sustains, and destroys the universe. Thus it appears that she is conceived to be the supreme deity, higher than all other gods, including Śiva. She is also said to be the material cause of creation, the great *māyā* or Parameśvarī having three *guṇas*.

159. Śiva Purāṇa, Vāyavīya-Saṃhitā 1.16.6–11.

160. Śiva Purāṇa, Rudra-Saṃhitā 1.9.45–48.

161. Śiva Purāṇa, Rudra-Saṃhitā 1.16.41–42: "Having become Satī, Śivā was married by Śiva. At her father's sacrifice, having cast off her body, which she did not take again, she went back to her own region. And Sivā incarnated again as Pārvatī at the request of the *devas*. Having performed very severe austeries (*tapas*), she again attained Śiva."

162. Śiva Purāṇa, Rudra-Saṃhitā 2.24.35 and 3.6.45.

163. Śiva Purāṇa, Vāyavīya-Saṃhitā 1.16.15–1.17.2.

164. Śiva Purāṇa, Vāyavīya-Saṃhitā 1.16.18–20.

165. Śiva Purāṇa, Vāyavīya-Saṃhitā 1.17.1–2.

166. As Brown notes in *Triumph of the Goddess* (pp. x, 10, 145–147, and *passim*), the ninth book of the Devī-Bhāgavata Purāṇa corresponds closely to the Prakṛti-Khaṇḍa of the Brahmavaivarta Purāṇa, except that Devī replaces Viṣṇu as supreme deity. Because the mythological material is substantially the same in both Purāṇas, we will not address this portion of the Devī-Bhāgavata Purāṇa.

167. See, for example, Devī-Bhāgavata Purāṇa 1.2.4–5, 1.2.8, 1.2.19.

168. See, for example, Devī-Bhāgavata Purāṇa 1.2.10, 1.8.40, 1.12.51, 3.7.4–7, 3.25.39, 12.8.75.

169. See, for example, Devī-Bhāgavata Purāṇa 1.5.48.

170. Devī-Bhāgavata Purāṇa 7.29.7, 12.12.12.

171. Devī-Bhāgavata Purāṇa 3.3.37–40. See also Brown's discussion of this passage in *Triumph of the Goddess,* pp. 206–212.

172. Devī-Bhāgavata Purāṇa 1.5.58–61.

173. Devī-Bhāgavata Purāṇa 1.2.19–20. See also 3.24.36–38. The correlation of *guṇas* and goddesses parallels that of *guṇas* and gods given in the Garuḍa Purāṇa, where *sattva* is associated with Viṣṇu (Lakṣmī's consort), *rajas* with Brahmā (Sarasvatī's consort), and *tamas* with Śiva (Kālī's consort). See the discussion of the Garuḍa Purāṇa above.

C. Mackenzie Brown discusses this passage in relation to the "Triśakti-Māhātmya" of the Varāha Purāṇa and two of the six "limbs" attached to the Devī-Māhātmya. See Brown, *Triumph of the Goddess,* pp. 136–142.

174. Devī-Bhāgavata Purāṇa 1.2.21–22. 1.4.46–48 associates the

same three *śaktis* with the same gods, and asserts that the male divinities would be unable to fulfill their functions without their *śaktis*. See also 3.30.30, 3.30.34, and 5.19.2.

175. Devī-Bhāgavata Purāṇa 1.2.6–8.

176. 7.32.1–4. This chapter forms part of the Devī-Gītā, which comprises chapters 31–40 of the seventh Skandha. Brown discusses the Devī-Gītā at length in *Triumph of the Goddess,* pp. 179–200.

177. Devī-Bhāgavata Purāṇa 7.32.7, 7.33.1.

178. Devī-Bhāgavata Purāṇa 7.32.8. The term used, *samavāyitva,* usually indicates an intimate or inherent relation existing between or among entities. The term *samāvāyikāraṇa,* however, can indicate a material or substantial cause. In this context, the force of *samavāyitva* is probably the same as that of *samāvāyikāraṇa.*

179. Devī-Bhāgavata Purāṇa 7.33.1. See also 12.8.67.

180. Devī-Bhāgavata Purāṇa 7.32.42–43.

181. Devī-Bhāgavata Purāṇa 12.8.69–70.

182. Devī-Bhāgavata Purāṇa 3.10.15 and 3.3.51.

183. Devī-Bhāgavata Purāṇa 3.5.6, 12.8.76.

184. Devī-Bhāgavata Purāṇa 7.33.22–39. This description of the cosmos as the manifestation of the body of Brahman, here identified with the Goddess, parallels a similar description in Bhāgavata Purāṇa 2.6. Since the Bhāgavata Purāṇa is Vaiṣṇava in orientation, however, it identifies Brahman not as the Goddess but as Viṣṇu-Nārāyana. For more on some of the materials shared by the two Bhāgavatas, see Brown, *Triumph of the Goddess,* pp. 17–77.

Chapter Four. Concluding Remarks

1. Coburn, *Encountering the Goddess,* p. 172.

2. Kathleen Erndl, "The Goddess and Female Empowerment in Kangra, India," paper read at the American Academy of Religion Annual Meeting, San Francisco, Calif., November 21, 1992.

3. Cynthia Ann Humes, "Glorifying the Great Goddess or Great Woman? Interpretation of the *Devī-Māhātmya,* East and West," paper read at the Biannual International East Meets West Conference, Long Beach, Calif., April 9, 1993. See also Humes's article "Glorifying the Great Goddess or Great Woman? Hindu Women's Experience in Ritual Recitation of the Devi-Mahatmya,"

in *Women in Goddess Traditions,* edited by Karen King and Karen Torjesen (Minneapolis: Fortress Press, forthcoming).

4. Frederick M. Smith, "Indra's Curse, Varuṇa's Noose," in *Roles and Rituals for Hindu Women,* edited by Julia Leslie (London: Pinter Publishers, 1991), p. 26.

5. William S. Sax, *Mountain Goddess: Gender and Politics in a Himalayan Pilgrimage* (New York and Oxford: Oxford University Press, 1991).

6. This point was made by Erndl in her paper (cited above) and also by Mary McGee in the discussion following her paper "Domesticated Shakti: Empowerment through Marriage" read at the American Academy of Religion Annual Meeting, November 21, 1992.

7. See also Brown, *Triumph of the Goddess,* pp. 215–218.

8. See Kinsley, *Hindu Goddesses,* p. 144.

9. Kinsley, *Sword and the Flute,* p. 143.

10. Kinsley, *Hindu Goddesses,* p. 144.

11. Liṅga Purāṇa 1.106.20. See also Kinsley, *Hindu Goddesses,* p. 118.

12. See Kinsley, *Hindu Goddesses,* pp. 178–196. See also Diana L. Eck, "India's *Tīrthas*: 'Crossings' in Sacred Geography," *History of Religions* 20, no. 4 (May 1981): 323–344.

13. Wadley, "Women and the Hindu Tradition," p. 117.

14. Sherry B. Ortner, "Is Female to Male as Nature Is to Culture?" in *Women, Culture, and Society,* edited by Michelle Zimbalist Rosaldo and Louise Lamphere (Stanford, Calif.: Stanford University Press, 1974), pp. 73, 84.

15. It should also be noted that some *śākta* texts like the Devī-Bhāgavata Purāṇa offer a somewhat different interpretation of the Goddess's role in this regard, asserting that the Goddess offers both liberation from the world (*mukti*) and enjoyment of it (*bhukti*).

16. See also Mary Douglas, *Purity and Danger: An Analysis of the Concepts of Pollution and Taboo* (London: Routledge and Kegan Paul, 1966), pp. 94–96. Douglas notes that transitional states lie between states of order and, thus, represent disorder. Disorder, in turn, runs counter to culture, which depends on well-defined states of order. Because they threaten order, transitional states are both powerful and dangerous.

17. Veena Das, "Epilogue," in *Structure and Cognition,* 2d ed. (Delhi: Oxford University Press, 1982), pp. 143–144, cited in Frédérique A. Marglin, "Introduction," in *Purity and Auspiciousness in Indian Society,* edited by John B. Carman and Frédérique A. Marglin (Leiden: E. J. Brill, 1985), p. 4.

18. See T. N. Madan, "Concerning the Categories *Śubha* and *Śuddha* in Hindu Culture: An Exploratory Essay," Vasudha Narayan, "The Two Levels of Auspiciousness in Śrīvaiṣṇava Literature," and Frédérique A. Marglin, "Types of Oppositions in Hindu Culture," in *Purity and Auspiciousness in Indian Society,* pp. 24, 58, 79–80.

19. Marglin, "Types of Oppositions in Hindu Culture," pp. 80–81.

20. Lawrence A. Babb, *The Divine Hierarchy: Popular Hinduism in Central India* (New York: Columbia University Press, 1975), pp. 219–226.

21. David Shulman, *Tamil Temple Myths: Sacrifice and Divine Marriage in the South Indian Śaiva Tradition* (Princeton, N. J.: Princeton University Press, 1980), pp. 212, 223–226; and Wadley, "Women and the Hindu Tradition," pp. 118–119. Brown quotes both Babb and Shulman in his own discussion of this problem in *Triumph of the Goddess,* pp. 124ff.

22. Sax, *Mountain Goddess,* pp. 31–32.

23. Wendy Doniger O'Flaherty, *Women, Androgynes, and Other Mythical Beasts* (Chicago: University of Chicago Press, 1980), pp. 90–91.

24. See Brown, *Triumph of the Goddess,* pp. 122–125.

25. Stanley Kurtz, *All the Mothers Are One: Hindu India and the Cultural Reshaping of Psychoanalysis* (New York: Columbia University Press, 1992), pp. 20–26, especially pp. 24–25.

26. See also Wadley, "Women and the Hindu Tradition," pp. 118—19.

27. Manu-Smṛti 9.15.

28. I. Julia Leslie, *The Perfect Wife: The Orthodox Hindu Woman According to the Strīdharmapaddhati of Tryambakayajvan* (Delhi: Oxford University Press, 1989), p. 248.

29. Ibid., p. 320.

30. Sax, *Mountain Goddess,* p. 32.

31. O'Flaherty, *Women,* pp. 53–55.

32. See also Wadley, "Women and the Hindu Tradition," p. 115.

33. Ronald B. Inden and McKim Marriott, "Caste Systems," in *The New Encyclopaedia Britannica, Macropaedia,* 15th ed., vol. 3, s.v. "Caste Systems," p. 983b.

34. Wadley, "Women and the Hindu Tradition," pp. 117–119.

35. Mary McGee, "Desired Fruits: Motive and Intention in the Votive Rites of Hindu Women," in *Roles and Rituals for Hindu Women,* p. 78.

36. Vanaja Dhruvarajan, *Hindu Women and the Power of Ideology* (Granby, Mass.: Bergin and Garvey Publishers, 1989), p. 41.

37. Susan S. Wadley, "The Paradoxical Powers of Tamil Women," in *The Powers of Tamil Women,* edited by Susan S. Wadley, Foreign and Comparative Studies/South Asian Series, no. 6 (Syracuse, N. Y.: Maxwell School of Citizenship and Public Affairs, Syracuse University, 1980), p. 157.

38. See Wadley, "Women and the Hindu Tradition," pp. 122–123.

39. The formulation of the mother as residing at the threshold of nature and culture is that of Julia Kristeva. See, for example, her article "Hérétique de l'amour," *Tel Quel,* no. 74 (Winter 1977), reprinted as "Stabat Mater," translated by Leon S. Roudiez, in *The Kristeva Reader,* edited by Toril Moi (New York: Columbia University Press, 1986). See also Alison Ainley, "The Ethics of Sexual Difference," in *Abjection, Melancholia and Love: The Work of Julia Kristeva,* edited by John Fletcher and Andrew Benjamin, Warwick Studies in Philosophy and Literature (London and New York: Routledge, 1990), p. 58.

40. Wadley, "Women and the Hindu Tradition," p. 132.

41. Ibid., p. 134.

Bibliography

Primary Sources: Sanskrit Texts and Translations

Agni Purāṇa

Agnipurāṇa of Maharṣi Vedavyāsa. Edited by Achārya Baladeva Upādhyāya. Kashi Sanskrit Series, no. 174. Varanasi: Chowkhamba Sanskrit Series Office, 1966.

• *Translation:*

The Agni Purāṇa. Translated by N. Gangadharan. Ancient Indian Tradition and Mythology Series, vols. 27–30. Delhi: Motilal Banarsidass, 1984-1987.

Aitareya Āraṇyaka

The Aitareya Āraṇyaka. Edited and translated by Arthur Berriedale Keith. Oxford: Clarendon Press, 1909.

Aitareya Brāhmaṇa

The Aitareya Bráhmaṇa of the Ṛg-Veda, with the Commentary of Sáyaṇa Áchárya. Edited by Paṇḍit Satyavrata Sámaśramí. 4 vols. Bibliotheca Indica New Series, nos. 847, 849, 850, 852, and 861. Calcutta: Satya Press, 1895-1898.

• *Translation:*

Rigveda Brāhmaṇas: The Aitareya and Kauṣītaki Brāhmaṇas of the Rigveda. Translated by Arthur Berriedale Keith. Harvard Oriental Series, vol. 25. 1920. 2d Indian reprint, Delhi: Motilal Banarsidass, 1981.

Aitareya Upaniṣad

Aitareya Upaniṣad. In *Upaniṣatsaṅgrahaḥ,* edited by Paṇḍita Jagadīśa Śāstri. Delhi: Motilal Banarsidass, 1970.

• *Translations:*

Aitareya Upaniṣad. In *The Thirteen Principal Upanishads,* translated by Robert E. Hume. 2d ed., 4th impression. Delhi: Oxford University Press, 1988.

———. In *The Principal Upaniṣads,* edited and translated by S. Radhakrishnan. Sanskrit text with English translation. London: George Allen and Unwin, 1953.

Āpastamba Śrauta-Sūtra

The Śrauta Sūtra of Āpastamba, belonging to the Taittirīya Saṃhitā with the Commentary of Rudradatta. Edited by Richard Garbe. 2d ed. 3 vols. New Delhi: Munshiram Manoharlal, 1983.

• *Translation:*

Āpastamba Śrauta Sūtra. In *The Grihya-Sūtras,* translated by Herman Oldenberg and F. Max Müller. Sacred Books of the East, vol. 30. 1892. Reprint, Delhi: Motilal Banarsidass, 1964.

Atharva-Veda Saṃhitā

Atharva Veda Sanhita. Edited by R. Roth and W. D. Whitney. Berlin: Ferd. Dümmler's Verlagsbuchhandlung, 1856.

• *Translations:*

The Hymns of the Atharva Veda, Translated with a Popular Commentary. Translated by Ralph T. H. Griffith. 2 vols. Chowkhamba Sanskrit Series, no. 66. Varanasi: Chowkhamba Sanskrit Series Office, 1968.

Atharva-Veda-Saṃhitā. Translated by W. D. Whitney. Harvard Oriental Series, vols. 7-8. 1905. 2d Indian reprint ed., Delhi: Motilal Banarsidass, 1971.

Bhāgavata Purāṇa

Bhāgavata Purāṇa of Kṛṣṇa Dvaipāyana Vyāsa, with Sanskrit Commentary Bhāvārthabodhinī of Śrīdhārasvāmin. Edited by J. L. Shastri. Delhi: Motilal Banarsidass, 1983.

Śrīmad Bhāgavata Mahāpurāṇa, with Sanskrit Text and English Translation. Translated by C. L. Goswami. 2 vols. Gorakhpur: Gītā Press, 1971.

Brahma Purāṇa

Śrībrahmamahāpurāṇam. Edited by R. N. Sharma. 1906. Reprint, Delhi: Nag Publishers, 1985.

• *Translation:*

Brahma Purāṇa. Translated by a board of scholars. Ancient Indian Tradition and Mythology Series, vols. 33–36. Delhi: Motilal Banarsidass, 1985–1986.

Brahmāṇḍa Purāṇa

Brahmāṇḍa Purāṇa of Sage Kṛṣṇa Dvaipāyana Vyāsa. Edited by J. L. Shastri. Delhi: Motilal Banarsidass, 1973.

• *Translation:*

The Brahmāṇḍa Purāṇa. Translated by G. V. Tagare. Ancient Indian Tradition and Mythology Series, vols. 22–26. Delhi: Motilal Banarsidass, 1983–1984.

Brahma-Sūtra and Brahma-Sūtra Bhāṣya

Brahmasûtra Śânkara Bhâshya with the Commentaries Bhâmatî, Kalpatarû and Parîmala and with Index, etc. Edited by Pandit Vedanta Viśarada, Nurani Anantha Krishna Śastri, and Vâsudev Laxmaṇ Shâstrî Paṇsîkar. Bombay: Nirnaya Sagar Press, 1917.

• *Translation:*

Vedānta-Sūtras with the Commentary by Śaṅkarācārya. Translated by George Thibaut. Sacred Books of the East, vols. 34 and 38. 1904. Reprint, Delhi: Motilal Banarsidass, 1962.

Brahma-Sūtra Bhāṣya of Śaṅkarācārya. Translated by Swami Gambhirananda. 4th ed. Calcutta: Advaita Ashrama, 1983.

Brahmavaivarta Purāṇa

Brahmavaivartapurāṇa. Edited by Vināyaka Ganeśa Apte. 2 vols. Ānandāśrama Sanskrit Series, no. 102. Poona: Ānandāśrama Press, 1935.

• *Translation:*

The Brahma-Vaivarta Puranam. Translated by Rajendra Nath Sen. Sacred Books of the Hindus, vol. 24, parts 1 and 2. 1920–1922. Reprint, New York: AMS Press, 1974.

Bṛhadāraṇyaka Upaniṣad

Bṛhadāraṇyaka Upaniṣad. In *Upaniṣatsaṅgrahaḥ,* edited by Paṇḍita Jagadīśa Śāstri. Delhi: Motilal Banarsidass, 1970.

• *Translations:*

Bṛhadāraṇyaka Upaniṣad. In *The Thirteen Principal Upanishads,* translated by Robert E. Hume. 2d ed., 4th impression. Delhi: Oxford University Press, 1988.

———. In *The Principal Upaniṣads,* edited and translated by S. Radhakrishnan. Sanskrit text with English translation. London: George Allen and Unwin, 1953.

Chāndogya Upaniṣad

Chāndogya Upaniṣad. In *Upaniṣatsaṅgrahaḥ,* edited by Paṇḍita Jagadīśa Śāstri. Delhi: Motilal Banarsidass, 1970.

• *Translations:*

Chāndogya Upaniṣad. In *The Thirteen Principal Upanishads,* translated by Robert E. Hume. 2d ed., 4th impression. Delhi: Oxford University Press, 1988.

———. In *The Principal Upaniṣads,* edited and translated by S. Radhakrishnan. Sanskrit text with English translation. London: George Allen and Unwin, 1953.

Devī-Bhāgavata Purāṇa

Śrīmaddevībhāgavatam. Bombay: Veṅkaṭeśvara Press, 1918 or 1919.

• *Translation:*

The Sri Mad Devi Bhagavatam. Translated by Swami Vijnanananda [Hari Prasanna Chatterji]. Sacred Books of the Hindus, vol. 26, parts 1–4. 1921–1923. Reprint, New York: AMS Press, 1974.

Devī-Māhātmya

Devī-Māhātmya: The Glorification of the Great Goddess. Translated by Vasudeva S. Agrawala. Sanskrit text with English translation. Varanasi: All-India Kashiraj Trust, 1963.

Devi Mahatmyam (Glory of the Divine Mother): 700 Mantras on Sri Durga. Translated by Swami Jagadiswarananda. Sanskrit text with English translation. Madras: Sri Ramakrishna Math, n.d. [See also Coburn, *Encountering the Goddess,* below]

Garuḍa Purāṇa

Śrīgaruḍamahāpurāṇam. Edited by S. N. Sharma. 1906. Reprint, Delhi: Nag Publishers, 1984.

• *Translation:*

Garuḍa Purāṇa. Translated by a board of scholars. Ancient Indian Tradition and Mythology Series, vols. 12–14. Delhi: Motilal Banarsidass, 1978–1980.

Harivaṃśa

The Harivaṃśa, Being the Khila or Supplement to the Mahābhārata. Edited by Parashuram Lakshman Vaidya. Critical ed. 2 vols. Poona: Bhandarkar Oriental Research Institute, 1969–1971.

———. Bombay ed. Bombay: Veṅkateśvara Press, 1965.

• *Translations:*

Harivamsha, Translated into English prose from the original Sanskrit Text. Edited and translated by D. N. Bose. Dum Dum, Bengal: Datta Bose and Co., n.d.

Harivansa ou Histoire de la Famille de Hari, Ouvrage Formant un Appendice du Mahabharata, et Traduit sur l'Original Sanscrit. Translated into French by Simon A. Langlois. 2 vols. Oriental Translations Fund, no. 36. Paris: Printed for the Oriental Translation Fund of Great Britain and Ireland; London: Parbury, Allen, and Co., 1834–1835.

Jaiminīya Brāhmaṇa

Jaiminīya Brāhmaṇa (Complete) of the Sāmaveda. Edited by Raghu Vira and Lokesh Chandra. 3 vols. Sarasvati-Vihara Series. Nagpur: International Academy of Indian Culture, 1954.

• *Translations:*

Jaiminīya Brāhmaṇa I, 1–65. Translated by H. W. Bodewitz. Leiden: E. J. Brill, 1973.

The Jyotiṣṭoma Ritual: Jaiminīya Brāhmaṇa I, 66–364. Translated by H. W. Bodewitz. Leiden: E. J. Brill, 1990.

Kāṭhaka Saṃhitā

Yajurvedīya-Kāṭhaka-Saṃhitā. Edited by S. D. Sātavalekara. 4th ed. Pāraḍī: Svādhyāya Maṇḍala, 1983.

Kauṣītaki Brāhmaṇa

Śāṅkhāyana-Brāhmaṇaṃ [= Kauṣītaki Brāhmaṇa]. Edited by H. Bhattacharya. Calcutta Sanskrit College Research Series, no. 73. Calcutta: Sanskrit College, 1970.

• *Translation:*

The Rigveda Brāhmaṇas: The Aitareya and Kauṣītaki Brāhmaṇas of the Ṛg-Veda. Translated by Arthur Berriedale Keith. Harvard Oriental Series, vol. 25. 1920. Reprint, Delhi: Motilal Banarsidass, 1971.

Kūrma Purāṇa

Kūrma Purāṇa, with English Translation. Edited by Sri Anand Swarup Gupta, translated by A. Bhattacharya, S. Mukherji, V. K. Varma, and G. S. Rai. Varanasi: All India Kashi Raj Trust, 1972.

Lakṣmī Tantra

Lakṣmī-Tantra: A Pāñcarātra Āgama. Edited by Pandit V. Krishnamacharya. Adyar Library Series, vol. 87. Madras: The Adyar Library and Research Centre, 1959.

• *Translation:*

Lakṣmī-Tantra: A Pāñcarātra Text. Translated by Sanjukta Gupta. Leiden: E. J. Brill, 1972.

Liṅga Purāṇa

Liṅgapurāṇam. Edited by J. L. Shastri. Delhi: Motilal Banarsidass, 1980.

• *Translation:*

The Liṅga-Purāṇa. Translated by a board of scholars. Ancient Indian Tradition and Mythology Series, vols. 5–6. Delhi: Motilal Banarsidass, 1973.

Mahābhārata

The Mahābhārata. Edited by Vishnu S. Sukthankar, S. K. Belvalkar, and P. L. Vaidya. Critical ed. 19 vols. Poona: Bhandarkar Oriental Research Institute, 1933–1959.

• *Translations:*

The Mahabharata of Krishna-Dwaipayana Vyasa. Translated by Pratap Chandra Roy. 2d ed. 12 vols. Calcutta: Oriental Publishing Co., 1883–1896.

The Mahābhārata. Edited and translated by J. A. B. van Buitenen. Books 1–5. 3 vols. Chicago: University of Chicago Press, 1973–1978.

Maitrāyaṇī Saṃhitā

Maitrāyaṇī Saṃhitā: Die Saṃhitā der Maitrāyaṇīya-Śākhā. Edited by Leopold von Shroeder. Wiesbaden: Franz Steiner Verlag GmbH, 1972.

Maitri Upaniṣad

Maitri Upaniṣad. In *Upaniṣatsaṅgrahaḥ,* edited by Paṇḍita Jagadīśa Śāstri. Delhi: Motilal Banarsidass, 1970.

• *Translations:*

Maitri Upaniṣad. In *The Thirteen Principal Upanishads,* translated by Robert E. Hume. 2d ed., 4th impression. Delhi: Oxford University Press, 1988.

———. In *The Principal Upaniṣads,* edited and translated by S. Radhakrishnan. Sanskrit text with English translation. London: George Allen and Unwin, 1953.

Manu-Smṛti

Manu-Smṛti, with the 'Manubhāṣya' of Medhātithi. Edited by Gaṅgānātha Jhā. Bibliotheca Indica, no. 256. Calcutta: Asiatic Society of Bengal, 1932–1939.

• *Translation:*

The Laws of Manu, Translated with Extracts from Seven Commentaries. Translated by G. Bühler. Sacred Books of the East, vol. 25. 1886. Reprint, Delhi: Motilal Banarsidass, 1988.

Mārkaṇḍeya Purāṇa

The Mārcaṇḍeya Purāna. Edited by K. M. Banerjea. Bibliotheca Indica. Calcutta: Bishop's College Press, 1862.

• *Translation:*

Mārkaṇḍeya Purāṇa. Translated by F. Eden Pargiter. Bibliotheca Indica, New Series nos. 700, 706, etc. 1904. Reprint, Delhi: Indological Book House, 1969.

Matsya Purāṇa

Matsyamahāpurāṇam. Edited by Puṣpendra Śarman. 1895. Reprint, New Delhi: Meharchand Lachhmandas, 1984.

• *Translation:*

The Matsya Purāṇam. Translated by B. C. Majumdar, S. C. Vasu, H. H. Wilson, Bentley, Wilford, and others. Edited by Jamna Das Akhtar. Sacred Books of the Aryans Series. Delhi: Oriental Publishers, 1972.

Mīmāṃsā-Sūtra

The Mímámsá Darśana or *The Aphorisms of the Mimámsa by Jaimini, with the Commentary of Śavara-Svámin.* Edited by Paṇḍita Maheśachandra Nyáyaratna. 2 vols. Bibliotheca Indica, no. 45. 1873–1889. Reprint, Osnabrück: Biblio Verlag, 1983.

• *Translation:*

The Mīmāṃsā-Sūtras of Jaiminī. Translated by Pandit Mohan Lal Sandal. Sanskrit text with English translation. Sacred Books of the Hindus, vol. 27. 1923–1925. Reprint, New York: AMS Press, 1974.

Nārada Purāṇa

Śrīnāradīyamahāpurāṇam. 1923 or 1924. Reprint, Delhi: Nag Publishers, 1984.

• *Translation:*

The Nārada-Purāṇa. Translated by G. V. Tagare. Ancient Indian Tradition and Mythology Series, vols. 15–19. Delhi: Motilal Banarsidass, 1980–1982.

Nirukta

The Nighaṇṭu and the Nirukta: The Oldest Indian Treatise on Etymology, Philology, and Sementics [sic] Critically Edited from Original Manuscripts and Translated for the First Time into English, with Introduction, Exegetical and Critical Notes, Three Indexes and Eight Appendices. Edited and translated by Lakshman Sarup. 1920–1927. 2d reprint, Delhi: Motilal Banarsidass, 1967.

Nyāya-Sūtra

The Nyāya Sūtras of Gotama. Translated by M. M. Satisa Chandra Vidyābhūṣaṇa, revised and edited by Nandalal Sinha. Sanskrit text with English translation. Sacred Books of the Hindus, vol. 8. 1930. Reprint, Delhi: Motilal Banarsidass, 1981.

Padma Purāṇa

Padma Puranam. 2 vols. Gurumandal Series, no. 18. Calcutta: Manasukharāya Mora, 1957.

- *Translation:*

Padma-Purāṇa. Translated by N. A. Deshpande. Ancient Indian Tradition and Mythology Series, vols. 39–48. Delhi: Motilal Banarsidass, 1988–1992.

Pañcaviṃśa Brāhmaṇa

Táṇḍya Mahábráhmaṇa, with the Commentary of Sáyaṇa Áchárya [= Pañcaviṃśa Brāhmaṇa]. Edited by Ánandachandra Vedántavágíśa. 2 vols. Bibliotheca Indica, New Series nos. 170, 175, etc. Calcutta: Asiatic Society of Bengal, 1870–1874.

- *Translation:*

Pañcaviṃśa-Brāhmaṇa: The Brāhmaṇa of Twenty Five Chapters. Translated by W. Caland. Bibliotheca Indica, no. 255. Calcutta: Asiatic Society of Bengal, 1931.

Parātrīśikā-Vivarana

Parātrīśikā-vivarana: The Secret of Tantric Mysticism. Edited by Bettina Bäumer, translated by Jaideva Singh. Abhinavagupta's Sanskrit text edited by Swami Lakshmanjee. Delhi: Motilal Banarsidass, 1988. Published in the United States as *A Trident of Wisdom.* SUNY Series in Tantric Studies. Albany: State University of New York Press, 1989.

Praśna Upaniṣad

Praśnopaniṣad. In *Upaniṣatsaṅgrahaḥ,* edited by Paṇḍita Jagadīśa Śāstri. Delhi: Motilal Banarsidass, 1970.

- *Translations:*

Praśna Upaniṣad. In *The Thirteen Principal Upanishads,* translated by Robert E. Hume. 2d ed., 4th impression. Delhi: Oxford University Press, 1988.

———. In *The Principal Upaniṣads,* edited and translated by S. Radhakrishnan. Sanskrit text with English translation. London: George Allen and Unwin, 1953.

R̥g-Veda Saṃhitā

R̥ig-Veda-Samhitā, together with the commentary of Sāyaṇāchārya. Edited by F. Max Müller. 1st Indian ed. 4 vols. Chowkhamba Sanskrit Series, no. 99. Varanasi: Chowkhamba Sanskrit Series Office, 1966.

• *Translations*:

Der Rig-Veda aus dem Sanskrit ins Deutsche Übersetzt. Translated into German by Karl Friedrich Geldner. Harvard Oriental Series, vols. 33–36. Cambridge, Mass.: Harvard University Press, 1951–1957.

The Hymns of the Ṛg-Veda, Translated with a Popular Commentary. Edited by J. L. Shastri, translated by Ralph T. H. Griffith. Rev. ed. 2 vols. Delhi: Motilal Banarsidass, 1973.

Sāṃkhya-Kārikā

"The *Sāṃkhyakārikā* of Īśvarakṛṣṇa." Sanskrit text with translation. Translated by Gerald J. Larson. In Gerald J. Larson, *Classical Sāṃkhya* (see below).

Śāṅkhāyana Āraṇyaka

Śāṅkhāyanāraṇyakam. Edited by Bhim Dev Shastri. Critical ed. Vishveshvaranand Indological Series, no. 70. Hoshiarpur: Vishveshvaranand Vedic Research Institute, 1980.

• *Translation*:

The Śāṅkhāyana Āraṇyaka, with an Appendix on the Mahāvrata. Translated by Arthur Berriedale Keith. Oriental Translation Fund New Series, vol. 18. London: The Royal Asiatic Society, 1908.

Śāṅkhāyana Śrauta-Sūtra

Śāṅkhāyana-śrautasūtram, Together with the Commentary of Vardattasuta Ānartīya and Govinda. Edited by Alfred Hillebrandt. 2 vols. New Delhi: Meharchand Lachhmandas, 1981.

• *Translation*:

Śāṅkhāyana-Śrautasūtra. Translated by W. Caland, edited by Lokesh Chandra. Sarasvati-Vihara Series, vol. 32. Nagpur: International Academy of Indian Culture, 1953.

Śatapatha Brāhmaṇa

The Śatapatha-Brāhmaṇa in the Mādhyandina-Śākhā, with Extracts from the Commentaries of Sāyaṇa, Harisvāmin, and Dvivedaganga. Edited by Albrecht Weber. 2d ed. Chowkhamba Sanskrit Series, no. 96. 1855. Reprint, Varanasi: Chowkhamba Sanskrit Series Office, 1964.

• *Translation*:

The Śatapatha-Brāhmaṇa According to the Mādhyandina School. Translated by Julius Eggling. Sacred Books of the East, vols. 12, 26, 41, 43, 44. 1882–1900. Reprint, Delhi: Motilal Banarsidass, 1963.

Śiva Purāṇa

Śivapurāṇam. Bombay: Veṅkaṭeśvara Press, 1906.

• *Translation:*

The Śiva-Purāṇa. Translated by a board of scholars. Ancient Indian Tradition and Mythology Series, vols. 1–4. Delhi: Motilal Banarsidass, 1969–1970.

Ślokavārttika

Ślokavārttika of Śrī Kumārila Bhatta, with the Commentary Nyāyaratnākara of Śrī Pārthasārathi Miśra. Edited and revised by Svāmī Dvārikādāsa Śāstrī. Prāchyabhārati Series, no. 10. Varanasi: Tara Publications, 1978.

• *Translation:*

Slokavartika. Translated by Gaṅgānātha Jhā. 2d ed. Sri Garib Das Oriental Series, no. 8. Delhi: Sri Satguru Publications, 1983.

Śvetāśvatara Upaniṣad

Śvetāśvatara Upaniṣad. In *Upaniṣatsaṅgrahaḥ,* edited by Paṇḍita Jagadīśa Śāstri. Delhi: Motilal Banarsidass, 1970.

• *Translations:*

Śvetāśvatara Upaniṣad. In *The Thirteen Principal Upanishads,* translated by Robert E. Hume. 2d ed., 4th impression. Delhi: Oxford University Press, 1988.

———. In *The Principal Upaniṣads,* edited and translated by S. Radhakrishnan. Sanskrit text with English translation. London: George Allen and Unwin, 1953.

Taittirīya Saṃhitā

The Sanhitā of the Black Yajur Veda, with the Commentary of Mādhava Āchārya. Edited by E. Röer and E. B. Cowell (vol. 1), E. B. Cowell (vol. 2), Maheśacandra Nyāyaratna (vols. 3-5), Satyavrata Sāmaśramī (vol. 6). Bibliotheca Indica, no. 26. Calcutta: Asiatic Society of Bengal, 1854–1899.

• *Translation:*

The Veda of the Black Yajus School Entitled Taittiriya Sanhita. Translated by Arthur Berriedale Keith. Harvard Oriental Series, vols. 18–19. 1914. Reprint, Delhi: Motilal Banarsidass, 1967.

Taittirīya Upaniṣad

Taittirīya Upaniṣad. In *Upaniṣatsaṅgrahaḥ,* edited by Paṇḍita Jagadīśa Śāstri. Delhi: Motilal Banarsidass, 1970.

• *Translations:*

Taittirīya Upaniṣad. In *The Thirteen Principal Upanishads,* translated by Robert E. Hume. 2d ed., 4th impression. Delhi: Oxford University Press, 1988.

———. In *The Principal Upaniṣads,* edited and translated by S. Radhakrishnan. Sanskrit text with English translation. London: George Allen and Unwin, 1953.

Vaiśeṣika-Sūtra

The Vaiśeṣika Sūtras of Kaṇāda [with the Commentary of Śaṅkara Miśra and Extracts from the Gloss of Jayanārāyaṇa, Together with Notes from the Commentary of Candrakānta and an Introduction by the Translator]. Edited by Major B. D. Basu, translated by Nandalal Sinha. Sanskrit text with English translation. Delhi: S. N. Publications, 1986.

Vājasaneyi Saṃhitā

The Vājasaneyi-Saṃhitā in the Mādhyandina and the Kānva Śākhā with the Commentary of Mahidhara. Edited by Albrecht Weber. 2d ed. Chowkhamba Sanskrit Series, no. 103. Varanasi: The Chowkhamba Sanskrit Series Office, 1972.

• *Translations:*

The Yajur Veda. Edited and translated by Devi Chand. Sanskrit text with English translation. New Delhi: S. Paul and Co., 1965.

Yajurveda Saṃhitā. Edited and enlarged by Surendra Pratap, translated by Ralph T. H. Griffith. Sanskrit text with English translation. Delhi: Nag Publishers, 1990.

The White Yajur Veda, Translated with a Popular Commentary. Translated by Ralph T. H. Griffith. Varanasi: E. J. Lazarus and Company, 1899.

Vākyapadīya

Vākyapadīya of Bhartṛhari with the Commentaries, Vṛtti and the Padhhati of Vṛṣabhadeva, Kāṇḍa I. Edited by K. A. Subramania Iyer. Deccan College Monograph Series, no. 32. Poona: Deccan College Postgraduate and Research Institute, 1966.

Vākyapadīyam (Brahmakāṇḍa) of Shri Bhartṛhari. Edited by Satyakam Varma. With Trilingual Commentary. New Delhi: Munshiram Manoharlal, 1970.

The Vākyapadīya: Critical Text of Cantos I and II [with English Translation, Summary of Ideas and Notes]. Edited and translated by K.

Raghavan Pillai. Studies in the Vākyapadīya, vol. 1. Delhi: Motilal Banarsidass, 1971.

• *Translations:*

The Vākyapadīyā of Bhartṛhari with the Vṛtti, Chapter I. Translated by K. A. Subramania Iyer. Deccan College Building Centenary and Silver Jubilee Series, no. 26. Poona: Deccan College Postgraduate and Research Institute, 1965.

The Vākyapadīya of Bhartṛhari, Chapter III, part i. Translated by K. A. Subramania Iyer. Deccan College Building Centenary and Silver Jubilee Series, no. 71. Poona: Deccan College Postgraduate and Research Institute, 1971.

The Vākyapadīya of Bhartṛhari, Chapter III, part ii. Translated by K. A. Subramania Iyer. Delhi: Motilal Banarsidass, 1974.

The Kālasamuddeśa of Bhartṛhari's Vākyapadīya (Together with Helārāja's Commentary Translated from the Sanskrit for the First Time). Translated by Peri Sarveswara Sarma. Transliterated Sanskrit text with English translation. Delhi: Motilal Banarsidass, 1972.

Vāmana Purāṇa

Vāmana Purāṇa, with English Translation. Edited by Anand Swarup Gupta, translated by S. M. Mukhopadhyaya, A. Bhattacharya, N. C. Nath, and V. K. Varma. Critical ed. Varanasi: All India Kashiraj Trust, 1968.

Varāha Purāṇa

Varāhapurāṇa. Edited by Ananda Swarup Gupta. Critical ed. 2 vols. Varanasi: All India Kashiraj Trust, 1981.

• *Translation:*

The Varāha Purāṇa. Translated by S. Venkitasubramonia Iyer. Ancient Indian Tradition and Mythology Series, vols. 31–32. Delhi: Motilal Banarsidass, 1985.

Vāyu Purāṇa

Srīvāyumahāpurāṇam. Delhi: Nag Publishers, 1983.

Vāyupurāṇam. Edited by Hari Nārāyaṇa Apte. Ānandāśrama Sanskrit Series, no. 49. 1905. Reprint, Poona: Ānandāśrama, 1983.

• *Translation:*

The Vāyu Purāṇa. Translated by G. V. Tagare. Ancient Indian Tradition and Mythology Series, vols. 37–38. Delhi: Motilal Banarsidass, 1987–1988.

Viṣṇu Purāṇa
Śriviṣṇupurāṇa. Gorakhpur: Gītā Press, 1967.
• *Translation:*
The Vishnu Purāṇa: A System of Hindu Mythology and Tradition. Translated by H. H. Wilson. 3d ed. Calcutta: Punthi Pustak, 1961.

Yoga-Sūtra
Patañjalayogadarśinam, tattvavaiśaradīsaṃvalitavyāsabhāṣyasametam [*Patañjali's Yoga Philosophy, with the Tattvavaiśaradī and the Commentary of Vyāsa*]. Edited by Ram Shankar Bhattacharya. Varanasi: Bhāratīya Vidyā Prakāśan, 1963.
Translation:
Yoga Sūtras. In *Yoga Philosophy of Patañjali,* translated with annotations by Swāmi Hariharānanda Āraṇya. Rev. ed. Albany: State University of New York Press, 1983.

Secondary Sources

Agrawala, Vasudeva. *Sparks from the Vedic Fire: A New Approach to Vedic Symbolism.* Varanasi: Banaras Hindu University, 1962.

Ainley, Alison. "The Ethics of Sexual Difference." In *Abjection, Melancholia, and Love: The Works of Julia Kristeva,* edited by John Fletcher and Andrew Benjamin. Warwick Studies in Philosophy and Literature. London and New York: Routledge, 1990.

Alper, Harvey P., ed. *Understanding Mantras.* SUNY Series in Religious Studies. Albany: State University of New York Press, 1989.

Baartmans, Frans. *Āpaḥ, The Sacred Waters: an Analysis of a Primordial Symbol in Hindu Myths.* Delhi: B. R. Publishing Corporation, 1990.

Babb, Lawrence A. *The Divine Hierarchy: Popular Hinduism in Central India.* New York: Columbia University Press, 1975.

Bailey, Greg. *The Mythology of Brahmā.* Delhi: Oxford University Press, 1983.

Banerjea, J. N. *Paurāṇic and Tāntric Religion (Early Phase).* Calcutta: University of Calcutta, 1966.

Banerji, S. C. *A Brief History of Tantra Literature.* Calcutta: Naya Prokash, 1988.

Beane, Wendell Charles. *Myth, Cult, and Symbols in Śākta Hinduism: A*

Study of the Indian Mother Goddess. Leiden: E. J. Brill, 1977.

Bennett, Lynn. *Dangerous Wives and Sacred Sisters: Social and Symbolic Roles of High-Caste Women in Nepal.* New York: Columbia University Press, 1983.

Bharati, Agehananda. *The Tantric Tradition.* London: Rider and Company, 1965.

Bhattacharji, Sukumari. *Literature in the Vedic Age.* 2 vols. Bagchi Indological Series, no. 3. Calcutta: K. P. Bagchi and Company, 1984.

Bhattacharyya, Narendra Nath. *History of the Śākta Religion.* New Delhi: Munshiram Manoharlal, 1974.

———. *Indian Mother Goddess.* Calcutta: Indian Studies Past and Present, 1971.

Biardeau, Madeleine. *Cosmogonies Purāṇiques.* Études de Mythologie Hindoue, tome 1. Publications de L'École Française D'Éxtrême Orient, vol. 128. Paris: École Française D'Éxtrême Orient, 1981.

Bilimoria, Puruṣottama. *Śabdapramāṇa: Word and Knowledge.* Dordrecht; Boston; London: Kluwer Academic Publishers, 1988.

Bodewitz, H. W. "The Waters in Vedic Cosmic Classifications." *Indologica Taurinensia* 10 (1982): 45–54.

Bose, D. N., and Hiralal Haldar. *Tantras: Their Philosophy and Occult Secrets.* 3d ed. Calcutta: Oriental Publishing Co., 1956.

Brooks, Douglas Renfrew. *The Secret of the Three Cities: An Introduction to Hindu Śākta Tantrism.* Chicago: University of Chicago Press, 1990.

Brown, C. Mackenzie. *God as Mother: A Feminine Theology in India; An Historical and Theological Study of the Brahmavaivarta Purāṇa.* Hartford, Vt.: Claude Stark and Co., 1974.

———. "Purāṇa as Scripture: From Sound to Image of the Holy Word in the Hindu Tradition." *History of Religions* 26, no. 1 (August 1986): 68–86.

———. *The Triumph of the Goddess: The Canonical Models and Theological Visions of the Devī-Bhāgavata Purāṇa.* SUNY Series in Hindu Studies. Albany: State University of New York Press, 1990.

Brown, W. Norman. "Agni, Sun, Sacrifice, and Vāc: A Sacerdotal Ode by Dīrghatamas (Rig Veda 1.164)." *Journal of the American Oriental Society* 88, no. 2 (April–June 1968): 199–218.

———. "The Creation Myth of the Rig Veda." *Journal of the American Oriental Society* 62, no. 2 (June 1942): 85–98.

———. "The Creative Role of the Goddess Vāc in the Rig Veda." In *Pratidānam: Indian, Iranian and Indo-European Studies Presented to Franciscus Bernardus Jacobus Kuiper on his 60th Birthday*, edited by J. C. Heesterman, G. H. Schokker, and V. I. Subramoniam. Janua linguarum, Series maior, no. 34. The Hague: Mouton, 1968.

———. "Theories of Creation in the Rig Veda." *Journal of the American Oriental Society* 85, no. 1 (January–March 1965): 23–34.

Bumiller, Elisabeth. *May You Be the Mother of a Hundred Sons: A Journey among the Women of India.* New York: Fawcett Columbine, 1990.

Chakrabarti, Samiran Chandra. *The Paribhāṣās in the Śrautasūtras.* Calcutta: Sanskrit Pustak Bhandar, 1980.

Chakravarti, Prabhat Chandra. *Doctrine of Sakti in Indian Literature.* Patna: Eastern Book House, 1940.

Chattopadhyāya, Debiprasad. *Lokāyata: A Study in Ancient Indian Materialism.* New Delhi: People's Publishing House, 1959.

———. *What Is Living and What Is Dead in Indian Philosophy.* New Delhi: People's Publishing House, 1976.

Coburn, Thomas B. "Consort of None, *Śakti* of All: The Vision of the *Devī-Māhātmya.*" In *The Divine Consort: Rādhā and the Goddesses of India,* edited by John S. Hawley and Donna Marie Wulff, pp. 153–165. Berkeley: Berkeley Religious Studies Series, 1982; reprint, Boston: Beacon Press, 1986.

———. *Devī-Māhātmya: The Crystallization of the Goddess Tradition.* Delhi: Motilal Banarsidass, 1984.

———. *Encountering the Goddess: A Translation of the Devī-Māhātmya and a Study of Its Interpretation.* SUNY Series in Hindu Studies. Albany: State University of New York Press, 1991.

———. "The Study of the Purāṇas and the Study of Religion." *Religious Studies* 16, no. 3 (September 1980): 341–352.

Coomaraswamy, Ananda K. *Yakṣas.* New Delhi: Munshiram Manoharlal, 1971.

Coward, Harold G. *Bhartṛhari.* Twayne's World Authors Series, no. 403. Boston: Twayne Publishers, 1976.

Danielou, Alain. *The Gods of India: Hindu Polytheism.* New York: Inner Traditions, 1985.

Das, S. K. *Śakti or Divine Power.* Calcutta: University of Calcutta, 1934.

Das, Veena. *Structure and Cognition.* 2d ed. Delhi: Oxford University Press, 1982.

———. "The Goddess and the Demon—An Analysis of the Devi Mahatmya." *Manushi,* no. 30 (1985): 28–32.

Dasgupta, S. B. *Aspects of Indian Religious Thought.* Calcutta: Firma KLM, 1977.

———. *Obscure Religious Cults.* Reprint of the 3d ed. Calcutta: Firma KLM, 1976.

Dasgupta, Surendranath. *A History of Indian Philosophy.* 5 vols. 1922. Reprint of the Indian ed., Delhi: Motilal Banarsidass, 1988.

Deussen, Paul. *The System of the Vedānta.* Translated by Charles Johnston. New Delhi: Akay Book Corporation, 1987.

Deutsch, Eliot. *Advaita Vedānta: A Philosophical Reconstruction.* Honolulu: University of Hawaii Press, 1969.

Dev, Usha. *The Concept of Śakti in the Purāṇas.* Purāṇa Vidyā Series, no. 2. Delhi: Nag Publishers, 1987.

Devanandan, Paul David. *The Concept of Māyā.* Lutterworth Library, vol. 31. Missionary Research Series, no. 13. London: Lutterworth Press, 1950.

Dhal, Upendra Nath. *Goddess Laksmi: Origin and Development.* New Delhi: Oriental Publishers, 1978.

Dhruvarajan, Vanaja. *Hindu Women and the Power of Ideology.* Granby, Mass.: Bergin and Garvey Publishers, 1989.

Dikshit, Sadanand K. *The Mother Goddess.* New Delhi: Published by the author, 1957.

Dimmitt, Cornelia, and J. A. B. van Buitenen, eds. and trans. *Classical Hindu Mythology: A Reader in the Sanskrit Purāṇas.* Philadelphia, Pa.: Temple University Press, 1978.

Douglas, Mary. *Purity and Danger: An Analysis of the Concepts of Pollution and Taboo.* London: Routledge and Kegan Paul, 1966.

Dyczkowski, Mark S. G. *The Aphorisms of Śiva: The Śiva Sūtra with Bhāskara's Commentary, the Vārttika.* SUNY Series in Tantric Studies. Albany: State University of New York Press, 1992.

———. *The Doctrine of Vibration: An Analysis of the Doctrines and Practices of Kashmir Shaivism.* SUNY Series in Kashmir Shaivism. Delhi: Motilal Banarsidass, 1989. Printed in the United States by State University of New York Press, 1987.

Eck, Diana. "India's *Tīrthas*: 'Crossings' in Sacred Geography." *History of Religions* 20, no. 4 (May 1981): 323–344.

Eco, Umberto. *Postscript to "The Name of the Rose."* Translated by William Weaver. San Diego: Harcourt Brace Jovanovich, 1984.

———. *Role of the Reader: Explorations in the Semiotics of Texts.* Bloomington: Indiana University Press, 1979.

Edgerton, Franklin. *The Beginnings of Indian Philosophy: Selections from the Rig Veda, Atharva Veda, Upaniṣads, and Mahābhārata.* Cambridge, Mass.: Harvard University Press, 1965.

Eliade, Mircea. *Patterns in Comparative Religion.* Translated by Rosemary Sheed. New York: New American Library, 1963.

———. *Yoga: Immortality and Freedom.* Translated by Willard R. Trask. 2d ed. Bollingen Series, no. 56. Princeton, N.J.: Princeton University Press, 1969.

Erndl, Kathleen M. "The Goddess and Female Empowerment in Kangra, India." Paper read at the American Academy of Religion Annual Meeting, November 21, 1992.

———. *Victory to the Mother.* New York and Oxford: Oxford University Press, 1993.

Falk, Marlya. *Nāma Rūpa and Dharma Rūpa: Origin and Aspects of an Ancient Indian Conception.* Calcutta: University of Calcutta, 1943.

Falk, Nancy A., and Rita M. Gross, eds. *Unspoken Worlds: Women's Religious Lives in Non-Western Cultures.* San Francisco: Harper and Row, 1980.

Frauwallner, Erich. *History of Indian Philosophy.* Translated by V. M. Bedekar. 2 vols. Delhi: Motilal Banarsidass, 1973.

Gächter, Othmar. *Hermeneutics and Language in Pūrva Mīmāṃsā: A Study in Śābara Bhāṣya.* Delhi: Motilal Banarsidass, 1983.

Gatwood, Lynne E. *Devi and the Spouse Goddess: Women, Sexuality, and Marriages in India.* Riverdale, Md.: The Riverdale Company, 1985.

Gonda, J. *Change and Continuity in Indian Religion.* Disputationes Rheno-Trajectinae, vol. 9. The Hague: Mouton, 1965.

———. "The "Original" Sense and the Etymology of Skt. *māyā.*" In *Four Studies in the Language of the Veda.* Disputationes Rheno-Trajectinae, vol. 3. The Hague: Mouton, 1959.

———. *The Ritual Sūtras.* Vol. 1, fasc. 2 of *A History of Indian Literature.* Wiesbaden: Otto Harrassowitz, 1977.

———. *The Vision of the Vedic Poets.* 1st Indian ed. Delhi: Munshiram Manoharlal, 1984.

———. *Triads in the Veda.* Amsterdam: North-Holland Publishing Co., 1976.

Goudriaan, Teun. *Māyā Divine and Human.* Delhi: Motilal Banarsidass, 1978.

Gupta, Sanjukta. "The Pāñcarātra Attitude to Mantra." In *Understanding Mantras,* edited by Harvey Alper, pp. 224–248. SUNY Series in Religious Studies. Albany: State University of New York Press, 1989.

Gupta, Sanjukta, and Teun Goudriaan. *Hindu Tantric and Śākta Literature.* Vol. 2, fasc. 2 of *A History of Indian Literature.* Wiesbaden: Otto Harrossowitz, 1981.

Gupta, Sanjukta, Dirk Jan Hoens, and Teun Goudriaan. *Hindu Tantrism.* Leiden: E. J. Brill, 1979.

Harman, William P. *The Sacred Marriage of a Hindu Goddess.* Religion in Asia and Africa Series. Bloomington: Indiana University Press, 1989.

Hazra, Rajendra Chandra. *Studies in the Purāṇic Records on Hindu Rites and Customs.* 2d ed. Delhi: Motilal Banarsidass, 1975.

———. *Studies in the Upapurāṇas.* 2 vols. Vol. 1: *Śaiva and Vaiṣṇava Upapurāṇas.* Vol. 2: *Śākta and Non-Sectarian Upapurāṇas.* Calcutta Sanskrit College Research Series, nos. 2 and 22. Calcutta: Sanskrit College, 1958 and 1963.

Heesterman, J. C. "Veda and Dharma." In *The Concept of Duty in South Asia,* edited by Wendy Doniger O'Flaherty and J. Duncan M. Derrett, pp. 80–95. New Delhi: Vikas Publishing House, 1978.

Heimann, Betty. *Facets of Indian Thought.* London: George Allen and Unwin, 1964.

Holdrege, Barbara A. "Hindu Ethics." In *The Berkeley-Harvard Annotated Bibliography on Comparative Religious Ethics,* edited by Valerie DeMarinis and Douglas Mansager. Cambridge and New York: Cambridge University Press, 1991.

———. *Veda and Torah: Ontological Conceptions of Scripture in the Brahmanical and Judaic Traditions.* Ph.D. Dissertation. Cambridge, Mass.: Harvard University, 1987.

———. *Veda and Torah: Transcending the Textuality of Scripture.* Albany: State University of New York Press, forthcoming.

Humes, Cynthia Ann. "Glorifying the Great Goddess or Great Woman? Hindu Women's Experience in Ritual Recitation of the Devī-Māhātmya." In *Women in Goddess Traditions,* edited by Karen King and Karen Torjesen. Minneapolis: Fortress Press, forthcoming.

———. "Glorifying the Great Goddess or Great Woman? Interpretation of the *Devī-Māhātmya,* East and West." Paper read at the Biannual International East Meets West Conference, Long Beach, Calif., April 9, 1993.

Jacob, G. A. *A Concordance to the Principle Upanishads and Bhagavad Gītā.* 1891. Reprint, Delhi: Motilal Banarsidass, 1963.

Jhā, Gaṅgānātha. *Pūrva-Mīmāṃsā in Its Sources.* 2d ed. Varanasi: Banaras Hindu University, 1964.

———. *The Prābhākara School of Pūrva Mīmāmsā.* 1911. Reprint, Delhi: Motilal Banarsidass, 1978.

Johnston, E. H. *Early Sāṃkhya: An Essay on its Historical Development According to the Texts.* Prize Publication Fund, vol. 15. London: Royal Asiatic Society, 1937.

Kaelber, Walter O. *Tapta Marga: Asceticism and Initiation in Vedic India.* Albany: State University of New York Press, 1989.

Keith, Arthur Berriedale. *The Karma-Mīmāṃsā.* The Heritage of India Series. Calcutta: Association Press, 1921.

———. *The Religion and Philosophy of the Veda and Upaniṣads.* Harvard Oriental Series, vols. 31–32. Cambridge, Mass.: Harvard University Press, 1925.

Khan, Mohammad Israil. *Sarasvati in Sanskrit Literature.* Ghaziabad: Crescent Publishing House, 1978.

Kinsley, David. *Hindu Goddesses: Visions of the Divine Feminine in the Hindu Tradition.* Berkeley and Los Angeles: University of California Press, 1986.

———. *The Sword and the Flute: Kālī and Kṛṣṇa; Dark Visions of the Terrible and the Sublime in Hindu Mythology.* Berkeley and Los Angeles: University of California Press, 1975.

Kramrisch, Stella. "The Indian Great Goddess." *History of Religions* 14, no. 4 (May 1975): 235–265.

Krishnaswamy, Shantha. *Glimpses of Women in India.* New Delhi: Ashish Publishing House, 1983.

Kristeva, Julia. *Le Texte du Roman: Approche Sémiologique d'une Structure Discursive Transformationnelle.* Approaches to Semiotics, no. 6. The Hague: Mouton, 1970.

———. *Powers of Horror: An Essay on Abjection.* Translated by Leon S. Roudiez. New York: Columbia University Press, 1982.

———. "Stabat Mater." Translated by Leon S. Roudiez. In *The Kristeva Reader,* edited by Toril Moi. New York: Columbia University Press, 1986. Translation of "Hérétique de l'amour." *Tel Quel,* no. 74 (Winter 1977).

Kuiper, F. B. J. "Cosmogony and Conception: A Query." *History of*

Religions 10, no. 2 (November 1970): 91–138.

Kumar, Pushpendra. *Sakti Cult in Ancient India.* Banaras: Bharatiya Publishing House, 1974.

Kunhan Raja, Chittenjoor. *Some Fundamental Problems in Indian Philosophy.* Delhi: Motilal Banarsidass, 1960.

Kurtz, Stanley. *All the Mothers Are One: Hindu India and the Cultural Reshaping of Psychoanalysis.* New York: Columbia University Press, 1992.

Lahiri, Ajoy Kumar. *Vedic Vṛtra.* Delhi: Motilal Banarsidass, 1984.

Lal, S. K. *Female Divinities in Hindu Mythology and Ritual.* Poona: University of Poona, 1980.

Larson, Gerald J. *Classical Sāṃkhya.* 2d ed. Delhi: Motilal Banarsidass, 1979.

———. "Reason in Early Indian Philosophy: Matter and Consciousness in Early Indian Philosophy." *Bulletin of the Ramakrishna Mission Institute of Culture* 41, nos. 8, 9, and 10 (August, September, and October 1990): 171–174, 206–210, 235–238.

———. "The Aesthetic (*rasāvāda*) and the Religious (*brahmāsvāda*) in Abhinavagupta's Kashmir Śaivism." *Philosophy East and West* 26, no. 4 (October 1976): 371–387.

———. "The Sources for Śakti in Abhinavagupta's Kāsmīr Śaivism: A Linguistic and Aesthetic Category." *Philosophy East and West* 24, no. 1 (January 1974): 41–56.

Larson, Gerald J., and R. S. Bhattacharya, eds. *Sāṃkhya: A Dualist Tradition in Indian Philosophies.* Vol. 4 of *Encyclopedia of Indian Philosophies.* Delhi: Motilal Banarsidass, 1987.

Larson, Gerald J., Pratapaditya Pal, and Rebecca P. Gowen. *In Her Image: The Great Goddess in Indian Asia and the Madonna in Christian Culture.* Santa Barbara: UCSB Art Museum, 1980.

Layle, P. G. *Studies in Devī Bhāgavata.* Bombay: Popular Prakashan, 1973.

Leitch, Vincent B. *Deconstructive Criticism: An Advanced Introduction.* New York: Columbia University Press, 1983.

Leslie, I. Julia. "Strīsvabhāva: The Inherent Nature of Women." In *Oxford University Papers on India,* vol. 1 part 1, pp. 28–58. Delhi: Oxford University Press, 1986.

———. *The Perfect Wife: The Orthodox Hindu Woman according to the Strīdharmapaddhati of Tryambakayajvan.* Delhi: Oxford University Press, 1989.

Macdonell, A. A. *Vedic Mythology.* 1898. Reprint, Delhi: Motilal Banarsidass, 1974.

McGee, Mary. "Desired Fruits: Motive and Intention in the Votive Rites of Hindu Women." In *Roles and Rituals for Hindu Women,* edited by Julia Leslie, pp. 71–88. London: Pinter Publishers, 1991.

———. "Domesticated Shakti: Empowerment through Marriage." Paper read at the American Academy of Religion Annual Meeting, November 21, 1992.

Madan, T. N. "Concerning the Categories *Śubha* and *Śuddha* in Hindu Culture: An Exploratory Essay." In *Purity and Auspiciousness in Indian Society,* edited by John B. Carman and Frédérique A. Marglin, pp. 11–29. International Studies in Sociology and Social Anthropology, vol. 43. Leiden: E. J. Brill, 1985.

Marglin, Frédérique A. "Introduction" and "Types of Oppositions in Hindu Culture." In *Purity and Auspiciousness in Indian Society,* edited by John B. Carman and Frédérique A. Marglin, pp. 1–10, 65–83. International Studies in Sociology and Social Anthropology, vol. 43. Leiden: E. J. Brill, 1985.

Miller, Jeanine. *The Vision of Cosmic Order in the Vedas.* London: Routledge and Kegan Paul, 1985.

Mitter, Sara S. *Dharma's Daughters: Contemporary Indian Women and Hindu Culture.* New Brunswick, N.J.: Rutgers University Press, 1991.

Monier-Williams, Sir Monier. *A Sanskrit-English Dictionary.* Rev. ed. Delhi: Motilal Banarsidass, 1988.

Mookerji, Ajit. *Kālī, the Feminine Force.* New York: Destiny Books, 1988.

Muir, J., comp. and trans. *Original Sanskrit Texts on the Origin and History of the People of India, Their Religion and Institutions.* 2d ed. 5 vols. 1872–1874. Reprint, Amsterdam: Oriental Press, 1967.

Müller, F. Max, and H. Oldenberg, trans. *Vedic Hymns.* Sacred Books of the East, vols. 32, 46. 1891. Reprint, Delhi: Motilal Banarsidass, 1964.

Muller-Ortega, Paul Eduardo. *The Triadic Heart of Śiva.* SUNY Series in the Shaiva Traditions of Kashmir. Albany: State University of New York Press, 1989.

Narayan, Vasudha. "The Two Levels of Auspiciousness in Śrīvaiṣṇava Literature." In *Purity and Auspiciousness in Indian Society*, edited by John B. Carman and Frédérique A. Marglin, pp. 55–64. International Studies in Sociology and Social Anthropology, vol. 43. Leiden: E. J. Brill, 1985.

O'Flaherty, Wendy Doniger. *Women, Androgynes, and Other Mythical Beasts.* Chicago: University of Chicago Press, 1980.

O'Neil, L. Thomas. *Māyā in Śaṅkara: Measuring the Immeasurable.* Delhi: Motilal Banarsidass, 1980.

Ortner, Sherry B. "Is Female to Male as Nature Is to Culture?" In *Women, Culture, and Society,* edited by Michelle Zimbalist Rosaldo and Louise Lamphere, pp. 67–87. Stanford, Calif.: Stanford University Press, 1974.

Padoux, André. *Vāc: The Concept of the Word in Selected Hindu Tantras.* Translated by Jacques Gontier. SUNY Series in the Shaiva Traditions of Kashmir. Albany: State University of New York Press, 1990.

Pandeya, R. C. *The Problem of Meaning in Indian Philosophy.* Delhi: Motilal Banarsidass, 1963.

Patni, B. *Śiva Purāṇa: A Poetic Analysis.* Delhi: Ajanta Publications, 1980.

Payne, Ernest A. *The Saktas: An Introductory and Comparative Study.* 1933. Reprint, New York and London: Garland Publishing, Inc., 1979.

Pfleuger, Lloyd William. "God, Consciousness, and Meditation: The Concept of Īśvara in the Yogasūtra." Ph.D. Dissertation. University of California, Santa Barbara, 1990.

Pintchman, Tracy. "Deciphering the Goddess: The Rise of the Feminine Principle in Brahmanical Hindu Cosmogony and Cosmology." Ph.D. Dissertation. University of California, Santa Barbara, 1992.

———. "Creation and the Great Goddess in the Purāṇas." *Purāṇa* 35, no. 2 (July 1993): 146–170.

———. "The Ambiguous Female: Conceptions of Female Gender in the Brahmanical Tradition and the Roles of Women in India." In *Ethical and Political Dilemmas of Modern India,* edited by Ninian Smart and Shivesh Thakur, pp. 144–159. New York: St. Martin's Press, 1993.

Potter, Karl H., ed. *Advaita Vedānta up to Śaṃkara and His Pupils.* Vol. 3 of *The Encyclopedia of Indian Philosophies.* Princeton, N.J.: Princeton University Press, 1981.

Preston, James J., ed. *Mother Worship, Theme and Variations.* Chapel Hill: University of North Carolina Press, 1982.

Przyluski, J. "The Great Goddess of India and Iran." *Indian Historical Quarterly* 10, no. 3 (September 1934): 405–430.

Rajwade, V. K. "Asurasya Māyā in Ṛgveda." In *First Oriental Conference, Poona, Procs. and Trans.* Vol. 1, 1920, pp. ix–xiii.

Ramanujan, A. K. "On Folk Mythologies and Folk Purāṇas." In *Purāṇa Perennis: Reciprocity and Transformation in Hindu and Jaina Texts,* edited by Wendy Doniger, pp. 101–120. Albany: State University of New York Press, 1993.

Regnaud, Paul. "La Maya et le Pouvoir Createur Des Divinités Védiques." *Revue de L'Histoire Des Religions* (1885): 237–245.

Renou, Louis. "Les Connexions entre le Rituel et la Grammaire en Sanskrit." *Journal Asiatique* 233 (1941–1942): 105–165. Reprinted in *A Reader on the Sanskrit Grammarians,* edited by J. F. Staal, pp. 435–469. Cambridge, Mass.: MIT Press, 1972.

———. *The Destiny of the Veda in India.* Edited and translated by Dev Raj Chanana. Delhi: Motilal Banarsidass, 1965.

———. "Sur La Notion de Brahman." *Journal Asiatique* (1949): 7–46.

Reyna, Ruth. *The Concept of Māyā from the Vedas to the Twentieth Century.* London: Asia Publishing House, 1962.

Rocher, Ludo. *The Purāṇas.* Vol. 2, fasc. 3 of *A History of Indian Literature.* Wiesbaden: Otto Harrassowitz, 1986.

Ruegg, David Seyfort. *Contributions à L'Histoire de la Philosophie Linguistique Indienne.* Publications de L'Institut de Civilisation Indienne, Série IN-8. Paris: E. de Boccard, 1959.

Santucci, James A. *An Outline of Vedic Literature.* The American Academy of Religion Aids to the Study of Religion Series, no. 5. Missoula, Mont.: Scholars Press, 1976.

Sarma, K. Madhava. "Vāk before Bhartṛhari." *Poona Orientalist* 8 (1943): 21–36.

Sarma, Rajendra Nath. *Verbal Knowledge in Prabhākara-Mīmāṃsā.* Sri Garib Dass Oriental Series, no. 60. Delhi: Sri Satguru Publications, 1990.

Sastri, Gaurinath. "Monism of Bhartṛhari." In *Beiträge zur Geistesgeschichte Indiens: Festschrift für Erich Frauwallner.* Leiden: E. J. Brill, 1968.

———. *The Philosophy of Word and Meaning: Some Indian Approaches with Special Reference to the Philosophy of Bhartṛhari.* Calcutta Sanskrit College Research Series, no. 5. 1959. Reprint, Calcutta: Sanskrit College, 1983.

Sax, William S. *Mountain Goddess: Gender and Politics in a Himalayan Pilgrimage.* New York and Oxford: Oxford University Press, 1991.

Schrader, F. Otto. *Introduction to the Pāñcarātra and the Ahirbudhnya Saṃhitā.* 2d ed. Madras: The Adyar Library and Research Centre, 1973.

Sharma, Chandradhar. *A Critical Survey of Indian Philosophy.* Delhi: Motilal Banarsidass, 1987.

Shastri, P. D. *The Doctrine of Māyā in the Philosophy of the Vedānta.* London: Luzac and Co., 1911.

Sheridan, Daniel P. *The Advaitic Theism of the Bhāgavata Purāṇa.* Delhi: Motilal Banarsidass, 1986.

Shulman, David. *Tamil Temple Myths: Sacrifice and Divine Marriage in the South Indian Śaiva Tradition.* Princeton, N.J.: Princeton University Press, 1980.

Siddhantashastree, Rabindra Kumar. *Vaiṣṇavism Through the Ages.* New Delhi: Munshiram Manoharlal, 1985.

Singh, Renuka. *The Womb of Mind: A Sociological Exploration of the Status Experience of Women in Delhi.* New Delhi: Vikas Publishing House, 1990.

Sircar, D. C., ed. *Foreigners in Ancient India and Lakṣmī and Sarasvatī in Art and Literature.* Calcutta: University of Calcutta, 1970.

———. *The Sakta Pithas.* 2d rev. ed. Delhi: Motilal Banarsidass, 1973.

———. *The Sakti Cult and Tara.* Calcutta: University of Calcutta, 1967.

Smith, Brian K. *Reflections on Resemblance, Ritual, and Religion.* New York and Oxford: Oxford University Press, 1989.

Smith, Frederick M. "Indra's Curse, Varuṇa's Noose." In *Roles and Rituals for Hindu Women,* edited by Julia Leslie, pp. 17–45. London: Pinter Publishers, 1991.

Staal, J. F. "Sanskrit Philosophy of Language." In *Linguistics in South Asia.* Vol. 5 of *Current Trends in Linguistics,* edited by Thomas A. Sebeok, pp. 499–531. The Hague: Mouton, 1969.

Van Buitenen, J. A. B. "Akṣara." *Journal of the American Oriental Society* 79, no. 3 (July–September 1959): 176–187.

———. "Studies in Sāṃkhya (I)." *Journal of the American Oriental Society* 76, no. 3 (July–September 1956): 153–157.

———. "Studies in Sāṃkhya (II)." *Journal of the American Oriental Society* 77, no. 1 (January–March 1957): 15–25.

———. "Studies in Sāṃkhya (III)." *Journal of the American Oriental Society* 77, no. 2 (April–June 1957): 88–107.

———. "The Large Ātman." *History of Religions* 4, no. 1 (1964): 103–114.

Van Kooij, K. R. *Worship of the Goddess According to the Kālikāpurāṇa, Part I.* Orientalia Rheno Traiectina, vol. 14. Leiden: E. J. Brill, 1972.

Varma, K. S. "The Doctrine of Māyā." *Agra University's Journal of Research,* 1 (November 1952): 33–41.

Wadley, Susan S. *Shakti: Power in the Conceptual Structure of Karimpur Religion.* The University of Chicago Studies in Anthropology Series in Social, Cultural, and Linguistic Anthropology, no. 2. Chicago: The University of Chicago Department of Anthropology, 1975.

———. "Women and the Hindu Tradition." In *Women in India: Two Perspectives,* edited by Doranne Jacobson and Susan S. Wadley. Columbia, Mo.: South Asia Books, 1977.

———, ed. *The Powers of Tamil Women.* Foreign and Comparative Studies/South Asian Series, no. 6. Syracuse, N.Y.: Maxwell School of Citizenship and Public Affairs, Syracuse University, 1980.

Winternitz, Maurice. *A History of Indian Literature.* Translated by V. Srinivasa Sarma and Subhadra Jha. 3 vols. Delhi: Motilal Banarsidass, 1985–1988.

Woodroffe, Sir John. *Introduction to Tantra Śāstra.* 7th ed. Madras: Ganesh and Co., 1980.

———. *Śakti and Śākta.* 7th ed. Madras: Ganesh and Co., 1969.

———. *The Garland of Letters: Studies in the Mantra-Śāstra.* 8th ed. Madras: Ganesh and Co., 1985.

———. *The World as Power.* 6th ed. Madras: Ganesh and Co., 1981.

Index

Aditi
as a cow, 32
and Dakṣa, 34
equated with the earth, 33, 47
equated with Vāc, 47
levels of identity of, 32
as a mother goddess, 32–33
as a universal being, 33–34, 47
Ādityas, 32
Adṛṣṭa, 101, 102–103, 104, 230n. 91
Advaita Vedānta, 90–97
influence on Purāṇic cosmogonies, 126, 131–137, 156, 157, 158, 175, 181–182
Agni/*agni* (god of fire; fire). *See also* Gross Elements
as son of the waters, 24, 25
as source of the waters, 66
Agni Purāṇa, 128, 130
Ahaṃkāra (egoity), 73, 84
in the Purāṇas, 129, 139, 155, 158, 173
identified with *mahat*, 135
Aitareya Brāhmaṇa, 49
Aitareya Upaniṣad, 54–55
Ajā (unborn female/she-goat), 68, 69, 71–72, 95
the Goddess as, 173, 174
ambhas. See Waters
ap. See Waters
Apūrva, 101, 103, 104
Āraṇyakas, 8, 9
Asuras (demons), 35, 36, 220n. 46
Aśvins, 41
Atharva-Veda Saṃhitā, 9
Aditi in, 33
earth in, 30–31, 32
Sarasvatī in, 40
Vāc in, 38
Virāj in, 35–37, 219–220nn. 43, 44, 46
the waters in, 25
Ātman
in the Purāṇas
identified with *mahat*, 135
as the source of *prakṛti* and *puruṣa*, 162
in the Upaniṣads
as personal creator, 54–55, 57
as ultimate principle, 54
Auspiciousness/Inauspiciousness, 202
Avidyā (ignorance)
in Advaita Vedānta, 94, 228–229n. 70
in the Purāṇas, 156–157, 158, 182, 198, 240n. 103
Avyakta (the unmanifest)
equated with *māyā*, in Advaita Vedānta, 94–95
and *prakṛti*
in classical Sāṃkhya, 84, 85 86
in the Mahābhārata, 73, 80, 81